Shadow Mountain

❖ ❖ ❖

Shadow Mountain

❖ ❖ ❖

A Memoir of Wolves,
a Woman, and the Wild

Renée Askins

DOUBLEDAY

New York   London   Toronto   Sydney   Auckland

PUBLISHED BY DOUBLEDAY
a division of Random House, Inc.
1540 Broadway, New York, New York 10036

DOUBLEDAY and the portrayal of an anchor with a dolphin are
trademarks of Doubleday, a division of Random House, Inc.

BOOK DESIGN BY AMANDA DEWEY

TITLE PAGE PHOTOGRAPH BY
MONTY SLOAN/WOLFPHOTOGRAPHY.COM

See page 321 for permission acknowledgments.

Library of Congress Cataloging-in-Publication Data
Askins, Renée.
Shadow Mountain : a memoir of wolves, a woman, and the wild /
Renée Askins—1st ed.
p. cm.
1. Wolves—Reintroduction—Yellowstone National Park.
2. Nature—Psychological
aspects. 3. Askins, Renée. I. Title.
QL737.C22 A8 2002
639.9'79773'0978752—dc21
2001055800

ISBN 0-385-48222-1

August 2002
First Edition
1   3   5   7   9   10   8   6   4   2

For Siena Aurora Askins Rush

and

For Natasha
In all her mystery and incarnations

Contents

❖ ❖ ❖

Prologue   *ix*

CHAPTER ONE   *1*

CHAPTER TWO   *7*

CHAPTER THREE   *21*

CHAPTER FOUR   *27*

CHAPTER FIVE   *37*

CHAPTER SIX   *51*

CHAPTER SEVEN   *61*

CHAPTER EIGHT   *75*

CHAPTER NINE   *87*

CHAPTER TEN   *95*

CHAPTER ELEVEN   *107*

CHAPTER TWELVE   *117*

CHAPTER THIRTEEN   *127*

CHAPTER FOURTEEN   139

CHAPTER FIFTEEN   151

CHAPTER SIXTEEN   159

CHAPTER SEVENTEEN   165

CHAPTER EIGHTEEN   177

CHAPTER NINETEEN   185

CHAPTER TWENTY   195

CHAPTER TWENTY-ONE   209

CHAPTER TWENTY-TWO   223

CHAPTER TWENTY-THREE   231

CHAPTER TWENTY-FOUR   239

CHAPTER TWENTY-FIVE   251

CHAPTER TWENTY-SIX   259

CHAPTER TWENTY-SEVEN   271

CHAPTER TWENTY-EIGHT   281

EPILOGUE   289

Select Bibliography   295
Sources, Resources,
    and Suggested Reading   299
Websites   301
To Help Support Wolf Recovery   303
Notes   305
Acknowledgments   309

Prologue

❖ ❖ ❖

URING THE YEARS of writing *Shadow Mountain* people would ask me, "What is your book about?" I found that each time I would answer differently depending upon what chapter I was working on, or my mood that moment. "This book is about . . . keeping a promise, living a passion, loving an animal, not giving up, hope, living from hope to hope, heartbreak, incandescent joy, wolves, wildness lost, wildness found, wildness within, healing, wounding, restoring, common experience, uncommon experience, a place called Shadow Mountain, a wolf named Natasha." I now realize that all these were true, each a vital ingredient of the story of *Shadow Mountain.*

With many undertakings, especially those that are drawn out over years and involve self-examination, one finds that the person who began the journey is someone quite different from the one completing it. When I crested Togwotee Pass in 1981, glimpsing the panorama of Jackson Hole and the Tetons in the swirling mists of an early winter snowstorm, I wondered if the restoration of wolves to Yellowstone would take a full year. Fourteen years later I learned the answer: yes—and thirteen more. It's rather odd to wake up one morning and realize that nearly a decade and a half has slipped by in the pursuit of a passion, one that you never intended to become your mission, or even your career, certainly not your identity. Likewise, when I began writing this book I thought it would be simple; I would just tell the story of returning wolves to Yellowstone, A to Z, but I soon realized I was uninterested in chronicling the Kafkaesque drama of meetings, memos, political wrangling, and philanthropy that I had lived for so long. I was far more interested in why, than I was in just who, what, and when. How, after all, had I come to this; or had it come to me? Did those years make a difference? Were they worth the cost and compromises?

The thread of a life is not stretched taut between two points. It twists in unexpected and mysterious ways, not so much weaving—as poets would have us believe—as snarling and catching, creating the tangles and knots which hold our stories and the keys to our understanding them. I at first thought this process would lead me to revelations that would be laid out like bright Easter eggs here and there along the path of my history. It turned out that I didn't discover the answers to my questions by systematically sleuthing through the calendar of my life. Rather, I found the truth buried beneath the surface of the story—not the intellectual, rational, ordered truth, but the deep, resonant, singular truth of my heart.

I had a fantasy that followed me through many of the years I worked on Yellowstone wolf recovery—when it was over, when I was released from this frenetic, consuming mission, I would send a letter home to all the people I loved explaining everything: why I had been so silent, so absent, so out of touch, gone for so long; why calls and letters had gone unanswered, baby presents unsent, weddings unattended, and why there had been times I wasn't there to listen, to comfort, to congratulate. I would explain that I had been swept away by events that flowed from a promise made to an animal I loved, and it had been a long, long journey back. It wasn't that I needed to apologize, rather I needed to tell my story: I needed to reconcile who I had been before the journey with who I had become during it. It was a need to express that a life lived devoted to the truth of one's heart reaches beyond either/or choices, that there are circumstances in which we must sacrifice some of now for later, trusting that everything has a right time, meaning, and place.

So *Shadow Mountain* is what came of my wonderings and wanderings among wolves and word these last twenty years. This book contains the stories of my travels, written with a compulsion to discover, through a maze of memories, the meaning of these many years. Written from the truth of my heart, it is my letter home.

Renée Askins
Wilson, Wyoming
February 5, 2002

*Whatever you do will be insignificant
and it is very important that you do it.*

MOHANDAS GANDHI

One

On this cold night
winter's last rally
rakes across the fledgling breast
of spring like claws. The last white bear
turns, hungering,
northward.
We put on layers of sweaters again
and light a circle of lamps
deep in the heart of the house. But
we are restless, keep listening.
You are the first to get up.
You pace a few silent steps
then go. Upstairs I find you
perched at the window,
an early stork
staring from the slender chimney
of your bones down
at icy slivers of teeth
slicing into tender garden growth.

Without thinking why
we gather the afghans
and carefully fold our long limbs
down into them.
With a soft ritual clicking of bills,
necks twining, wings rising,
we begin
the ancient migration
back to the place
of our birth.

MARCIA CASEY, "Storks"

MY FIRST MEMORIES are of meadows. Evening meadows, when the sun's honey-warm rays turned the long grasses and birch borders into an enchanted and radiant secret. It is the light I mostly remember, when the dark was seducing the day and the shadows would flicker and splinter in a spectacle of courtship. It was the hour of whimsy and expectation. Perhaps it was the melon light that beckoned the deer. They emerged like druids from the forests, miragelike in the tall shimmering grass, unable to resist those last lingering moments of summer sunlight to warm their shadow-cooled backs.

My mother would count them. Two, three, four, ten, twenty-six, twenty-seven, twenty-eight. My older sister Robin and I would listen and watch, two small daughters perched beside their mother on the liver-colored seat of a plump black Volkswagen Bug. There was no television in our remote cottage in the Thunder Bay State Forest of northern Michigan, and my father had to travel for his work, leaving my mother in the silence of those white pine forests for days at a time.

That's how the summer evenings of my early childhood passed, our

Volkswagen parked alongside some meadow, with its nose edged into the tall summer grass like a huge Lab sniffing the dirt, with my mama counting the deer. It's also how I learned to count, but for years I would be confused about what numbers really followed others because my mother's voice would drift off at fourteen or thirty-seven, like the sun slipping behind a darkened cloud into some secret shadowed place that concealed the loneliness of a young mother, and then suddenly her voice would reemerge brilliant and warm on twenty-six or forty-three. I doubt that it mattered to her how many deer there were, the numbers were only a mantra to give order to the loneliness, to arrange an eternal evening according to a knowable rhythm. Occasionally she would remark on how large a fawn had gotten, or on the limp of a doe, but mostly she would just count, thirty-eight, thirty-nine, forty . . . and the light would fall and her voice would trail off and the deer would slip back into the shadows.

It was in this way the wild would be made intimate, the outside wariness transformed into some sort of interior attentiveness. In my early childhood I unconsciously absorbed the notion of reciprocity—the idea that as we enter the realm of animals, offer our presence, and bear witness to the lives of creatures, they in turn offer their own gifts, their own example and accompaniment through the loneliness of our human existence. For millions of years animals lived without humans, but we have never lived without animals. Edwin Muir said, "Long before man appeared on earth he existed as a dream of prophecy in the animal soul."

Even four decades later those early images of long grasses and the arch of evening light, the silhouettes of deer melting into a darkened border of shadowed trees, the comfort and caress of my mother's voice, and the warmth of my sister's body pressed against me illuminate my life like moonlight through stained glass. Partly due to the clarity of hindsight and partly because the power of my childhood experiences with the wild still resonates in my life today, I have grown to appreciate how important, how formative, childhood contact with the natural world can be. It is the foundation that is laid by early interactions with the wild that give us an understanding of "otherness," and a context beyond one's self. Early contact with animals and wild places can help to develop a matured empathy and capacity for human relationships, for our connection with a sense of place and landscape, all of which are critical to the unfolding of our personalities and our feelings of belonging to a greater planetary community of creatures, places, and people.

As I believe in the power of wildness and wild things to guide us, so have I come to believe in the importance of place and its potency in our lives. I feel with certainty that everything follows from place, that place makes us who we are, that landscape carves out a certain character and community, and that ultimately the places in which we choose to live govern the unfolding of our lives. And so it was, nearly thirty years after leaving Thunder Bay National Forest, I would discover a place that provided a counterpoint, an adult analogue, to the enchantment of those lovely Michigan meadows. For ten years I lived there with my lover, and came to cherish it. It was my shelter, my solace, my home. It was a place called Shadow Mountain.

Our little log house nestled into a stand of aspens at the base of the mountain like a child leaning into the soft folds of a young mother's skirts. Shadow Mountain was a sensuously curved goddess of a mountain in comparison to the hard-lined granite pinnacles encircling our valley in northwest Wyoming. The forests of pine and aspen that draped down her gentle slopes fell like long unruly tresses, spilling from her shoulders into the sage meadows at her base in a resplendent cascade of arboreal curls and crescents. She stood like a solemn guardian behind the north shoulder of our home, her shadow engulfing us at dawn. As the sun rose behind her it first lit the western horizon of the Tetons, enveloping the peaks in shades of coral and crimson. Cascading down the dim slopes, the sunlight raced toward us across the hazel meadows of Antelope Flats like a wave of radiance. We would often sit drinking our morning tea as the dawn light melted the lingering pool of darkness around us, ushering in the day.

Our little compound at Shadow Mountain, which was comprised of our home, a few tiny cabins, sheds, and an old barn, had become a gathering place for wild animals, from badger to bald eagle, coyote to curlew. Fifty yards from our door the bison had created massive wallows which in time had became watering holes. Except at the height of winter, it was rare for a day to pass without having at least one and often several hundred bison drift through the yard. Sometimes during rut they would gather for days, their rutting growls so deafening it was impossible to sleep, a circumstance only made worse by their habit of rubbing on the log ends of the house, which made it rock like a boat in a storm. A weekly chore, listed between vacuuming and emptying the garbage, was the cleaning of bison snot off the plate-glass windows where the ever-curious bovines stared in and the slightly anxious hominids stared out. Our animal visitors included mule deer, an occasional moose with a gangly legged calf, black bears, a few grizzlies, weasels, once a great gray owl, ravens, coyotes—the list reads like a passenger manifest for the Ark. During the spring and fall migrations there were large gatherings of antelope and herds of elk that numbered in the thousands. The winter before we left the wolves arrived, but therein lies the story to come.

The place was aptly named. There I was forced to confront and accept the dark side of the wild, a concept that seldom clouded my Michigan childhood. The luminosity and grace of Shadow Mountain's wildness were matched by her ferocious darkness, harshness, and isolation. Glorious nights of falling stars were countered by wildfires that almost swept away our home. The delights of gentle summer evenings, being lulled to sleep by the songs of coyotes and awakened to a dazzling morning by the clatter of sandhill cranes, were often forgotten in the hardship of subzero temperatures and blizzards that shut us off from the world for weeks at a time.

Living at Shadow Mountain taught me about both "the nature of shadow" and "the shadow of nature." Recognizing and embracing the darkness that accompanies light is at the heart of understanding the wild. During the time I lived at Shadow Mountain I gave my heart to working for wolves and the wild. When I left there I discovered how Shadow Mountain had given me the wild wisdom of its heart.

Two

❖ ❖ ❖

The future enters into us,
in order to transform
itself in us, long before it happens.

RAINER MARIA RILKE

I WILL START IN the middle, because often it is in the middle that we see that there is an emerging shape to things, that there was at some point a beginning, that events are unfolding toward a still uncertain end. The thread of life bends back over itself, and connections are made. In the midst of the amorphous flow of daily events we sense patterns beginning to form, we realize there is a resonance to certain things that went before, and try to peer through the murk to discern the shape of what is to come.

Just as the faint dawn rays pierce the lingering dark of an interminable April night, I awaken to the snuffling, searching wet muzzle of a six-day-old wolf puppy burrowing under my chin. Cramped and aching, I lift my head up from the long wooden plank that forms the desk at which I'd been working, and over which I'd slumped into a guilty sleep. With mild dismay I notice I've drooled all over the papers strewn across the desk's well-worn surface, carved and stained over the years to a comforting patina. Natasha, the mouse-size wolf puppy, had been asleep on the frayed remnants of a favorite Egyptian cotton towel wound and plumped into a sumptuous, albeit thread-worn and frayed pastel nest at the corner of the desk.

Sometime in the night the puppy had abandoned the cotton bowl I had painstakingly created, and instinctively scuttled across the plank to nestle into the cranny of my sleeping chin. She had been awakened by the sound of her own pack stirring and stretching outside the little shack we occupied. The sounds of canine reveille were broadcast inside our glass-sided hut by a sophisticated system of microphones mounted throughout the one-and-a-half acre enclosure surrounding us.

Bleary and sleep-clumsied, I reach for my thermos of warmed Esbilac, an infant animal formula, and a tiny nursing bottle. Now fully awake, Natasha's wee body is squirming and rooting in a frantic nipple-search, and I struggle to hold her and fill the narrow-necked bottle simultaneously. After dipping my little finger in the formula to check its temperature, I offer her the fingertip, which she latches on to, sucking voraciously while I attempt to pour the creamy substance into the bottle with the other hand. Inevitably, it spills and warm milk spreads across the drool-smeared ink on my once neat pages of data. I curse; the art of combining science and suckling surpasses my capacities. I grab the beloved towel to mop up, remembering at that moment to flip the switch which turns on red-tinted lights in the enclosure. The scene outside, bathed in the warm merlot glow of the red bulbs, is dreamlike. I stop to stare. Natasha, still attached to my little finger, doesn't. Barely discernible long-legged wolf silhouettes unfurl from shallow hollows of cool earth. The alpha male stands and bows, his rump arched high and front legs locked in a long stretch that curves his belly in a furry crescent, echoing the silver moon's shallow smile in the dawning night sky behind him. Scratching and scuffling noises fill the hut, followed by the canine meow-grumble of an early morning yawn.

As Natasha greedily gulps and suckles at the tiny bottle, I watch her pack moving around us outside the hut. I can make out the great pendulum swings of the yearling wolves' lowered tails sweeping wide suspended arcs as they crowd the alpha male in their morning greeting rites. The rest of the pack rises stiff-legged and dew-damp to join the yearlings, forming the canine version of a football huddle. I hear the snuffles and high-pitched whines, the hushed swish of hair rubbing hair as the wolves lean into each other and brush past one another like courting cats.

I have come to think of these greeting ceremonies as part of the grace of this wild creature's habits; called "rallies" by behaviorists, they precede most activities of consequence within a wolf pack: waking, hunting, leaving, returning, reunion of almost any sort. In this ancient and wild canine culture, ritual marks the intricacies of bonding and surviving. We humans are not unlike them—witness our snuggling, squirreling behavior with our lovers in the early dawn. Our kisses, hello and good-bye, our hugs and hovering and hand-holding, our calling out and coming out and letting go and leaving. The ritual of greeting and parting is woven through both canid and human species.

I had been guiltily fighting to stay awake for the last few hours as the wolves slept. Obviously I had failed. I am awed that even at six days old, blind and still deaf, this small creature demonstrated such sensitivity to the stirrings of her own kind and, thankfully, had awakened me. Was it the speaker vibrations? Scent? I don't know, but I'm relieved that the wolves are up, putting an end to the monotonous waiting. Throughout most of my watch the wolves had been inactive, making the night's long hours stretch endlessly. As I tumble into the day I can't help but mimic their languorous stretching and yawning, settling back in at the observation table, Natasha now in a sling hung from my shoulder, to record what I see and wonder at what I don't.

I am a college student, recently arrived at this wolf research facility to complete my undergraduate thesis. This part of my job is to record the interactions and individual activities of the different pack members on an ethogram, essentially a catalog of behaviors detailed enough to record interesting behavioral anomalies and specific individual interactions between the wolves. My low student standing assures me the graveyard observation shift. Although the hours are exhausting, I love the early morning solitude. Watching the wolves awaken and play in the predawn light, courting and tackling each other, makes this the premier observation period.

All that I had neatly planned for my research thesis had already dissolved in the weeks preceding this dawn vigil. I had arrived from Kalamazoo College less than a month before, twenty-one years old, a crisp-cornered research study in hand and an enchantment with wolves that rivaled that of the most ardent of animal lover. The focus of my research project was supposed to have been the pack's alpha female, an eight-year-old snowy white wolf named Cassie. My first lesson in sanguinary wolf society had been delivered when the pack had, without warning, fatally attacked Cassie, their uncontested leader of nearly a decade. My doe-eyed idealism about peaceable wolves, along with my meticulously planned research design, was eviscerated that day with Cassie and the six unborn puppies she carried, in the aptly named midwestern village of Battleground, Indiana.

It happened in the early afternoon of April 3, 1980—the wolves were milling about and agitated, about to be fed. On that particular morning Tom Huffman, the groundskeeper and on-site photographer, had dragged the carcass of a road-killed deer into the enclosure holding the pack. The usual snarls and snaps and yelps ensued as the lower-ranking wolves tried to persuade the alpha animals to share the bounty. Tensions were high anyway because Cassie was about to whelp, and the pack sensed the change in her behavior. The birth of pups often creates a void in leadership and a temporary destabilization of the social order within a pack.

In spite of the unpredictable nature of the whelping period, what came next was a shock to everyone, especially to Dr. Erich Klinghammer, the founder and director of Wolf Park, and Pat Goodman, the park's head research associate, both of whom had been observing the pack for nearly eight years and had not detected any weakening in Cassie's authority. Cassie approached her daughter, Alexa, a slender fine-boned wolf who was the lowest-ranking female in the pack, while she was tearing at a deer hock. Alexa, who normally would have submitted, was cornered against the back fence and, in a desperate act of self-defense, lunged back at Cassie. An explosion of canine fur and teeth and growls ensued, leaving Alexa with a good hold on her mother, who, uncharacteristically, yelped in response to the bite.

Perhaps it was hearing a yelp from their invincible leader, or perhaps the tension was so great that any event could have triggered the brawl that ensued—no one knows why, but in a split second the pack erupted in a gang attack on their unchallenged leader of eight years. Two minutes later Cassie was left barely breathing and paralyzed from a spinal bite. She was euthanized by the grief-stricken staff later that day.

Cassie's death was the first of many humbling lessons in the wild's volatility and unpredictability I was to receive in the years to come, offered both from wild creatures and from my own domestic animal companions. My strutting into the lives of these wolves with a neatly designed study titled "Contribution and Interaction of Individuals from a Captive Wolf Pack with a Single Litter of Pups at Wolf Park, Battleground, Indiana, 1980" was mockable in light of the chaos that occurred at Wolf Park that spring. I learned that our assumptions, expectations, wisdom, and presumed knowledge are only a construct that allows us to believe we can both control and predict the nature of nature, when its essence is as fleeting and mysterious as life itself. That, in the end, was my lesson: honor and allow the mystery, love the questions and the otherness; it is from that wild unknown that any resolution to our environmental crisis must come.

The surprises didn't stop with Cassie's death. A few days later first Venus, the new alpha female, and then Alexa gave birth to pups. Oddly, no one had detected their pregnancies. Although it had occasionally happened in the wild when there was an abundant food supply, according to the literature in the early eighties, it was relatively rare for more than one female, even in captive wolf packs, to conceive at the same time.

The prevailing assumption was that, because of a wild pack's inability to support a large number of pups, a variety of factors operate to limit each pack to a single litter. No one really knew what specific mechanism translated into the de facto birth control, but several theories were put forth. One was that the alpha female's aggression toward other females throughout breeding season creates tremendous stress in the lower-ranking females and, although those subordinate wolves come into estrus and even might be bred, the significant stress they endure from harassment by the higher-ranking females acts to suppress conception.

Some researchers also speculated that the alpha female may produce pheromones that could prevent other females from coming into full estrus, thus limiting the possibility of pregnancy. None of those mechanisms functioned at Wolf Park in the spring of 1980, because three separate litters were conceived in the main pack that winter at Battleground's wolf reserve.

Events such as the breakdown of a social structure in captivity provide insight into why it is so difficult to justify keeping wild animals in captivity in order to study their behavior "so we can better protect them in the wild," which is the rhetoric used by many zoos and wild animal parks. Rarely is it appropriate to extrapolate what we witness in captive situations to the wild because behaviors are radically altered by the adaptations and stresses inherent in captivity. It would be much like putting a human child in solitary confinement, without social contact or nurturing, and assuming that the behavior exhibited under those circumstances represents the full spectrum of what it is to be human.

With two new litters of pups born to the main pack, it was indeed a fascinating time to be at Wolf Park. All the wolves were tremendously curious and interested in the puppies. The younger wolves, especially, found the infant newcomers irresistible. In the wild it is up to the mother to protect the pups until they are old enough to interact with the rest of the pack. Most of the pack members are reluctant to go too near the den site for fear of reprisal from the mother. But if she is a low-ranking female—rarely the case in the wild—she poses little threat to intruders and therefore is less able to defend her young.

Because of her low standing in the pack's hierarchy, Alexa, the female who had initiated the attack on Cassie, was virtually incapable of protecting her two puppies. When she was at last driven by thirst to leave the shallow burrow where she gave birth, a grizzled black yearling male named Faust immediately darted in and grabbed one of the infant pups. He carried the puppy around for a few minutes, then rolled over, nudging it toward his inguinal area as though some deep impulse to nurse struck him even without mammary or milk. Then Faust's brother Mephisto, driven by curiosity and playfulness, darted in to grab the new toy. The brothers played a brief game of tug-of-war and the day-old puppy died almost instantly from the trauma. Dr. Klinghammer was forced to go in and remove the other pup lest she meet the same fate as her unfortunate sibling.

When Dr. Klinghammer entered the observation hut I was sitting alone at the desk. Not one to waste words or offer explanation, he handed me the furry little bundle, smaller than my fist, with four words that would change my life: "You will raise her." He turned and left. After a few stunned, frozen moments my maternal instincts overcame my bewilderment, and I set out in search of Pat Goodman, den mother to us all, wolves and volunteers alike. She helped set me up with bottles and Esbilac, and taught me how to clean and care for the tiny canid.

Anyone who has ever tended orphaned creatures knows that there is a basic bonding that drives you to rise every few hours to bottle-feed and nurture a new being in the world, but right from the beginning my relationship with Natasha was different from those I had had with any of the other creatures I had raised or rescued, from baby birds to orphaned kittens. I had a nose for neediness, and my childhood mothering experiments ranged from taking care of abandoned puppies and bunnies to reptilian rescues of snakes and tadpoles. My experience with Natasha was entirely unlike any which preceded.

To say she was special or singular seems pathetically inadequate in describing the acuity and force with which she asserted her own identity right from the beginning.

For years I have tried to capture in words exactly how Natasha was different from my other animal wards. The clearest description I can offer is that she had an essence of "other," rather than underling. I felt accompanied rather than ascendant. Even as I carried her around in a sling against my belly, bottle-fed her, stimulated her with a damp cloth to urinate and defecate as her mother's tongue would have done, and slept with her curled against me, even in the face of her utter vulnerability and dependence, I did not feel like her mother, but rather like her companion. It is difficult to articulate how such a tiny being was capable of conveying such an independent presence, but it was distinctive and determinate in the nature of our relationship.

I kept notes on her as she grew; when I sat eyeing her and recording comments in my journal, I felt she was doing the same to me. No paper, no ink, but an observation and record so indelible and accurate that our entire race might be re-created from this creature's perception. It was the first time I felt the utter limitations of language, and the first time I truly began to face and fathom the capacity of another species.

The emotion associated with this recognition is even more difficult to describe. It is a breathless sensation, as though your brain were gasping, sucking in an "insight" like thirst gulps water. It is as though something is yawning inside you and your entire body needs to expand to accommodate "seeing" in a different dimension. One can feel one's mind stretching to encompass and absorb the recognition, the idea of such a thing—of such an otherness. This creature is simultaneously different and familiar. She is of her own nature and yet I recognize my own impulses in her actions. I see reflected in her my hungers and fears, my curiosity and contentment—through her I begin to fathom an ancient relationship with the wild. My strength, for this moment, is greater than hers. Nonetheless, her senses surpass mine. Her diminutive presence connects me, includes me, and I recognize that I am, like her, merely a pulse in the rhythm of the world.

Inevitably one's sense of stature and importance is diminished in such exercises, and yet simultaneously one is engulfed by a sense of belonging, of living a purpose of incalculable possibility. That is how "recognizing" Natasha made me feel, that is what she forced me to fathom—animal as other, not underling. With this recognition came a sense of communion and belonging, an emotion which made me see how exiled I had felt, cornered by an unconscious belief in a typically Western, hierarchical universe. Somehow, guided by fate and serendipity, I had stumbled upon my place in what poets called "the family of things."

As a part of my thesis at Wolf Park I watched the pack for eight to ten hours a day and helped to socialize several litters of pups. But before any of the other puppies were removed from the pack for socialization, Natasha and I spent long hours in the observation hut, surrounded by the movement and murmurs of the pack filtering in through the microphones. I'd sit with my chin on the table where she was curled, nose to nose, looking into her eyes, and hum to her the first song I ever learned as a child, Dr. Dolittle's "If we could talk to the animals, learn their languages. . . ."

These are the moments when the nature of childhood seeps into the most profound aspects of our adult lives. My formative years were spent among animals and my development was facilitated, like that of many children, by echoing and mimicking the creatures that roamed the terrain of my youth. Animals profoundly influenced who I would become.

When the other litters of puppies from various pairs and packs at the park reached the age where they required human socialization—so they could be handled as adult wolves by veterinarians and the staff—they joined Natasha and me. I bottle-fed them all and slept on a mattress on the floor with them, sometimes with puppies burrowed everywhere, under my armpits and chin, in the crook of my elbow and behind my knee, in the arch of my foot and the small of my back. For a three-month period I was immersed in wolf society, sleeping, feeding, observing, and nurturing these wolves and their pups.

Paradoxically, it was the privilege and opportunity afforded me by the wolves' captivity at Wolf Park that led me to realize the degree to which their lives had been compromised by that captivity. As I watched and lived with these wolves hour after hour, day after day, a cognizance of *what* I was watching (and being watched by) began to slowly infiltrate my consciousness. And as I began to fathom the extraordinary sentient capacity of these animals, their intelligence, imagination, sensitivity, and sophistication, the compromise implicit in their captivity became nearly unbearable for me. This feeling was particularly acute with regard to Natasha, with whom I had deeply bonded.

Natasha's sacrifice was absolute, as is the sacrifice of all wild things caged for the amusement or education of humans. Although Natasha was captive, her whole being retained the resonance of the wild. In her pacing and her panting, in her own bittersweet way she taught me of another world, another existence, in which the animals spoke through their roaming and their roaring, their howling and their prowling. Through the sheer force of her being, her autonomy and will, through her *otherness* Natasha began to reveal a story. It was the story of the loss of wildness in our world, and its truth was inescapably affirmed by the circumstances of her life in captivity.

Natasha, like most captive-born wolves, was destined for a life behind chain-link fences, both because she had been habituated to humans and because she had not received the necessary stimulus and training in her formative months for survival in the wild. At the same time, like most wild creatures raised in captivity, she would never be "tame" in the sense that a dog or cat is tame. She was wild by nature (and by genetics) and no veneer of domestication would ever change that—she would never be, nor want to be, a dog. She was a wild thing and from the very beginning she hated confinement.

She was always the first to try to escape. As an infant she gnawed at the cardboard box which held her; as she got older she chewed on the chain-link fencing until her gums were bloodied; she was the first to charge a gate or a door if it was slightly ajar, or to attempt scaling a confinement wall. I suspect she knew right from the beginning that these walls meant death to her. In the end she was right, and because of that I will be forever haunted by wild things held captive.

I had always assumed that Natasha would grow up and grow old among her littermates and the pack, a life that fell unspeakably short of a wild existence, but was superior to most captive circumstances. However, toward the end of my thesis work Erich informed me of the decision to send Natasha, along with several other pups I had socialized, to a research facility in North Dakota. His announcement that Natasha would be taken not only from me but from a life in the relative comfort of Wolf Park was conveyed in the same clipped and emotionless tone he used when she was delivered to me. This was not because he was a cruel or unfeeling man. In fact, I suspect quite the opposite. His brusqueness served to stiffen his resolve in the face of hard decisions, of having to find his way between his deep love for these creatures and the considerable demands of sustaining a captive research facility.

The topic of reproduction presents a conundrum for the majority of captive animal facilities. Most claim that reproduction and the behavior associated with whelping and raising young are important to researching and observing behavior. (Whether the facility is doing valid research, and how valuable that research might be to the general knowledge about the species, is an entirely different question.) Captive facilities relish the presence of baby animals. Although most administrators are reluctant to state it directly, it is nearly universally true that, from a marketing standpoint, the presence of baby animals provides a key attraction for the paying and donating public, which is the primary source of income for most captive animal facilities.

The administrators of many of these facilities view the presence of baby animals as a means of survival. The problem is that the captive facilities can't support the exponential increase in animal numbers that new litters generate every year. Administrators are forced to "place" some of the young from each litter with other start-up captive facilities, animal parks, or zoos. Each of those facilities, in turn, need baby animals to enable and justify their own existence, and the cycle perpetuates itself. Breeding continues year after year and the number of wild creatures destined to lives in captivity continues to increase. In the case of wolves alone, we have thousands held in captive facilities, a very small number of which are really used for valid research, education, or conservation purposes.

To say I railed against Erich's decision to send Natasha away would be an understatement, but my pleading and begging fell on deaf ears. I was a mere intern; hundreds had preceded me and as many would follow after I left. Many of them had probably fallen "in love" with pups they had helped raise, and I'm sure many had felt invested in the future of their wards. Erich was resolute. The decision had been made.

I was crazed with pain. I contemplated kidnapping Natasha, or turning all the wolves loose in the hope she might find her way among them. I imagined all kinds of escapes and schemes and possibilities, but in the end I submitted. There are few things I regret in life, but not finding a better future for Natasha is one of them. I wish I had been more radical, more fierce, more insistent. Even though I had no jurisdiction, legal right, or ownership, I wish I had not acquiesced. But I did. In the end Erich's will prevailed.

The prospect of Natasha's spirit, her being, her essence behind chained walls or concrete, without even pack mates to soften the monotony, filled me with despair. In the heart of that despair I resolved that I would find a way to make up to her species what I had failed to do for her.

Only in the last dark weeks before Natasha was taken away from Wolf Park would a shimmering possibility arise as to how I might act on that resolve. One afternoon I was sitting in the hut on observation duty, watching the pack, when a young biologist named John Weaver arrived from Wyoming. He had come to consult Dr. Klinghammer about behavioral issues related to an effort, just beginning to gain momentum, to restore wolves to Yellowstone National Park. As chance would have it, Dr. Klinghammer chose to hold his discussion with Weaver in the observation hut during my watch. Weaver had just finished his master's research on the historical presence of wolves in the Yellowstone area, and felt passionately about the injustice and insanity of their extermination sixty years before. There was a movement afoot to restore the predator to the park, and he was quickly becoming one of its driving forces.

With Natasha, then several months old, curled on my lap, I listened intently to Weaver and Klinghammer's discussion. The mention of Yellowstone had aroused my interest immediately, so strong had been my response to the place nearly two years earlier when I had first visited it. As I stroked Natasha an idea began to form. As Weaver was leaving I shyly approached him to express interest and enthusiasm for his work, and asked if I might get involved once I graduated. He gave me his address and encouraged me to write him when I finished my degree.

It was a fortuitous meeting because years later Weaver would turn out to be my first mentor on the Yellowstone wolf project. Although rarely credited, he really provided the spark that ultimately got the bureaucratic fires burning on the restoration of wolves to Yellowstone. Not long after Weaver's departure, another young biologist named Timm Kaminski, an associate of Weaver's who was in the process of pursuing his master's research on wolves in the West, came to visit Wolf Park. He, too, urged me to contact them after I had finished college.

Just before I left Wolf Park an envoy, a young woman, arrived and Natasha and several other puppies from that year's litters were loaded into kennels for the trip to North Dakota. I remember I could hardly speak to her. I felt a vengeful helplessness, a hatred and despondency so dark and overwhelming that I just stood by, paralyzed. I wish desperately I had fought harder, refused to turn her over, done anything but what I did—surrendered. I let Natasha go.

The car pulled out into the dry dirt lane lined with budding poplars and dust-covered shrubs. I should have blocked it, I should have pounded on the car, chained myself to the gate. Instead I ran to a favorite perch on a hill overlooking the enclosure and watched the car disappear into the wavy mirage of the horizon. I turned back to the pack, swallowing my sobs, and howled. Then an uncommon thing happened. Despite the heat of midday, a period when the wolves hardly moved, let alone howled, that day they joined in. Each member of the main pack and many of the separated pairs, one by one, called out in the long, graceful wail that is the code of their species. Their own had been taken. I had no doubt they knew.

The car disappeared in the distance, the searing sun glinting on chrome through a haze of lingering dust. All I had in the echoing emptiness of Natasha's departure was hope, and from that came a promise—a young girl's promise, made innocently and idealistically out of a need to make sense of a loved one's suffering, and, perhaps, to alleviate my own. I promised Natasha that I would do something that would give back in some small way what we had so wantonly taken from her and her wild ancestors, that I would fight for wolves in the wild. Although I didn't know it at the time, making that promise set the course for the next two decades of my life. From my hillside overlook I vowed to her, *"You will not be forgotten, little one, what you have taught me will make a difference. I promise you it will make a difference."*

Three

To tell the story . . . is to let the place itself speak through the telling.

DAVID ABRAMS, *Places of the Wild*

I T WAS THE spring of 1978, two years before my experience at Wolf Park. I had just finished my first year of college, and I set out to see the West with a backpack, sleeping bag, pair of binoculars, bird book, virtually no money, and a case of wanderlust as ripe and hungry as a fine, dark wine. It was a rather feral phase in my life; all I needed I carried on my back, and I was ready to let the winds of fate unfurl the future. I left Michigan hitchhiking with a friend, Chris Clark, an ardent bird-watcher and fellow student, headed for some unknown destination on the Pacific coast. Our plan, if we had one, was to search for western birds and summer jobs. The trip's only imperative was that we see Yellowstone National Park on the way.

On a late spring evening on the second or third day of our trip westward, Chris and I were dropped off in the cradle of the Teton Mountain Range. According to our map, the location was in the southern region of the Greater Yellowstone Ecosystem. It was nearing nightfall so we decided to camp. We hiked up off the road through the dusk-blessed winking of aspen stands and lush grasses woven with the magenta pink of blossoming fireweed. The scoured scent of fresh sage and the pressing cool of the impending dark enveloped us as we picked our way up a steep slope overlooking the valley. We fell silent when we turned to find the last sliver of a fiery sun sinking behind the cathedral-lit peaks that spanned the western horizon. That night we set up camp illegally, unbeknownst to us, just within the northern boundary of Grand Teton National Park. I had no way of knowing that a few years hence destiny's thread would loop around, rooting my life in this landscape. This valley called Jackson Hole, where the mountains leaned against a dusky blue sky, would become my home and the place from which I would work for nearly fourteen years in an effort to fulfill a promise to an animal I loved.

We arose the next morning to the twittering of tanagers and pine siskins. Savannah sparrows hopped about the dew-covered balsam root that had created a saffron blanket upon which our sleeping bags were spread. An opalescent dawn melted over the Gros Ventre mountains to the east of us, bathing the Tetons to the west in a blushing alpenglow, nudging us back down the hillside to the road. Our first ride that morning was a rusted, mustard-colored pickup truck from Arkansas. We clambered into the back, propping our packs as backrests, and headed north for what was to be my first encounter with the most enchanted land on earth—Yellowstone National Park. It was early spring and a delicious, sun-sparkled morning. Thankfully, there were very few cars around to disturb the park's serenity. It was a marvelous blessing that our driver was as eager and wide-eyed as we were and willing to stop and even explore any vista, falls, riverbank, geyser basin, soaring bird, or wildlife sighting that beckoned us. Never have I been so taken with the sheer power and potency of a place as I was upon first seeing Yellowstone.

From the southern entrance of the park the road wound through dense needle-green tunnels of subalpine fir and lodgepole pines, the trunks as straight and seamless as river reeds. We passed by the Lewis River Canyon, a dramatic gorge through which the Lewis River (named for Meriwether Lewis, cocaptain of the Lewis and Clark expedition) cuts on its way to join the Snake River to the south. The splintered morning light spread to a warm brightness as the road opened up, paralleling the cloudless calm of Lewis Lake's eastern shore. As we moved into the park's interior, the shadowed dense forests gave way to vast meadows of golden sedges and willow-bordered marshes harboring a mélange of birds. My notes list seeing, in the span of a few hours, loons, mergansers, sandhill cranes, marsh hawks, bald eagles, pelicans, and swans.

Roaming the mysterious steaming geyser basins was like stepping through a secret passage into some kind of primordial vision. Hot springs bubbled and frothed, a steamy fog caressed our faces and hands, enveloping us in an ethereal wonderland. The mist would one minute obscure everything in an eddy of vapory veils and then suddenly shift to reveal translucent turquoise and emerald green pools that looked like the secret spas of the gods. Tiny ocher, tangerine, copper, and terra-cotta rivulets seeped from the edges of the pools, creating a collage of algae gardens that spread in lovely swirls throughout the basin.

Bear, moose, bison, mule deer, antelope, and coyote appeared along the meadows and hillsides, in willow stands and sage flats, as though they were on a secret march to the Ark. Bighorn sheep emerged like soldiers from the craggy camouflage of their habitat, staring intently at our mustard yellow truck. I'd never before encountered such a diversity and abundance of wildlife. Even the hillsides, charred from flash wildfires, offered a hushed beauty ruffled only by the flashing red of a hairy woodpecker or the sudden orange of a startled flicker, its dipping flight tracing a fineness of line through the stark trunks as beautiful and delicate as Japanese calligraphy.

Discovering my nation's first national park was an experience both visceral and provocative. Like so many visitors, I was overcome by the scale and yet drawn into the intimate terrain of this legendary land. The names of places in the park rang like word chimes for me: Absaroka, Gibbon, Shoshone, Harlequin, Tanager, Obsidian, Bannock—lovely words that would linger on the tongue just as the grand vistas and piercing clarity of the air would settle in one's mind.

The driver indulged me in one other way that first day in Yellowstone: he would pull over when we came to the thick broad meadows that defined much of the inner landscape of the park. Huge herds of elk grazed, oblivious to onlookers, their tannin coats shimmering in the spring sun. There, perched on the pickup bed with my binoculars, I would count the elk, evoking memories of childhood meadows. The mantra of numbers was a way of acknowledging each animal, the act of counting giving order and familiarity to this place and its unfathomable abundance of creatures. The counting brought the size of these elk herds into focus—there were literally thousands! Chris and I were amazed by their docility and proximity to the road, given the lack of cover. Indeed, these elk had been habituated to cars and humans for many decades, and those that stayed within the park had never been hunted by man. But what we didn't know was that for over sixty years these Yellowstone elk had been without their primary predator, the wolf.

It was not until two years later, while doing my senior thesis, that I learned Yellowstone still had every plant and animal species that was present when Europeans hit the shores of North America with the exception of one—the wolf. It is biologically evident that the absence of a keystone species like the wolf could have a significant effect on the intricate interworkings of a pristine ecosystem. How the wolf's absence affected these elk, or the myriad of other species, would become a question central to my work in the years to come. Right then, no one really knew. Researchers had pondered the question for several decades, and would continue to do so for several more.

The intense pride and protectiveness that I felt in recognizing the foresight of my grandparent's generation in protecting the Yellowstone area made me realize I was for the first time experiencing a place, a wild place, that my nation held sacred. Bill Moyers describes a sacred place as a landscape where we might feel the presence of all creation, sensing a belonging to something ancient and yet very much alive. Paul Shepard calls the intuition that we experience in a wild place "the deep current of pre-comprehension running silently beneath our spoken thoughts."

In some ways it is odd that a road trip though Yellowstone provided my first conscious experience of the wild. Most people on their first encounter with Yellowstone today find a paved, crowded, bumper-to-bumper parade of worming recreational vehicles and overweight, camera-loaded tourists. It can be that. But if one steps off the road, even a few hundred feet, and listens, there is a calm to the land, a certain wild rhythm that is closer to the surface than in most places. Geysers froth and spew, mud pots bubble and blink, elk bugle, bison grunt, antelope snort, coyotes howl—the language underneath our language becomes audible, like silence singing.

Yellowstone National Park is the heart of what many Americans think of as the wild. The movement of creature and creek, hawk and hardwood, water and wilderness become the sound of our breathing, the echo of what we already know but have largely forgotten.

Four

❖ ❖ ❖

*We humans fear the beast within the wolf because
we do not understand the beast within ourselves.*

GERALD HAUSMAN, *Turtle Island Alphabet*

For MILLENNIA WOLVES had been abundant throughout the area now defined as Yellowstone National Park and the surrounding states of Wyoming, Montana, and Idaho. But in the span of less than fifty years man had systematically, consciously, intentionally killed every wolf in the West, including those within park boundaries. The haunting question is— why? The scope of the killing, the method, the madness, leaves some of us troubled and shamed even today. Hundreds of thousands of wolves were killed—some in the name of protecting livestock, some for their pelts, some because we believed it was our inalienable right, and some just out of cold, hard vengeance and cruelty, a cruelty we so often attribute to the wolf.

With the massive movement west in the mid-1800s, colonizers were brought into intimate contact with vast herds of game animals, which they promptly decimated. In particular, a whole economy emerged around the harvesting of bison hides and tongues, providing an extremely lucrative trade for skilled hunters. Records indicate that between 1850 and 1880 over 75 million buffalo were killed, the majority of them for their hides. The sudden increase in available buffalo carcasses, usually missing only hide and tongue—free protein—led to an explosion in predator numbers. And as the huge game herds disappeared, virtually overnight, they were replaced by homesteading ranchers and domestic livestock. In the absence of their natural prey, wolves quite naturally shifted to killing cattle and sheep in order to survive. Also quite naturally, the homesteaders responded to livestock depredations by initiating a bounty system, and thus began the war on predators. Meanwhile, because of their robust population and the relative scarcity of other wildlife (and the incentive of the bounties), wolves also became a favorite target for trappers—an easy target, because of the effectiveness and efficiency of poisons. A single carcass laced with strychnine could easily wipe out a whole pack, not to mention large numbers of eagles, foxes, coyotes, and any other scavengers that might be in the area.

The first wave of wolf killing took place in the 1870s. Historical records indicate a take of 100,000 wolves a year between 1870 and 1877 in the state of Montana alone. Man's effectiveness at wiping out such immense native wildlife populations in short periods of time is truly shocking. Our virtual extermination of the bison and the wolf, in particular, is sadly reminiscent of the way in which we drove to extinction the passenger pigeons whose vast flocks once darkened the skies on their migratory routes as bison had the western plains.

On March 1, 1872, Congress established Yellowstone National Park, ordering the Department of the Interior to "provide for the preservation . . . of all timber, mineral deposits, natural curiosities, or wonders within said park . . . in their natural condition . . . and to prevent wanton destruction of fish and game." Unfortunately, in the view of early managers wolves were not "game," and they threatened the preservation of "game"; therefore they were poisoned, trapped, and shot with a vengeance even within park boundaries where there was a mandate for protection. By the early 1900s, wolves had almost been eliminated from Yellowstone. Then, between 1914 and 1926, we finished the job. In that time span 136 wolves were killed, including 80 pups. The wolf was gone.

The history of wolves in the West (and elsewhere—the story repeats itself almost anywhere "civilized" man and wolf have overlapped) provides a glimpse into our history of ambivalence toward the wild. Greed and the desire for conquest are clearly evident in our early treatment of wolves, but, tellingly, that treatment also exposes our deepest fear—*the dread of the uncon-*

trolled. With Manifest Destiny and the westward movement of settlers came the assumed right to control and dominate, and with that attitude came the predator wars. Predator control in the late 1800s and early 1900s was more than dealing with a nuisance animal that occasionally killed livestock and competed with man; it was a symbolic war. The wolf was a cultural symbol for wild, untamable, uncontrolled nature.

The pattern of killing wolves in the West followed that of the elimination of predators throughout most of the rest of the continent with one notable difference. Viciousness and malice saturated the wolf extermination efforts in the West, which emphasized not so much the killing as the conquering of the creature. Perhaps as relevant as the killing itself, the methods of extermination reveal a great deal about our values and our attitudes toward wolves and the wild.

Our forefathers didn't *just* want to control wolves, they wanted to conquer them. They didn't *just* kill wolves, they tortured them. They lassoed animals and tore them apart by their limbs, they wired their jaws shut and left them to starve, they doused them with gasoline and ignited them.

Perhaps our method does betray the secret of our madness. What hunger did torture satisfy that a bullet would not? What fear was soothed or vengeance realized by the suffering of these animals that a painless death could not have accomplished? What is it in ourselves that we had to kill in the wolf? The answer is, of course, wildness. And even though we killed the wolf, every last one of them in the West, we never extinguished the wild—we only became more deeply alienated from it. In the panic of our alienation we attempted to control what we feared; when we couldn't control it we tried to extinguish it. But the wild is not controllable, or even extinguishable, so inextricably is it bound to the force of life itself. It flickers on—without us, within us, and between us—its nature buried in the mystery of our origins.

It is far too easy to assume that this behavior, these barbaric acts, could have been committed only by our ignorant predecessors, that, given our enlightened ecological understanding, such things could never happen in the twenty-first century. The troubling truth is, of course, that they do. Animals, particularly predators, continue to be killed, some brutally. In fact we spend over half a million of our tax dollars annually to rid ourselves of an estimated one-and-a-half million "nuisance" animals nationwide, and a great deal of this killing takes place on our public lands. Our techniques include poisoning, trapping, snaring, denning, and aerial gunning. Depending on how they are utilized, any of these methods can be extremely cruel and involve terrible suffering. They can also result in the loss of many nontarget species (what the military likes to call "collateral damage").

Inevitably, our first response to this level of historical and current carnage is to assume it is someone else's evil doing. We retreat into the familiar "us versus them" construct and condemn the act, whether it be the torturing of lab animals or the poisoning of thousands of coyotes on western lands, with the assumption that evil people (the "them" part of the blame equation) are responsible for the savagery.

If we want to explore what's behind the extinctions we have caused, or our frightening descent toward environmental collapse, we must start by examining this dark side of human nature, whether it relates to our treatment of animals, the destruction of wild places, or the atrocities of war. We need to recognize that we are *all* capable of this kind of behavior, that within each of us lies the capacity to be both destructive and creative, good and bad, saint and sinner, lover and liar. The darkness and rage that drove us to torture and exterminate wolves in such hideous ways is part of the dark wildness present in each of our hearts, even today. Until we each own and embrace that truth with compassion for our own terrors and failings we will continue, generation after generation, to project it onto innocent animals, or our ever-present enemies, be they members of a different race, religion, sex, or species.

> Goodness will reign in the world not when it triumphs over evil, but when our love of goodness ceases to express itself in terms of triumph over evil. Peace [and environmental restoration] if it comes, will not be made by people who have rendered themselves into saints, but by people who have humbly accepted their condition as sinners.

Perhaps we can explore the true origin of the word *wild* and its meaning in our lives by slashing through the tangled etymology of the word itself, admittedly a task that even the experts find "bewildering." (I use that word not as a pun, but as an example of the many ways the idea of wildness lurks in our language, rarely contemplated or discussed.) A few have, however, cleared the way into the heart of wildness.

Henry David Thoreau was one of the first to ponder the complexities of the meaning of wildness in his prodigious nineteenth-century collection of essays and journals, followed in the twentieth century by Gary Snyder and Jack Turner, in their books, respectively, *The Practice of the Wild* and *The Abstract Wild.* Snyder's describes the word's etymology as follows:

> The word *wild* is like a gray fox trotting off through the forest, ducking behind bushes, going in and out of sight. Up close, first glance, it is "wild"—then farther into the woods next glance it's "wyld" and it recedes via Old Norse *villr* and Old Teutonic *wilthijaz* into a faint and pre-Teutonic word *ghweltijos* which means still, wild and maybe wooded (*wald*) and lurks back there with possible connections to *will,* to Latin *silva* (forest, sauvage) and to the Indo-European root *ghwer,* base of Latin *ferus* (feral, fierce . . .).

Both Snyder and Turner frequently refer to Thoreau's use of "wildness" and its connection to "will," or "self-willed." Inherent in the core meaning of wildness are the notions of autonomy, freedom, and self-determination. However, most definitions reach far beyond the idea of an individual's experience to encompass the theory of a system that is self-informing and self-organizing.

"Wildness" is most often used to describe wilderness, as innocence might describe childhood. Too often "wildness" is a glib and artificial catchall term for the rather glib and artificial emotion associated with packaged "wild" scenery and animals, whether in a zoo, on a television show, or in a glossy conservation magazine. Sometimes people don't even differentiate between wildness and wilderness at all, and the words are even transposed, as is often done with Thoreau's declaration "In *wildness* is the preservation of the world."

Snyder notes that "wild" is defined in most dictionaries by what it is not. For example, in the *Oxford English Dictionary,* wild is not tame, not cultivated, not civilized, not restrained or subordinate. What it *is* is left for us to arrive at as we chip away at what it is not, in a process not unlike that of chiseling a figure from marble. It is difficult to capture the quality of something by describing its attributes rather than its essence; the result is similar to a description of a personality rather than a person.

The word "wilderness" need not be limited to describing a place or an experience; it can be used to capture a more elusive idea, as for example, in the phrase "the wilderness of the soul." "Wildness" is sometimes used to describe the fierce, elemental spirit that lives in us, underneath our civilized facades (which is not to imply that its meaning is "crude" or "primitive," but rather that it refers to a part of us that remains undomesticated or unaltered from our original state).

Some believe the wild is only accessible when one is teetering on the brink of survival, danger and adrenaline flushing away any flickerings of self-consciousness. I disagree. Experiencing the wild does not require conquest or challenge. Pitting one's wits and brawn *against* mountain, river, or creature is an approach that can separate rather than integrate. I believe experiencing the wild is a process of allowing our senses to infiltrate, not overwhelm, the self. Our sense of self does not disappear, for we, too, are of the wild; it is simply intermingled with a sensibility that is larger than we are, creating a vivid alertness and attentiveness. I think of it as being breathed by the world. Certainly, recognizing the wild involves a certain relinquishing of control, which is why so many believe we must renounce the symbols of control to experience it. I believe it is not so much the leaving as the letting go. We can experience wildness as truly through being vividly conscious during sex or a symphony as we can by venturing to the most remote regions of the planet. Wildness resides in us, around us, and between us.

We haven't killed the wild, but we have, over time, successfully repressed our consciousness of how important it is to us, buried it like a distant but seminal childhood experience. Its presence still expresses itself in every element of our being, however—our longings, rages, melancholies, pathologies, and especially our dreams. Its repression only strengthens its power to haunt us. James Hillman wrote, "Our dreams recover what the world forgets."

We still hunger for the wild as we do for our fleeting childhoods. The longing is expressed in our obsession with Native American traditions: we build our sweat lodges and clutch our animal fetishes, we hang our dream catchers. We watch our nostalgic movies. We buy exotic pets, and own wolf hybrids and wear T-shirts with our favorite animals painted on them. We mount antlers and pelts and game trophies on our walls. We are reaching for something representative of the wild that we fear is slipping away, and we think if we mount it or wear it or own it we will embody it. Because we intuitively know, as Gary Snyder wrote, "A world without wildness is a world beyond its capacity to heal."

It is not that our ability to experience wildness has been lost, but rather that it has been buried and unrealized in a world in which our senses have been cauterized by the constant din of industry and entertainment. The reciprocity between wild nature and the wild in our selves, between knowledge of the wild and knowledge of the self, still exists but lies dormant. It is *this* wild that Natasha had revealed to me, a wild she both possessed and reflected. My experience with her created a context for me to discover what already existed.

An Ethiopian proverb says, "He who conceals his disease cannot be cured." To heal we must first learn the nature of our wounds. Again, we can find clues in the origins of words. The linguistic root of *health* is associated with *whole*. To be whole we need to embrace the light and the dark elements of who we are rather than create an enemy to bear our rejected enmity. Jung referred to it as holding the tension of the opposites—acknowledging the shadow as integral to the light, or the evil (even unenacted) as accompanying the good. Honoring both dimensions may not eliminate the darkness we all fear within ourselves, or dissolve the shadow that has darkened our troubled planet, but it can change our relationship with that darkness. Acceptance can give rise to compassion, both for ourselves and our "others."

For centuries our search for wholeness has led us back to the animals, to our origins, to our history. Something mysterious happens when we look into the eyes of an animal, whether it be a panther or a poodle—we see something familiar looking back. Ourselves? Yes, but we also see an "other." We see something that is in us and yet without us, something we recognize and yet is unfamiliar, something we fear but for which we long. We see the wild. The animals have always been a part of our survival and healing, and we, sometimes, theirs. At a time when our relationship to land and soil and place has been diminished, we still turn to our animals, domestic and wild, as a conduit to healing. And through our animals—those of our childhood, those in our homes, and those in the wild—we can begin to find our way back to being whole.

Five

Expose a child to a particular environment at his susceptible time and he will perceive in the shapes of that environment until he dies.

WALLACE STEGNER, *Wolf Willow*

I'VE ALWAYS WONDERED what the transition must have been like for my mother when she went from a busy Detroit social life in the forties and fifties to the isolated existence of young motherhood in Thunder Bay State Forest. My mamma was a great beauty in her day. She had perfect fair skin with just a sprinkling of freckles that matched her auburn waves of hair. Her blue eyes hinted toward green or lavender, depending on the sometimes mercurial moods my daddy attributed to her redhead lineage. Her wrists and her waist, even after bearing two babies, had the slender lines of the fine-boned deer we counted.

She has always claimed that she was too busy tending her beloved babies to miss the social whirl of the big city. I can't imagine how she managed, especially when I study the pictures of my sister and me as infants and toddlers, knowing that our enviable wardrobes, from the soft white flannel diapers to the "twin" princess-waisted chiffon and lace dresses with matching bonnets, immaculately fitted and pressed, were all hand sewn. Only our little boots were from a mail-order catalog. Everything in our layette was hand stitched—from the terry-cloth bibs to the delicately flowered crib sheets—

and Mamma had to hand wash it all, feeding our clothes through one of those hand-cranked wringers to mush the water out. She hung the laundry on a line near the back door of the cottage, a task she had to accomplish while keeping a close eye on the two of us scrambling, quick as weasels, every which way. Apparently snakes were fond of settling on the sun-warmed cement steps going up to the cottage. Not just a few, but lots of them, and almost every warm day. In fact the only thing I ever heard my mama complain about were those snakes and the tiny black beetles that loved to congregate on our snowy white flannel diapers drying on the line. The beetles were a mere nuisance. The snakes, however, provoked Mamma's ire. She kept a six-foot ice spud near the end of the clothesline with which she would dispatch the reptilian threats to her babies in typical redheaded fashion.

I might never have known about my mother's glamorous city life had it not been for the discovery of a cedar trunk containing Mamma's city clothes. When we were a little older that trunk kept my sister and me entertained with dress-up games for hours. We would stagger about in the skin-soft high heeled pumps and ankle-strapped toeless platform shoes my mother wore "before she was married." There was a bustle-backed tapered black crepe dress and a deep aqua-green silk shift that changed colors like sunlight on water. A faint sweet perfume hung on the finely tailored wool suits with labels from Saks Fifth Avenue and Hughes and Hatches. I would wind my braids under the fur-trimmed pillbox hat and, with a long creamy cape slung around my shoulders, pretend I was floating across the ballroom, twirling and dipping, probably looking more like a courting whooping crane than a ballroom dancer. Sometimes my mamma would tell us stories about dancing the cha-cha and jitterbug to Woody Herman and Glenn Miller at the Greystone Ballroom on Woodward or the Vanity Ballroom on Grand River. After days spent in swamps catching toads and snakes I would go to sleep dreaming of sparkling city lights and big band melodies melting like caramel in a musical swirl.

In 1960 my brother Craig, who was to become my inseparable comrade, was born and we moved from the cottage into a small farmhouse on the border of the forest. My mother stopped counting deer in the meadows, but still the animals came, the gauzy ghosts of my childhood, bringing my second distinct memory. My daddy carried me out into a splintering cold moonlit winter night to show me a snowy owl perched in a scrub oak near our barn. I remember the yellow eyes, iridescent in the moonlight, the fawnlike spots falling down the back of the owl like ashen snowflakes, and how startled I was when it launched forward off the branch, its huge sheltering wings wrapping around the air like my daddy's arms around me. I shivered and leaned into the broadness of my father's chest and he whispered that this would be an occasion I would remember. And I did. A few years later it was under that owl tree that Sambo's first litter of kittens were buried.

Sambo, properly Black Sambo, was a lean and worldly female calico cat. She appeared in our yard approximately an hour after our family physician, Doc Rousseau, brought me a young male cat for my fifth birthday. I unimaginatively christened him "Peter Pan." There was only one problem that marred the introduction of feline felicity to my childhood menagerie—my father was terribly allergic to cats—or so I was told. I figured the doc knew it, too, but I surmised that allergies, in Doc Rousseau's mind, were insignificant in the face of a young child's yearnings and the doc's own predicament of having a huge litter of kittens in his den at home. The doc enjoyed certain privileges with my family, given that he took care of our sick rabbits and chickens as well as ailing family members. Sambo and Pan got on well and quickly, and it wasn't long before they had a batch of kittens, born under the chicken plucker in our pump house.

The pump house was a barn-shaped building with whitewashed adobelike walls and an avocado green roof made of asphalt tiles. It was filled with old machinery and dusty hunks of leather, creaky harnesses, and big oil drums, and it always had the delicious aroma of black walnuts gathered from a nearby tree, kept in bushel baskets and preserved by the cool of the thick adobe walls. My brother and I would occasionally raid the stash, shattering the shells with some dusty old tool from the jumble of junk, sucking and prying to get at the meaty centers. This was a forbidden practice because the walnuts were precious and saved for special occasions, mainly Christmas when my mama would make heavy dark fudge with thick chunks of black walnuts floating in it like buried treasures in a chocolate sea.

Our pump house was larger than most because the former owner of the farm used it for raising fryer chickens. My brother and I loved picking through the old harnesses and greasy treasures, but undoubtedly the object that held the most fascination for me there was the chicken plucker. It was a machine the size of a jukebox with a studded metal belt that had bits of feather and dried blood clinging to it from the days when the pump house sheltered chickens—or rather didn't shelter chickens. Although long out of use, it still seemed alive as a monument to a grizzly function. I was both mesmerized and horrified by the thing. I sometimes had nightmares about it, that is, until I found the kittens.

I didn't even know Sambo was pregnant until early one spring morning I padded sleepy-eyed into the kitchen in my fleecy plastic-soled pajama suit to overhear my father saying quietly to my mother as she turned the sizzling bacon on the stove that he'd "taken care of" the kittens from the pump house under the scrub oak. Scrub oak meant "owl tree" to me. I'm not sure I understood at all what he was talking about, but the minute I heard the word "kittens" I turned and raced out the porch door, the little soles of my pj's crunching on the frost-crusted grass, in a dead sprint to the pump house to search for Sambo, leaving the screen door slapping behind me like hesitant applause.

I found Sambo that morning under the chicken plucker, curled in a little nest of rags and straw that looked empty. But when I reached back under the low metal shield into the very womb of the plucker where no adult male hand could have gone, I pulled out three wee kittens the size of small mice. I raced in glee to tell my parents of the discovery. My father, in particular, seemed very surprised, slapping his hand to his forehead and wagging his head. My mother laughed and said something like, "How wonderful, honey." There were two black-and-white "twin" kittens, which we ultimately gave to some neighbors who had twin daughters; the third was a tabby I named Tinker, short, of course, for Tinkerbell.

I guess Doc Rousseau didn't know how to do neuters and spays because Sambo, Pan, and Tinker outsmarted all population control efforts. I remember having thirteen cats at one point. In my wise child's way, to keep track of all my feline wards, I would count them over and over in the same tone my mother counted the deer. It must have been around that time I began to think it was my duty and calling to offer animals refuge from the misguided actions of grown-ups. I don't know when I actually absorbed the fact that my father culled that first kitten litter, but I do remember being haunted by the knowledge as a child.

My father is a gentle man. Square-jawed, solemn, handsome, he was mostly soft-spoken—remote, it seemed to me, not by choice, but by nature. He bore the sort of distance an only child develops when raised without the hubbub of extended family or neighborhood frolic, his quiet driven deeper by a heritage of Catholic schools and well-meaning but perhaps overzealous nuns who frightened a fine but shy spirit into hiding. My father carried a deep and residing moral code, but I fear his natural whimsy, which as a child I would see emerge from time to time like a nocturnal creature curious about the day, had fallen victim to an arcane private school system that doled out ample correction and meager reward. I think "doing what had to be done," as he put it, must have been difficult for him. He seemed to take pleasure in the plethora of animals in our midst—the chickens and rabbits, the cats (in spite of his allergies), and a young Brittany spaniel pup named Tammy. Years later I got up the nerve to ask my father how he had "taken care of" the unwanted kittens. I assumed he must have broken their necks or drowned them, as was the country way back then. There was a long, stunned silence—he had no idea that I had known—and he said in a low, apologetic voice, "carbon monoxide." He sounded so distant and sad, explaining that "animal shelters didn't exist." He felt he had to do something to "control the situation" and it seemed the only option available.

It must have been heartbreaking to him, just as it is to the thousands of volunteers and employees of animals shelters across this country who are forced to kill the five to six million cats and dogs abandoned at shelters every year because today we still haven't figured out how to "take care of the situation." Our treatment of these animals is the shadow side of our love of pets. Our betrayal of them is both harsh and hideous. In the end the atrocity of putting so many to death, animals born out of our simple unwillingness to spay and neuter, blasphemes not only the spirits of these creatures but the spirit of love this nation proclaims for animals.

Much of my early childhood was spent roaming the Thunder Bay State Forest with a boy five years my senior, named Stephen Alexander. He was a lean and shy youth who spent most of his days hunting, fishing, or wandering the forest. With Robin and Craig occupied with Stephen's brother and sister, who were precisely my siblings' ages, I was left to explore on my own. I learned that if I was quiet and uncomplaining Stephen would often endure my tagging along on his forest forays. He rarely talked, but he was a kind and patient guide and teacher, always pausing to show me how he was baiting the hook or setting the trap. He'd point out deer tracks, beaver dams, squirrel nests with a nod or a prolonged silent stare until I would find the object of interest with my own searching. Now and then, if I found something he'd missed he would pat my pigtailed head approvingly. Thus I spent the most important years of my childhood crawling through swamps, climbing trees, catching critters that we would use in any number of ways to frighten our siblings.

It was a snapping turtle that brought that enchanted period to an end. My unquestioning trust and adulation of Stephen was severed as abruptly as the falling of a blade. We had been out checking one of Stephen's traplines and returned home with several dead rabbits and a huge snapping turtle that was very much alive. I carried the rabbits slung like an animal necklace around my shoulders, stroking their smooth mouse-brown coats and whispering to them that I was sorry they had died and I hoped it hadn't hurt, as I scrambled panting after Stephen. He carried the algae-covered turtle, its head retracted but claws extended, kneading the empty air as he held it suspended in front of him. Back at the house, Stephen set the turtle on a large flat-topped stump. He taunted the turtle with a stout stick until it clamped on one end. I was told to pull with all my might on the other end of the stick "to see how long his neck was." So preoccupied was I with the strength of the turtle I didn't notice as Stephen picked up an ax. The blade came down squarely on the turtle's neck, blood spewed like a hydrant all over me as I fell backward, clutching the stick—to which the turtle's head was still clamped—to my blood-soaked chest.

There were several seconds of stunned silence as I tried to assimilate what had happened. Toppled, bewildered, and bloody, I started screaming. I was not sure what had happened, whether I'd lost a hand or a finger, where all the blood had come from. I lay there wailing, soaked in turtle gore; the turtle's head and I were still clutching the stick when the adults arrived. Stephen was scolded, and I was carried off in some sort of shock to a warm bath and my mother's soothing coos.

Stephen felt terrible—he had not intended a prank; he was simply readying the turtle for its fate as the evening meal, not realizing how traumatic the event might be for me. Yet my hero had fallen. I had not been prepared for the turtle's execution, nor was I prepared for its consumption. I refused the "chicken" soup that evening, my child intuition telling me that it was the broth of the beheaded turtle. I also refused the gamy dark meat of our roasted rabbits that Stephen had spent the rest of the afternoon skinning out.

The blood christening from the turtle's death had both confused me and connected me to the hunting, killing, and eating of animals, and would echo throughout my life. I have been both a vegetarian and a meat eater at different times. From my earliest childhood I participated in the offerings made to animals both wild and domestic. Deer grazed on our farm fields, birds came to our feeders, small creatures to our gardens, and, simultaneously, I was fed, clothed, and comforted by the offerings animals made to us. To eat and be eaten is a sacred cycle of reciprocity that once defined human consciousness, but, sadly, that exchange has been interrupted, if not obliterated, by our habit of consuming animals without grace or gratitude, without care for or consciousness of their lives or origins.

Several years after the turtle incident, my father, who was a bow hunter, brought home a young buck. There is a picture of him in front of the pump house steps holding its head up. I remember the day the picture was taken. I was sitting on the steps, a five-year-old child trying to contain the confused and stormy emotions of witnessing my father's pride (at least postured pride—there were other men there) and my own grief over the dead deer. I remember being so overcome that I ran down the steps and threw my arms around the neck of the deer, sobbing and sobbing. I had to be pried away. I always wondered whether that was one of the deer my mama counted, in her sweet melancholy voice, thirty-eight, thirty-nine, forty . . . when my daddy was away.

We ate mostly venison that winter. The deer's hide was sent off to some tannery and it came back a soft and supple sheet the color of dry meadow grass. That year for Christmas each child received golden deer-hide mittens. My mother received gloves, chocolate brown like the black-walnut fudge. She wore them to church on Sundays. I developed the habit of absently stroking my cheek with the back of my deer mittens, like some children finger the silken edge of their baby blanket for comfort.

At about the same time I started asking for a pony. My prayers and wheedling went on for years and years. During this period Sambo, Pan, and Tinker all passed on and a raucous parakeet named Tina joined the household. (Tina Turner had infiltrated rural existence by then.) We moved from the farm on the edge of Thunder Bay State Forest across the fingers of our mitten-shaped state to a log house on the edge of a meadow in northwest Michigan. Night after night my parents would patiently explain all the reasons we couldn't have a pony—space, money, practicality. (Years later I would hear the same arguments used against returning wolves to Yellowstone.) So I waited, wished, prayed, argued, and willed. Maybe I was just stubborn, but somehow I had come to believe that anything was possible.

It was 1969 and I was ten years old when my family made a visit to my grandparents in Nashville, Michigan, to celebrate the town's centennial. There were parties and parades and floats, horse-drawn carriages and carts, people dressed up in heirloom bustles and top hats, hot dog and cotton candy stands, and an air of excitement everywhere. One afternoon my grandfather and I were sent downtown on some errand contrived just to get us out from underfoot. We walked hand in hand down the cracked sidewalk of Main Street till we reached the gas station. Grandpa had to ask the attendant some question and I stood outside reading the window posters. Drawn immediately to a Polaroid picture of a pony, I read that a raffle was to be held on Saturday night and the grand prize was a PONY!!! The tickets were fifty cents. I was an adored and persuasive grandchild and I walked away with one hand in Grandpa's and three raffle tickets, one for each grandchild, clenched in the other. I had a chance and a goal.

Saturday evening came as slowly as Christmas morning, but there I was perched in the bleachers, indifferent to popcorn, cotton candy, clowns, and all the other annoying distractions. Holding my breath, I waited, never having wanted anything as much as I did that night. At last the drawing came. My name was not drawn. Shattered. The stars, sky, moon, and God all fell at once. I was inconsolable. Nothing had prepared me for this disappointment; I just went numb and was carried home in a godless, dark universe.

Somehow I was stuffed into my Sunday clothes and dragged off to church the next morning, sullen, silent, and brokenhearted. We were all lined up in one long pew, my father positioned, as always, between my brother Craig and me to discourage our endless horsing around, which was not a threat that morning because I could only stare at my toes, so dejected did I feel about God's obvious rejection. Before the mass proper was to begin, one of the congregation's elders went up front to give a summary of the centennial events. He droned on for a long time and at last my child ears heard the change in pitch and rhythm that announced the end of a grown-up's monologue. He started to walk back to his pew and mid-step remembered a forgotten announcement. "Oh, and by the way—Mr. Kelly, who won the pony, doesn't want it. Since I'm the one giving the pony away I thought we'd have another drawing after church today."

The words were frozen in the air. The man giving the pony away was right here in church. Someone didn't want it! Unfathomable to my young mind, but irrelevant since he said he was still giving it away! To this day my father says he could feel something palpable rise around him in church that morning. I don't doubt him. Positioned between my brother and me, given the sheer force and ardency of our prayer, Craig's for me and mine for the pony, my father was caught in the eye of a supplicatory hurricane.

We stood out on the church steps after mass in a hushed silence as a hand plunged into a basket, a ticket was drawn out, and a man's voice sliced through the air—Craig—Craig Askins. Craig and I screamed and squealed and cried and whooped and jumped, and underneath our hysteria I still remember, almost in slow motion, my father's characteristic response. His hand rose and clapped his forehead, followed by the slow wagging of his head as he groaned "Oh no!" over and over again. He smiled feebly as well-wishers slapped him on the back and pumped his hand in congratulations. My mother stood next to him smiling, holding him up, I suspect, more than anything. I beamed up at them as if to remind them that there might not exist a clearer example of divine intervention than what had just happened. The name had, after all, been drawn from a basket on the *church* steps.

It made no difference to me that my brother's name and not mine had been drawn. It went uncontested that my brother was the angel among us, and of course God would just do it that way since Craig was a much better conduit for holy acts. Typically, Craig was so happy for me he didn't seem to notice whose name had been called either. That afternoon we went to visit our new pony. He was a compact chestnut three-year-old who had just been gelded a few weeks before. He was aptly named "Thunder." Yet unbroke and volatile as one of those handheld sparklers with which I had written the phrase in the night air "PLEASE GOD LET ME WIN THIS PONY" some hundred times the evening before, he bucked and twisted in a gleeful gallop around the corral. Here we were 250 miles from home with an unbroke, newly gelded, three-year-old unruly pony.

I remember my father off in one corner of the pasture berating his father for buying those raffle tickets. The staccato words were indistinguishable in the distance, but their intent was recognizable because of the accompaniment of wild gesticulations, strained stomping and pacing back and forth, and the periodic slap of my father's hand to his furrowed forehead. My grandpa just stood quietly looking up at his son with a bemused smile, not at all unpleased with his own part in God's mirthful deed.

With a few pies and her persuasive charm, my mother got permission from all the neighbors to have a pony in our meadow—we weren't exactly on property zoned for horses. My daddy, despite his early skepticism, cheerfully built a corral and shed, and soon we managed to get Thunder to northern Michigan and installed in his new quarters. For the first few weeks we just talked. I followed Thunder around telling him my life story and he obligingly listened as he munched on the endless supply of hay, grass, apples, carrots, or sugar lumps I brought him. That I had never ridden a pony and that this pony had never been ridden didn't strike me as a problem at the time. We would learn together. I had no bridle or saddle and wouldn't have known what to do with them if I had. I started out leaning on him often, then hanging over his back, then at last straddling him.

Once I got the sense of bareback balance, Thunder and I roamed the country far and wide. I spent most of that summer reading Nancy Drew stretched across his back while he grazed in abandoned apple orchards and wildflower-swept meadows. I laid tummy down with my bare feet hitched over his withers and my chin on his rump poring through pages while he grazed the lush grasses of northern Michigan. I was thrown once, early on, when a dog ran out and spooked him. So I taught Thunder to chase dogs that charged us. After the first few ventures it became a game that he loved, and many a Michigan mongrel lived in terror of Thunder's thundering hooves.

Thunder was also my secret partner in crime. It all started in a Christmas tree plantation high on Hill Road overlooking the blue distance of Lake Charlevoix. Thunder loved to play slalom through those trees, and we would dash headlong, weaving in and out of the perfect rows, ducking errant branches and leaping downed trees like Robin Hood and his trusty steed escaping the wicked king's horsemen. When we tired of our fantasy we would wander down the hillside to a beautiful stand of mature pines. Those pines held tremendous mystery for me. Nowhere else could we ride through trees of such grandeur, under dark and towering boughs which created a tunnel-like and hushed canopy for our silent passage over the forest's needled floor. It was an enchanted place, perfect for the fantasies and imagination of a young girl. One day we discovered that the pine stand backed up against the dog pound. It was an innocent discovery. I kneeled on Thunder's back and peered in through the dusty windows to see a half dozen mournful canine faces peering back.

I somehow knew it was a dog pound. These dogs were definitely impounded—that is, seized, retained, and held against their will. I know because I asked them. I don't think it occurred to anyone in those days that dogs had wills; that's why these places were still called "pounds" rather than "shelters." I was quite young then, but old enough to feel an injustice was taking place. Clever enough to read the definition of "pound" in the dictionary: "a public enclosure for the confinement of 'stray' animals." Insightful enough to recognize the word "stray" as painfully descriptive of how I felt myself—"to wander beyond established limits; roam, to become lost, to meander, to go astray, to digress, to be out of place, lost, scattered, or separate." And even innocent enough to believe that one small act could actually make a difference.

So it was at that dog pound, with the help of Thunder, that I committed my first crime, that I first went—as did all the dogs—astray. The first release was unplanned; subsequent ones required more subversive tactics. It was at that dog pound that I experienced the exhilaration of releasing the controlled back into the wild. Mind you, beagles, Brittanys, and matted-haired mutts aren't wolves and straight dark rows of managed pine stands aren't exactly wilderness; but some seed, like a milkweed feather on a midsummer night's breeze, was set innocently afloat into my future when a motley collection of canine prisoners burst forth from a small concrete building on the highlands of a small northern Michigan town, and a girl, yipping like a banshee on her barebacked pony, went racing off into the shadows of evergreen boughs hot on the heels of a batch of freshly liberated, baying mongrels.

Six

My eyes already touch the sunny hill,
going far ahead of the road I have begun.
So we are grasped by what we cannot grasp;
it has its inner light, even from a distance——

and changes us, even if we do not reach it,
into something else, which, hardly sensing it, we already are;
a gesture waves us on, answering our own wave . . .
but what we feel is the wind in our faces.

RAINER MARIA RILKE, "The Walk"
Selected Poems of Rainer Maria Rilke
EDITED AND TRANSLATED BY ROBERT BLY

T HE THEORY THAT our childhood contact with the natural world and animals is critical to the development of a healthy human being has received growing attention and support in recent years. It is becoming increasingly apparent that the geography of our childhood may hold an important key to the unfolding of our adult psyche—our passions, our penchants, and even our sense of place. Whether we had contact or a relationship with animals, wild or domestic, zoo-kept, house-kept, or farm-kept, can be a tremendously influential part of who we become. Just as the intimate wild places that were accessible to us as children—the places into which we tunneled, climbed, crawled, or crept, the meadows, marshes, tree limbs, and caves (even the cubbyholes, corners, and crannies of abandoned parking lots, tenement gardens, and urban parks) that define the "sanctuaries" to which all children, including urban youth, turn to for solace, escape, discovery, and contemplation, from infancy to adolescence—may have an important impact on our sense of belonging, our personality, and our feelings of connection to the earth.

Although Stephen Alexander was my first nature guide and interpreter, it is to the companionship and accompaniment of my younger brother Craig that I owe a deep-rooted sense of intimacy and comfort with natural landscapes. When he was three and I was four, we discovered a long-abandoned gravel pit, beyond the stand of scrub oak in which the "owl tree" loomed, at our childhood farm. At the east edge of the backyard forest stand, the long grasses and the fluttering of birch leaves gave way to a disheveled meadow that wrapped around the northeast side of the property. It was a rocky little unkempt tract of land with rolling mounds and scrawny, unexpected pine trees sprouting here and there, clutching the earth like frightened settlers. Just a hundred feet from the forest stand, in the midst of the meadow, nearly invisible until you were right at its bank, lay the bowl of sand that held immeasurable delight for our childhood adventures.

Craig and I spent endless afternoons rolling, plunging, somersaulting, or lurching in the astonishing numbers of ways children can invent to catapult themselves down a deliciously sandy slope. One of our favorite methods was the "mummy roll." We'd lie down, wrap our arms across our chest and clutch the back of our shoulders, straitjacket style, press our ankles together, and position ourselves like lean cylinders at the lip of the gravel pit slope. Launching a downhill roll, once started, our bodies would gain momentum, spinning faster and faster, tumbling down the slope of the gravel pit like a splintering log bouncing down a mountain, until we hit the bottom in a tangle of body parts, arms and legs askew like rag dolls strewn in the sand. Grinning and sand-coated from head to toe, we would pull ourselves up like clownish marionettes, scramble side by side back up to the crest, panting and spitting sand, only to flop down and do it again.

The gravel pit slopes provided abundant opportunities for the construction of elaborate forts, or the burrowing of dens which we would line with long meadow grasses and cover with branches. We'd peer out from our little nests like fox kits, hiding from nothing but the bright light of a sunny afternoon, reveling in the dark press of cool sand and the sagey scent of fresh-plucked grass. Some days we would slither like oversize salamanders up to the edge of the gravel pit, feathers planted in our hair and stick tomahawks wedged in our elastic waistbands, to spy on our make-believe enemies, which ranged from black-hatted bandits to ornery grizzly bears, or maybe just Mama hanging out the laundry.

Our child bodies learned the taste, smell, and texture of the terrain from scuttling over its curves and ridges like little horseshoe crabs, careening down its slopes and digging into its sandy depths, dirt wedged for weeks under our teardrop-size fingernails. This exploration, I'm sure, provided a kind of trust in the way the earth can hold and shelter one's body, but more importantly it lay the foundation for a lifetime interest in the natural world. A decade and more later Craig would introduce me to another way of learning the land; this movement, however, required biped motion—the art of distance running.

My brother became one of the star cross-country competitors at our high school, and one of the finest runners in the state. Entering my third year of high school, I decided to also run cross-country. There was no women's team, so I had to compete on the men's. Craig was very supportive, but before the first practice he sat down with me, explained how difficult an undertaking distance running was, and asked me to promise him one thing—that I wouldn't quit. I was deeply offended, indignant that he thought I would even consider quitting, but after an elaborate and verbose speech denouncing his presumption, and much tossing of my ponytail, he remained insistent and I made the promise.

I thought I would die after the first day of practice. I never wanted to quit anything so badly in my life, not even my cherry-picking job when I was seven. But I had made a promise, and promises were sacred between my brother and me. There were many dimensions to the difficulty. One was being the only female on an all-male team in an all-male conference. Even though the boys on my home team were very civil and supportive, there were those among the competition who deeply objected to a girl competing in the sport and were enraged at being challenged, let alone potentially beaten, by a female. Concerning the latter, they didn't have too much to worry about.

Although I was a strong runner in practice, I was a mediocre to poor competitor. I never came in last in a race, but always somewhere toward the back of the pack. I was a decent athlete in other sports and thus a prideful young girl who believed that will and hard work could accomplish anything, which really means I was accustomed to winning, or at least being in control. For the first time in my life I was forced to acknowledge the limits of my will. No matter how hard I physically tried, I didn't have the stuff of the high-speed competitors. I didn't win. Ever. I thought the lesson was learning how to lose; instead it was learning how to relinquish control, how to not win and not quit. The price of that particular lesson was a pummeled ego race after race. The reward was a newly discovered humility, learning how to accept help, modify goals, and, perhaps most importantly, the development of the ability to sustain hope in the face of failure.

I will forever remember the hundreds of times I thought I couldn't take another step, let alone run another interval, reach the top of a hill, pass a competitor, run another mile, cross another finish line. I remember the sweat and the spit and my lungs gasping for air and the persistent, gut-wrenching spasms that made me want to vomit mid-race. I remember wanting to collapse along those courses, curl up in a fetal ball, and rock myself out of this hellish determination. Years later I learned I had a condition called exercise-induced asthma, a revelation that explained why the sprint starts demanded in the races were so debilitating for me. But at the time I only knew that no matter how I willed it, no matter how much I believed I was in control of the outcome, I couldn't run faster—even when there was a boy running neck and neck beside me toward the finish line, cussing with the thump of every footfall like a chant, "Bitch/fuckin'/whore/hussy, Bitch/fuckin'/whore/hussy . . ." and then, as he passed me, "I'm not gonna let no fucking bitch beat me!" And he didn't. It was a rough way to learn that "will" was not just a vehicle for ego, or for pride, but also a vehicle for humility.

Competing on that cross-country team both literally and figuratively brought me to my knees, and it was on my knees that I figured out promises often need to become prayers. Prayers teach patience and perspective, they teach mindfulness and attentiveness to the lessons at hand, they teach the humility needed to partition grandiose goals into pocket-size achievements. My brother helped me learn the lesson of the latter—apportioning goals—cultivating the patience that keeping future promises would require.

Craig would finish these cross-country races, often in first place, and then sprint back along the course to run next to me. Urging me on in a low chanting voice, he would break down the course with descriptions of what was ahead. "See the tree, aim for the tree, OK got the tree, now there's a little hill, it's nothin', though, we did twice its size in practice last week, aim for the crest, keep your eye on the crest, got the crest, see the rock, aim for the rock, go for the rock, come on, use your arms, one foot in front of the other, push it push it, OK finish is just round that bend, easy sprint, push it push it, keep going almost over, push there it is GO GO GO . . ." and we would cross the finish line together, Craig for the second time.

The promise to my brother, and the prayers pursuant to that promise, were all that kept one foot moving in front of the other that fall. I remember the relief of having finished a race, of having made it through another practice, of having lived by my word one more day. What Craig and my wonderful coach, Bob Wollenburg, taught me was "will training." What the will training taught me was how to pray, which in my mind was a spiritual rather than religious exercise. "Every natural fact is a symbol of some spiritual fact," Emerson asserted. My prayers produced no miracles, only the discovery that the way one trains will is not through huge, grandiose goals, but by tiny increments. It's just putting one foot in front of the other—another practice, another race, another day, another hour, another step. And even though you might be wanting, wishing, hungering to quit, you don't quit. You just aim for the next little goal and pray. Running cross-country prepared me for my future in ways that were incomprehensible at the time. Still, twenty years later, when people ask me what I think is the best training for conservation work, I suggest long-distance running.

Running was also my means of caressing the land, but running is just one means. What is important is that the repetition and rhythm of moving over the land, through the water, up a mountain, or down a river mediate a visceral exchange between the outer, physical geography and an inner, spiritual landscape. The outward reality, through the translator of motion and repetition, becomes a mirror for one's inner terrain. It is one of the ways I think the outer "wild" invokes a corresponding inner "wild." This bonding between land and spirit reached through physical movement seems to bypass the scrutiny of the intellect. I suspect that many athletes and outdoorsmen, whatever their medium—surfer and sea, climber and rock, skier and snow—experience this bonding, this unifying of place and person.

The writer John Haines captures the parallel sense of the wild in describing his experience living in Alaska.

The wilderness is out there, quiet under the brief, rose-gray twilight before the sun rises again. But the wilderness is in myself, also, like a durable shadow. I prowl my region of flesh, my forest of blood, muttering and sniffing, turning many times in search of my own best place.

Finding our inner geography through contact with the outward landscape echoes an ancient relationship with the land inherited from our hunter-gatherer ancestors. We often forget that our psyches were molded from nearly three million years of nomadic existence—a life in motion lived in intricate intimacy with landscape. Our existence and survival were once guided by stars, wind, water, scents, colors, and movement. We lived a reality in which every facet of our senses was used and invoked. Today we are virtually insulated from the natural world. We are cooled, warmed, fed, and entertained largely by artificial means, removed from the sources of our survival and from the stimulation and exchange that at one time defined not only what we were but who we were.

Today we are disoriented and alienated in a world whose changes have outpaced our ability to adapt. Is it so surprising that depression and despair are ubiquitous in a society in which we are removed from the very forces that once defined us? My original desire to understand the circumstances of Natasha's life led over the years to a cascade of questions. First, wondering how we were capable of exterminating wolves in such harsh, fanatical ways led to asking how we got so removed from the natural sympathy and reciprocity of our relationship to animals, which inevitably posed the question at the root of it all: How did we get so disconnected from the very things we are dependent upon for our survival?

Following these meandering fox trails led me to the work of Paul Shepard. In his visionary book *Nature and Madness,* Shepard asks, "Why do men persist in destroying their habitat when they are dependent upon it for their very survival?" His answers lead not only back to our ancestry but into our relationship with animals.

The elegance of Shepard's thinking lies in its simplicity—his basic premise is that we are Pleistocene beings trying to survive in non-Pleistocene conditions. He is not inclined to indulge in the nostalgic rhetoric of "we must go back to simpler times," but plainly asserts *we never really left.* Biologically, we are what we evolved to be for over thirteen million years. Our ability to adapt to the changes brought about by the advent of agriculture, industry, science, and technology beginning only ten thousand years ago is severely hampered by the exceedingly slow pace of evolution. We might physically be able to survive and even prosper in the face of those changes, but our psyches suffer from such dramatic shifts in societal structure. The human species is subjected to tremendous stress and chaos in a world that we have created but are increasingly ill equipped to navigate.

Our response to this state of dis-ease and disorientation is seen in the epidemic level of anxiety, depression, and debilitating mental illness in our culture today. Shepard asserts that much of our pain and many of our social problems, especially those related to the environment, arise from the fact that we are unable to recognize what we essentially are as biological entities, and thus we have failed to understand what we need in order to become whole.

To understand what it means to be whole, we must first look at what it means to be human—the secret of which lies far back in the unfolding of evolution. If we examine hunter-gatherer cultures, some of which still survive today, we can see how differently human needs were once recognized and met. Shepard suggests child-rearing practices, and the correlation between normal or healthy human ontogeny (the course of development of an individual) and early personal contact with animals and nature, might provide the basis for understanding what has been lost today. The heart and originality of Shepard's arguments lie in his assertion that contact with wild nature and contact with animals are two critical "cues" in our development, as essential to the maturation of the psyches of human beings as folic acid is to our neurological health.

There is a profound, inescapable need for animals that is in all people everywhere, an urgent requirement for which no substitute exists. This need is no vague, romantic, or intangible yearning, no simple sop to our loneliness or nostalgia for Paradise. As hard and unavoidable as the compounds of our inner chemistry, it is universal but poorly recognized. It is grounded in the way that animals are used in the growth and development of the human person, in those priceless qualities which we lump together as "mind." Animals have a critical role in the shaping of personal identity and social consciousness. Among the first inhabitants of the mind's eye, they are basic to the development of speech and thought. Later they play a key role in the passage to adulthood. Because of their participation in each stage of the growth of consciousness, they are indispensable to our becoming human in the fullest sense.

Without the presence of animals and the wild in our childhood we never achieve the capacity to recognize "other" and "self." "Other" provides the means of establishing self-identity. The process of witnessing "other" in the context of a place we, too, inhabit provides us with the foundation for kinship. It also provides the backdrop for our sense of belonging, of being part of a matrix that binds human to animal, animal to earth, and earth to human. When we are deprived of the experiences that lead us to recognize animals as brethren and the earth as home to both "other" and "self," we lose the capacity to understand our dependence on and interdependence with wild nature. Without the ability to recognize—not intellectually but intuitively—our relationship to animals and the land, to see them as an extension of ourselves, to understand that our health is derived from and dependent upon them, we become capable of the mindless (literally) exploitation which could lead to our own extinction.

I began to realize that what Natasha really taught me was not what we had done to wolves or to animals in general, but how animals might show us what we had done ourselves. The conditions of her existence—trapped, diminished, disconnected, and separated—were metaphors for mankind's existence. That we could sentence this creature, one of millions consigned to such a fate, to a life of concrete and cages, separated from her pack and natural habitat, was merely an expression of our own alienation. If our treatment of creatures like Natasha, domestic or wild, was as wounding to us as it was to her, then so might the gesture of inviting animals back into our lives, honoring their wildness and wild nature, their autonomy and distinctiveness, be a part of the journey toward reconnection and healing. The seed that John Weaver planted in his visit to Wolf Park, the idea of giving wolves back to Yellowstone and the wild back to wilderness, could represent one step on that journey toward restoration of our relationship with the natural world. And what Craig taught me had given me some of the most basic tools I would need to personally embark on that quest.

Seven

◇ ◇ ◇

I have the skins
my two
which are alike

What are they?

The bare ground
and the sky.

A MASAI RIDDLE

GRIEF-STRICKEN OVER THE loss of Natasha, I left Wolf Park and returned to Kalamazoo College for the summer quarter. Numb and restless, I fought a constant sense of helplessness. I understood it was imperative that I do something, but couldn't identify what it was. I paced with relentless uncertainty, attached to some faraway and feral being I truly loved. I went through the motions of attending classes and completing my thesis, but my heart wasn't in it. Instead it was in a concrete run, behind an anonymous chain-link fence, in some far-off town in North Dakota with Natasha.

In spite of my promise, my remorse shattered my sense of direction and purpose. Although I had made the decision the year before to forgo spending my junior year abroad, part of Kalamazoo's traditional offering, I decided at the last minute to take advantage of the foreign study option and go my senior year instead. It took some heavy administrative jockeying, but in less than two months I had a passport, a stuttering grasp of a dialect called Krio, and had set off with five other students for a tiny agricultural college in the remote regions of Sierra Leone, West Africa. It was my time in the third world that helped put our conservation crisis into some kind of perspective, and helped me realize that the attitudes that gave rise to Natasha's circumstances might lie in the midst of the most extreme expression of the problem.

In Sierra Leone, amid poverty, illiteracy, overpopulation, and devastated landscapes, I found some of the happiest, most whole human beings I will ever know. I was also forced to recognize that in my homeland, with its riches and sophisticated conservation rhetoric, existed some of the most devastated and alienated human beings on earth. In retrospect it was not without purpose that I chose to go to the most remote, most undeveloped, most politically volatile site available to Kalamazoo students, for it was into the utter wild of Africa that I was drawn to heal my own broken heart.

Upon arrival in Africa my feelings, deadened after Natasha's loss, were jolted awake by the incongruity of past and present. I never stopped thinking about her, but my senses were so assaulted by the novelty of Africa and the struggle to assimilate a culture so foreign that learning how to survive the months ahead demanded my complete attention. I was one of seven Americans, six of us women, all of us white, who arrived in the fall of 1980 at Njala Agricultural College. We were greeted by a student body of eight hundred, all black, only fifty of whom were women. It came as a surprise to learn that Njala was one of Kalamazoo College's "pilot" programs, which meant that, aside from some credits showing up on our transcripts back in the States, there was absolutely no rhyme or reason to our presence in Africa or Njala.

I admit not all my fellow American students shared my enthusiasm for the structureless existence and the academic freedom granted us, the lack of running water, the monotonous meals of rice and spinachlike cassava sauce served twice a day, or the free-roaming ocher-speckled geckos that scuttled across the walls and ceilings of our rooms day and night. As the resident biologist on the trip I pointed out that the geckos killed cockroaches, the other free-ranging wildlife in our rooms. My comrades remained skeptical. At least we had cement-block rooms—many of the students lived in the thatched-roof dirt huts in the nearby village. On a good day we even got bread for breakfast. Although the classes were supposedly taught in English, most were in fact taught in a combination dialect of the universal Sierra Leonian Krio with heavy influences of the Mende and Temne tribal dialects. Either language could be a barrier, or the lack of language an advantage, depending on what one had set out to learn.

I found the absence of structure and supervision tremendously liberating.

Having been a model student most of my life, I delighted in exploring the wicked corners of truancy. One day while hiking some of the trails around the local village I encountered a weathered old man, named Keena, on his way back to the village from one of the nearby fields. We started chatting. My Krio was limited, but we at least got through the greetings and some "small talk." I accepted his invitation to join him on the rickety watchtower the next day. After that I could be found on more than one afternoon playing hooky, sitting out on the high bamboo tower with Keena, whose sole job it was to keep the mynah birds off the corn. He accomplished this task by swinging a long leather sling, called a *bola,* in a whirring circle over his head. With a twist of his wrist he would fling the stone held in the centrifuge of the *bola's* pocketed base rocketing toward the avian thief. His marksmanship was nothing less than sublime. I perceived that my job up on our tower was to teach him American folk songs, a task which was challenging because I couldn't sing worth a damn. However, my lackluster abilities were considerably enhanced by the gourd of palm wine, locally called *poyo,* that he kept by his side. His job was to teach me how to be quiet, a skill with which the *poyo* offered little assistance.

Something about the silence and the sun heightened my interest in *poyo.* In fact, one of my accomplishments in Africa was to become a connoisseur of the evolving flavor of *poyo,* something I inventively called a "cultural subtlety" which was lost on all but the truly pathetic foreign visitors. A palm oil tree is tapped each morning by a young village boy who shinnies up the long trunk to drain the sap for the village's daily libations. Yeast is added to the juice to expedite fermentation. The interesting thing about palm wine (which I didn't know in the beginning but learned after a long day on the tower with Keena, a blistering bout of sunstroke, and a 105-degree fever that kept me delirious for longer than I want or am able to remember) is that it continuously ferments, its alcoholic content increasing exponentially as the day wears on; thus its evolving flavor—and effect. Maybe it was the palm wine, maybe it was the old man, but in Africa I did eventually learn, as the poet A. R. Ammons put it, "to be quiet in the hands of the marvelous."

To be quiet is as familiar an idea to Africans as it is alien to Americans, and it took me months to understand their ritual of visitation and silence. The Sierra Leonians would often pay each other visits in the evening, beginning with a warm greeting ritual in which usually greeter and greeted would hold hands rather than shake hands, sometimes for the duration of the meeting. After the elaborate greeting the visitor would be invited to sit and often the conversation would lapse into silence. Occasionally the silence would be punctuated with another hello, or a comment on the day. At other times the visitor would start speaking spontaneously, as though a mute button had been switched off, and the conversation that had been going the whole time could now be heard by human ears rather than the intuitive senses. After thirty minutes or an hour another greeting/farewell exchange would take place with the extended holding of hands, and the visitor would leave.

At first when people from the village I had met or fellow students would come to visit I would scurry about trying to gather something up to serve—oranges, ground nuts, a sliced banana, a bottle of Coke. I would then try to make polite conversation to "keep the flow going," feeling terribly inadequate as my guest would repeatedly fall silent. At last my African roommate, Edith, gently explained to me the ceremony of silent visitation. It wasn't that there wasn't anything to say, or that my visitors didn't know how to say it, it was that so much more was said in silence. The gift of presence was the act of intimacy, not the pretense of conversation. Furthermore, my act of leaving when she had visitors (which I'd always done out of politeness) was something of an insult, rather than an accommodation. Privacy, in Africa, was by no means preferable to presence. I remember my shock, then shame, then the fits of unstoppable giggles as we rolled around in our hammocks while she imitated my frenzy and effort with a visitor.

One weekend Edith took me home with her to her village. I was especially moved by the sheer joy of the people of rural Sierra Leone. A sort of infectious merriment inhabited most of the tiny villages that nestled in the hungry green of the countryside. People everywhere were spirited and friendly, a trait nearly universal among villagers regardless of tribal affiliation or social status. This good cheer seemed widespread in spite of the crushing hardship and political unrest that had begun to seep into the remote regions. As you walked by a village, children would call out a greeting, their voices chiming and clear like the song of a meadowlark. Many of them had open sores and the swollen bellies of malnutrition, yet they would run out to the trail to take your hand, skipping along happily chattering with curiosity about any *bwana* (white person) who happened to pass. The obligatory begging was part of every greeting, but most often it was not serious, and a handful of groundnuts or an orange section was met with cheerful acceptance.

The children of rural Sierra Leone exuded confidence and certainty, qualities that I believe are largely attributable to a culture based on large and loving extended families. Children are universally adored, and aunts and uncles, cousins and grandparents all play an active role in their education and upbringing. Rarely did I ever see a child crying or corrected for wrongdoing. This shared child rearing allows mothers both a broader role in community activities and discretionary time to spend in artistic efforts such as the creation of the local *gara,* a beautiful tie-dyed cloth produced throughout West Africa. Edith gave me a traditional Sierra Leonean dress that had been dyed in her village and sewn by her sister. She explained that the distinctive design made out of lovely tannin and indigo shades was extracted from the ubiquitous kola nut and plants of the *Indigofera* genus. The village women literally beat some of the dyes into the *gara* cloth, a drumming rhythm that resonated throughout many villages in the burbling evening hum as women gathered to work and gossip.

I became particularly interested in the child-rearing methods in Africa because I had never seen such happy, contented children. What I found was that the extended family structure also offered the children an expanded sphere of exploration and discovery. Community becomes nearly as important as direct family, and throughout the maturation process the child feels both the responsibility and safety of "belonging." Much of early childhood is spent exploring the forests and fields that surround the villages. The children not only have a direct relationship with the land, but if they are privileged enough to get occasional meat, it is invariably from an animal they have helped raise, feed, herd, and even kill and butcher, creating an immediacy of experience and connection with the natural world.

Rural Sierra Leone, when not war-ravaged, has a predominantly subsistence-level agricultural economy, and many children are raised in intimate contact with nature. Many have an intuitive and sophisticated knowledge of the rhythms of weather, animal behavior, plant identification, and even celestial systems. The Mendes, the predominant tribe in the vicinity of Njala, are known for their secret societies, called *bundu,* which employ elaborate initiation rituals. Children are trained for years in matters of tribal law, crafts, and ceremony. The result of this engagement both with community and with the land is young people who have an authentic sense of centered- ness derived from a feeling of belonging and connection to place. I don't cite this culture as a system that we should mimic or return to, clearly an impos- sible undertaking, but rather as an example from which we can gain insight about what child-rearing tactics might be effective in offering children con- nection to and engagement in the natural world.

Much of what I learned in Africa was, shall I say, "extracurricular." While Keena taught me the value of silence, perhaps my greatest lesson in Africa was taught by a very vocal group of students. The student body at Njala was both the intellectual center of and mouthpiece for political sentiments which were extremely threatening to Siaka Stevens, the Sierra Leonean dictator and leader at that time of the ruling party, the All People's Congress (APC) in Sierra Leone's capital, Freetown. The political opposition party, the Sierra Leone People's Party (SLPP), was centered in Njala. It was the party of the southern Mendes, largely representing the rural, agriculturally based, un- educated public. Mostly because I was a passable soccer player—and as a woman, something of a novelty in that capacity—I was befriended early on by some of the college's student leaders. Occasionally I would be invited to some secret, late night gathering of SLPP leaders where the students would sit around and debate and strategize upcoming political events or maneuvers. Because the talk was fast and furious and outpaced my language skills, partic- ularly after a gourd of palm wine had been passed around, I could only follow bits and pieces of the discussion; but the passion and commitment of these students and their willingness to risk everything for what they believed was very moving to me, especially since my political experience had been limited to a stint as president of my high school student council, where the topics of our debates rarely transcended a discussion of which band would be appropri- ate for the after-game dance.

Within the first few months of our stay, an entourage of political VIPs and staff from Siaka Stevens's office made a visit to Njala in seven white Mercedes buses. One of Njala's student activists had mysteriously disappeared while in the custody of the APC security people a few days before, and the students staged what was supposed to be a peaceful demonstration urging his release. Freetown-based APC thugs tried to break up the protest, and within minutes the situation exploded. Suddenly there were people running and screaming, and students overturning buses and setting them aflame, and guns going off everywhere. In the aftermath of the fighting I wandered among the burned-out buses, gutted metallic carcasses lying on their sides like dead rhinos. For the first time I truly felt the rage of people oppressed, exploited, and politically disenfranchised, sentiments that I would recognize years later in the faces of ranchers and hunters at antiwolf rallies.

After the rioting Njala was closed for an indefinite period, presumably to give the students an opportunity to cool off. With two other Americans, James Lindbeck and Debbie Price, I set off to do some exploration. We found ourselves on New Year's Eve in the village of Zorzor, Liberia. We had just gotten off of a lorry, a small truck used for public transport, when a drunk army captain with spooky bloodshot eyes began harassing, then beating our driver, who turned out to be from Mali and was indeed driving illegally in Liberia. The driver, however, spoke only French and didn't understand English and thus was helpless, and incapable of responding to his brutal interrogation. I intervened in hopes of distracting the captain from his preoccupation of kicking the driver's bloody face with the polished points of his steel-toed boots. It worked. The captain forgot about the driver and turned on us, shoving the muzzle of his American-made M-16 in our bellies and drilling us with questions about our passports and visas. That we were American students attending an agricultural college in the remote regions of Sierra Leone was utterly inconceivable to him. Thus, he concluded, we must be spies. I tried to explain that he was mistaken but he only got more angry and agitated. Then Debbie tried. He blew up, screaming at us both to shut up. In his country men need only speak to men. He turned to James, who, although valiant in his effort, failed as well.

We were arrested, our passports and papers confiscated, shoved in cars, and, with a military escort and sirens wailing, delivered to a crude jail. We were fingerprinted and shoved into a dank gray cell with a poster on the far wall. I commented as we entered that the dirt cubicle was a lot like the runs in the dog pound in my hometown, except those cells had no decoration. I volunteered in a sort of brittle cheer that perhaps that was because the dogs in my hometown couldn't read. As our eyes adjusted to the dark it became clear that the five-foot poster on our wall had no writing. Instead it was a grid divided into a hundred or more pictures, like the class pictures we took home in first grade. A closer look revealed that each picture was the face, sometimes beaten or at least swollen and gruesome, of a hanged or hanging prisoner.

It was a long night. Debbie and James were not completely appreciative of my act of valor on behalf of the illegal Malian driver. In self-defense I pointed out that we hadn't had any other plans for the evening, and no place to stay anyway. It was New Year's Eve, everything in Zorzor was probably filled up. Debbie wailed. Unquestionably we were all terrified, but like all good traveling companions enduring the rough terrain, we dug for the humor. In some cases, quite literally. That night James carved lines in the packed dirt floor and we sat most of the night in a cross-legged tournament of ticktacktoe. I, with my back to the poster, hummed songs from *The Sound of Music.* It's astonishing how many "favorite things" you can think of when you're in a third world prison cell. Just as dawn was breaking a new officer in full military regalia appeared. He thumbed through our visas and passports and, finding everything in order, released us with profuse apologies for the inconvenience, any delays, etc. I'm sure it was my own discretion rather than James's iron grip on my arm as he escorted me toward the door, but for once I kept my opinions to myself and we walked out into the morning light.

It took the third world to make me a committed believer in democracy. There would be times in the next fifteen years, facing the monumental political objections to restoring wolves to the West, when I would seriously contemplate subversive tactics. People would often suggest that with a bit of finesse and imagination we could sneak wolves into Yellowstone a whole lot quicker, a lot cheaper, and with a lot less grief. Oddly, it was this time in Africa that instilled both a resolute belief in the process of democracy and a contempt for its opposite. Fanaticism breeds totalitarianism, and that leads inevitably to army captains drunkenly kicking wounded victims. We were lucky to have escaped with a sleepless night. Most don't.

Africa offered me many valuable lessons that would be useful in surviving future wolf politics, but a few times I realized I had brought some lessons from wolves that would prove invaluable in surviving Africa. A few days after our prison escapade we found ourselves on the abandoned outskirts of a small city in the Ivory Coast. After a late night of terrific West African beer and "endurance dancing," as Debbie called it, to the hungry rhythms of West African reggae music, we took a taxi back to our hostel. Unfortunately, the taxi dropped us in the pitch black of night in the wrong place, an error that went unrecognized until he had driven away. We wandered around an abandoned suburb for hours looking for a way back to the central part of town. There were no people, no cars, only empty houses and huts. The place had the feel of an abandoned village hit by plague, past prosperity and sudden desertion echoing from the dust and thick mud walls.

At about three in the morning we rounded a walled corner to startle a pack of twenty or so feral dogs. West African dogs are treated as scoundrels and, sadly, are more often than not diseased and dangerous. Regaining their composure quickly, a few of the dogs started toward us, growling and dropping to the ground in a stalking slither. My heart began thudding, pumping adrenaline to my beer-dulled brain. Muscles tensed, skin prickled, I braced myself. I'd never witnessed dog behavior like this before. Nor had I ever felt fear in the presence of dogs, even very aggressive dogs, but in this instance terror coursed through every cell in my body. I had never heard of feral dogs attacking a group of humans, but there was no doubt in my mind about the intent of this clan.

It was all I could do to keep Debbie from running and triggering a predatory swarm. One day at Wolf Park I had been alone, cleaning the wolf enclosure, when I found myself cornered, being stalked by a yearling male. Sensing the mounting tension in the pack, with Cassie's fate clear in my memory, I had howled. It had worked to disarm and distract the wolves—in fact they joined my howls, and a rally ensued during which I was able to slip along the fence and out a gate. There in the middle of West Africa, facing a menacing pack of feral dogs, I did the only thing I could think of—I howled. It utterly bewildered the dogs, not to mention James and Debbie. Some of the dogs sat down on their haunches and howled back; others milled around in confusion, yapping and barking. Drawing on my childhood experience of being chased by dogs on Thunder, I figured there was only one way to defuse the situation. I hoped to hell it would work in Africa. I ran straight at the dogs, barking and yipping at the top of my lungs, waving my arms like a lunatic. The dogs scattered like pool balls, fleeing in all directions. With my heart pounding, my hands shaking, and a sheepish grin on my face, I returned to James and Debbie. James just rolled his eyes and slapped his hand to his forehead, wagging his head in disbelief.

Just then Debbie spotted the headlights of a car, the first in our nearly two hours of searching. She went running toward the headlights, waving her arms frantically. Debbie was very beautiful, and the man rolled down his window with cautious interest, staring blankly as she, by then in near hysteria, tried to explain our predicament in broken French. At last she was reduced to repeating over and over, "Les chats sont mal, sont mal." I gently tried to point out to her she was saying, "The cats are bad, are bad." In spite of Debbie's incoherent babble and the absurd hour, the kind African did deliver us to our hostel. In those few hours of early morning sleep, for the first time in my life I dreamt of wolves attacking me. I awoke drenched in sweat and terror. The memory of that night would enable me to listen years later with honest patience, in meeting after meeting, public hearing after public hearing, to westerners opposing the reintroduction of wolves because of some primal dread of wolf attacks. None of us escape from having evolved in the presence of predators. None of us.

After the experience with the feral dogs I could not get Natasha out of my mind. I was haunted by the thought of Natasha behind the coldness of crisscross chain link, in a metallic prison of glinting steel. The night I returned to Njala I sat up late into the night writing long résuméic letters by candlelight both to John Weaver and Timm Kaminski, the two biologists I had met while at Wolf Park. I asked, as I had nearly two years before, if there might be some way I could get involved with the effort to restore wolves to Yellowstone. The next morning, because nearly 60 percent of my mail never made it out of Africa, I sent the letters with a Peace Corps worker on his way to the States so I would be sure of their delivery.

My experience in Africa profoundly shaped not only my views on conservation but how I feel it must be practiced to be relevant as a model beyond the borders of my own country. By traditional measures of conservation, Sierra Leone is far from exemplary. By the late 1970s only 4 percent of the rain forests that once cloaked the whole country still existed. Unregulated hunting and numerous sorts of exploitation were rampant even before the wars of the late 1990s further ravaged the people and country. The grace and kindness of the Sierra Leonean people that I witnessed in the early eighties was shadowed a decade later with the outbreak of conflict and a growing civil war. Over the next decade the unfathomable reports of human atrocities and the sheer viciousness and senselessness of Sierra Leoneans killing each other left the world in shock and one of the most beautiful and potentially wealthy West African countries crippled—thirty thousand dead, thousands more mutilated, and much of the land and many of the villages now in ruins.

In no way do I want to idealize or minimize the anguish of poverty or the resultant plundering that has stripped West Africa of much of its native beauty. However, my experience there offered some measure of insight into what makes human beings whole. In spite of the hardships I witnessed, never have I seen a happier, more delightful people. Although this wholeness has done little to halt the desolation of overpopulation or the foreign extractive industries, there is still much to be learned from traditional people. If we see the conservation crisis as arising, in part, from a loss of both connection with the natural world and a conscious sense of one's context in nature, we can look to some of these traditional societies, marred as they might be, for hints on how to bring us back into some relationship with nature. We can learn much from people who still find themselves participants rather than spectators in a vibrant, natural world. It is from the melding of wisdoms, primitive and contemporary, scientific and traditional, that our answers will come.

Eight

◇ ◇ ◇

Our destiny exercises its influence over us even when, as yet, we have not learned its nature; it is our future that lays down the law of our today.

FRIEDRICH NIETZSCHE, *Human, All Too Human,* 1878

I RETURNED FROM Africa in the spring of 1981 and went on to graduate from Kalamazoo College. Even though months had passed since my letters had been sent, I received no response from John Weaver or Timm Kaminski. When I returned to the States I had attempted calling, but Weaver had left his position and no one could tell me for where or what, and Kaminski was no longer enrolled in school. It seemed the two had vanished without a trace. I contemplated heading west anyway, but I could find no one who knew anything about the Yellowstone wolf project except for vague notions that there existed an interest in wolf recovery in the park. Meanwhile I was being pressured by Dr. Lou Batts, one of my advisers at Kalamazoo, who had become a close friend and mentor of sorts, to consider law school, a much more practical career path. (He was, of course, a lawyer himself with an illustrious career as a founder of the Environmental Defense Fund, one of the finest environmental legal organizations in the country.) Dr. Batts argued convincingly that I could probably do "something" more significant and far-reaching for wolves if I had a law degree to supplement my biology degree.

I was quite dejected not having gotten a response from Weaver or

Kaminski, and stymied regarding what to do next—either find them or find some other way to facilitate getting involved with the Yellowstone project. I didn't know whether to interpret their silence as a polite rejection or whether they were just too busy to respond to all the students who wanted to get involved with a wolf project in Yellowstone. The law school route certainly seemed the safest and most clearly marked path, and there was no doubt as to my parents' opinion. Then a remarkable thing happened. Late in the evening the very night before I was to leave for Vermont where I hoped to establish residency to go to the Vermont Law School, my car sitting in the driveway packed for a dawn departure, I got a call from Timm Kaminski.

As it turned out, neither he nor Weaver had received my letters from Africa. (I later learned on a chance encounter in New Haven, Connecticut, with my mail-carrying Peace Corps friend that he had fallen ill with malaria on the way to Freetown and had been laid up for nearly three weeks. He had sent the letters via African mails from his sickbed, and obviously they had been lost.) Kaminski, by complete and remarkable coincidence, was calling to see if I was still interested in the Yellowstone wolf project. "Your name came up the other day, we figured you had graduated, and we wondered what had become of you. Weaver thinks you should come out, he might even have a job for you." That's all the urging it took.

For reasons that escape me I had decided to take my eighty-year-old paternal grandmother, who was experiencing the onset of Alzheimer's, on the trip west. We set out for Jackson Hole in the fall of 1981 in my intrepid Ford Maverick, freshly painted park-bench green by my daddy. I had recently acquired an eight-week-old husky-mix puppy named Bristol, who sat on my grandmother's lap a good deal of the trip being gently stroked by hands etched with veins like our map was with roads. I adored my grandmother and had often confided in her while growing up. So in spite of the Alzheimer's and the fact that I had told no one else my ambitious plan or the motivation behind it, I chose to tell Grams all about Natasha and my promise to her and that I was moving to Jackson to help bring the wolves back to Yellowstone.

My grandmother spoke a very "Germanized" English. Having come to the States late in her youth with little formal education in English, she would embellish words with extra vowels or *sha*'s at the end, or invert sentence structure in a way I found utterly charming. For instance, "I didn't know," or "I don't know," was "I know not." My name was always "Renéesha." The word "jump" was pronounced "yump," a source of great amusement for her grandchildren. Most animals, in my grandmother's lexicon, jumped rather than ran, so whether it be fox or ferret, it "yumped and yumped" to get around. When we were young, my brother and I would beg Grams to say the word. We would contrive specific questions like "What does the bunny do on Easter, Grandma?" At last she would humor us with wide eyes and arms flailing in large arcs. "On Easter, the bunny he will come, yumping and yumping." We would burst into fits of giggles, rolling around the floor and yumping and yumping across the kitchen linoleum like ecstatic frogs.

As we left the Midwest I would occasionally ask Grams, who had never been west of Chicago, if she remembered where we were going, and she would stop humming one of her old German folk tunes long enough to say, "Ya, ya, we go to the mountains where the woovs they will come yumping and yumping."

Grams brought a black patent leather shoe bag on that trip which she would not let out of her sight. When we stopped at a hotel or a restaurant Grams would insist on bringing her shoe bag in with her. I found this slightly bewildering, even irritating, and would try to explain to my grandmother that we would not be needing her good shoes on that particular venture into the restaurant for soup or into the gas station for a soda. Her stubbornness surpassed even my own, however, and that shoe bag went everywhere.

The Maverick broke down in Rapid City, South Dakota, and we were delayed for several days waiting for a part, so I was elated when we finally made it to Wyoming and neared Jackson Hole. I quickly sobered, however, when I realized we were wholly unprepared for the late fall snowstorm that forced us, with a rapidly dwindling tank of gas and no snow tires, to inch our way over Togwotee Pass, the 9,658-foot northwest gateway into Jackson. The Tetons appeared for a few minutes as we descended—my heart skipped a beat remembering the morning three years before when I had awakened to that view. How strange the turn of events seemed. I remember wondering as we descended the west side of the pass and the mountains came in and out of view through the strange swirls of fog and snow whether it would take a full year to get the wolves back. My grandmother hummed the whole way down the mountain as I skidded, lurched, swerved, and cursed in spite of our turtle-like pace. My little Maverick should have had ice skates. Grams just kept stroking Bristol, now and then exclaiming as though she were spotting them for the first time each time, "Look the mountains, the mountains!"

I hadn't budgeted for the extra days in Rapid City, nor had I planned on the costly car repairs, so when we arrived in Jackson after a five-hour ordeal on Togwotee I found myself in the difficult position of having only six dollars and thirty-eight cents, no place to stay, and no credit cards. I figured that it was enough cash to get my grandmother a cup of coffee and a piece of pie and me a drink, preferably a very strong one, and maybe I could beg a few scraps from the waitress for Bris. So off we went, my grandmother, her shoe bag, and I, to the Wort Hotel. Even though I knew Grams had no money with her, my father having insisted that if she carried a wallet she would lose it, I decided to confess my dilemma to her. I figured she would forget it ten minutes later and I might feel less burdened, and sharing our situation might also make me feel a little less alone. I knew it all had to work out somehow. I wasn't voted class optimist for nothing, right? I knew only one person in Wyoming, John Weaver, and he was, hopefully, to become my boss. I could hardly show up on his doorstep penniless, homeless, with my grandmother and a puppy.

In the restaurant at the Wort Hotel my grandmother, always drawn to examining linen by the fine needlepoint habits she learned during her German girlhood, fingered the nicely stitched corners of the pretty cotton napkins. They bore a Thanksgiving theme with "horns of plenty" spilling mounds of grapes and apples and plump pears onto the cloth. I couldn't quite manage to tell my grandmother that "plenty" wasn't what we had at that moment, but I halfheartedly joked that we might have to wash those napkins ourselves, or the pie plate she had eaten from, because we were so low on cash. She seemed surprised and uncomprehending, tilting her head like a dog listening to a curious sound. She said in her heavy accent, "Oh Renéesha, plenty of money have we, I knew not you needed it." She reached under the table and pulled out her shoe bag. I started to protest that she didn't need her shoes just this minute, which, as usual, went unacknowledged. She pulled out her shoes (my turn to tilt my head like a dog) and, reaching under the quilted lining of the shoe bag, started pulling out hundred-dollar bills. Half the gulp of gin and tonic I had just taken went down my windpipe, which precipitated a less than ladylike coughing and choking fit. The coughs dissolved into giggles, then tears. I was astonished, overjoyed, bewildered, and very, very relieved. I wiped away the tears with horn-of-plenty napkins, grateful we wouldn't be washing them, or the dishes, that evening. The waitress brought the check and my grandmother paid with a hundred-dollar bill.

That night in our hotel I counted the money from the shoe bag. Four thousand three hundred and sixty-three dollars. My grandmother would have happily given it all to me, but I accepted only a few hundred dollars to tide me over until my first payday. I had the rest made into a cashier's check. Knowing that the ravages of memory loss would blank all of this out for Grams and that she would panic upon discovering the cash missing, I wrote a note in big letters explaining what I had done. I put the note and cashier's check back in the lining of the shoe bag. My grandmother must have taken that note out and read it fifty times before she got on the plane a day later. The morning she left I got her settled into one of the bulk-head seats on the plane, her shoe bag in her lap, and leaned down to kiss her good-bye. She put her hand on my arm, beckoning me close to impart one of her many wisdoms that always had to be conveyed in urgent whispered tones. Kneading my arm and pulling me closer, she whispered, "Renéesha, don't ever give up, the woovs will one day be yumping and yumping in the mountains of Yellowstone."

The coincidences and themes that have repeated themselves throughout my experiences have given me faith that there exists a thread of destiny that runs through our lives. Sometimes it has been just the right person showing up at just the right time, or perhaps a specific incident that would guide me toward a certain decision or action, or the sudden appearance of financial help when it was most needed; these patterns convince me that life is inspired and driven by forces larger than our individual egos. At the same time I do believe will is a determinate force in shaping one's future. Both will and destiny court each other in an odd sort of dance, weaving synchronicities like Kaminski's call or the windfall of my grandmother's eccentricity into affirmations that one is headed in the right direction.

When I was younger I might have dismissed events like those described here as mere chance, but after experiencing so many mysterious congruities throughout the course of working for the return of wolves, an effort that would occupy the next fifteen years of my life, I believe that stronger forces are at play. When something corresponds so perfectly to a need or question, I have come to trust the strands of guidance. It is not that I believe that our fates are predetermined, but rather that a greater wisdom is available to us and, if we pay attention, can guide our lives.

My first months in Jackson however, felt anything but guided, so often did I stumble in trying to find my footing in the West. The paid biologist's technician position (translation: field gopher) that John Weaver had thought was secured for me disappeared in some sort of bureaucratic tangle and I had to scavenge for work. I attempted to support my "wolf habit," as my parents called it, with whatever odd jobs I could string together during that first year. My first job was waitressing at a Chinese restaurant called the Lame Duck. It was there that I met my first Wyoming friend, Tim-Bob Sandlin, who was the short-order cook, and to whom I am eternally grateful. It was his blessed soy-soaked soul that hauled me through that first winter of discontent by teaching me how to drink tequila, dance the Western Swing, and endure country and western music—in that order. Admittedly, the first helped considerably with the last. Little did I know at the time how each of those skills would become indispensable to me in a future of negotiating in countless after-meeting bars filled with wolf-hating cowboys.

I spent every spare moment I had volunteering for John Weaver, who by then had been appointed to serve on the Northern Rocky Mountain Wolf Recovery Team, the government-appointed body charged with developing a blueprint for restoring wolves to the Rockies. As a team member John was well positioned to coordinate many of the Yellowstone wolf-related efforts. In return for my volunteer work, John taught me a great deal about the history and status of the Yellowstone wolf project and mentored my entry into the wolf politics of the West. Because of his position on the team, John was asked to attend numerous meetings throughout the region to inform and educate members of various other state and federal entities about the wolf's potential presence and the progress of the recovery plan. John generously allowed me to tag along to many of these gatherings. On the long trips home from Missoula or Cheyenne we would have postmortem discussions about who said what, why they said it, what it really meant, and how it influenced the goal we cared about—wolves on the ground in Yellowstone.

Entering the wolf political arena was a bit like getting lost in a city with no art museums and blocks of gang-infested ghettos: none of the beauty, all of the danger. Like a visitor to a foreign land, I didn't understand the language or the signposts of this new habitat. In the West, particularly in the realm of state and federal bureaucracies and politics, the idea of returning wolves provoked passions completely disproportionate to the potential impact of the wolf's presence. It soon became clear that in most discussions wolves merely provided a pretext to talk about much deeper and more personal political views, invariably those having to do with control—control of land and control of animals. Who controlled the "rights" to the animals, who could kill the elk that the wolves would prey upon, who could kill the wolves that killed "too many" elk, who could control which prey species and which predators and where and when and how. In truth, all of it was a discussion about killing and control veiled in the professional shibboleth of "wildlife management." Wildlife management is, of course, an oxymoron. Animals that are truly "wild" are, by definition, not managed. Yet I would discover in the different jobs I would have over the next several years a troubling trend toward complete control or manipulation of many "wildlife" populations even within national parks.

I barely survived my first Jackson Hole winter. The transition from Africa's tropical heat to Wyoming's arctic minus 60 degree temperatures was a confused migration. I credit Bristol with getting me through the winter. Her husky-born, snow-swooned glee ceaselessly inspired me to love the snow and cold. Even though I shared a small brick house with two roommates and two other dogs, I struggled that first winter to meet the exorbitant rents in Jackson. When Weaver and his wife Terry offered to loan me their tepee for my first summer there I leapt at the opportunity. Another friend, Jeff Foott, offered his back pasture as a setup site.

The location had lyrical significance because years before the previous owner of the property, a filmmaker, had kept a captive pack of wolves on that same land. A small creek ran through the property and large Douglas firs arched over the edges of the lush green meadow. I had a small school desk in the tepee, the kind with the pencil slot on the top, a chair that swiveled, and a lid that lifted. I kept my journals tucked into the neat cradle of that desk. My books were stored in the red plastic milk crates that had once been Bristol's travel kennel, upon which sat a single-burner camp stove. A red plastic cooler (which, I will note, matched my bookcase) was tucked into an earthen hole in one corner of the tepee. On weeks that were blessed with a payday the cooler might hold perishable groceries or an opened can of dog food. A cot completed my collection of tepee furniture, serving as couch, chair, and berth. At night I slept in a thick cotton sleeping bag, its red flannel lining patterned with flying ducks and geese. I had used the same bag growing up at slumber parties and on family camping trips, so it brought a sense of home to Wyoming.

Bristol had grown to be a wild thing. From the beginning she was a mysterious dog—self-possessed, dignified, determined—without question, her own being. As she matured she developed a lovely strawberry-blond hue with snowy white highlights; her dark hazel-brown eyes were rimmed in a warm chocolate diamond that reminded me of my mother's Christmas fudge. Each ear stood erect about halfway up and then the tips flopped forward in a funny bow, giving her the tender look of the Flying Nun. Even as a puppy she chose her own quarters, preferring her makeshift kennel of the two red milk crates lashed together, a hot-water bottle, and a windup alarm clock with a hearty ticktock to almost any human lap, except my grandmother's.

It was a lean summer. I ate mostly peanut butter sandwiches, and in the evening Bris and I would share a package of ramen noodles. Sometimes they were on sale for nineteen cents and we would each get our own. I think that was the happiest summer of Bristol's life. She roamed freely in the forests behind the pasture. Down the driveway and across Fall Creek Road lay a llama ranch. For some reason the llamas enchanted Bristol. She had little interest in cows, sheep, or horses, but would spend hours sitting at the edge of the corral contemplating the llamas. They would in turn stare back at her, and what was conveyed in these long hours of meditation between dog and llama I will never know.

Several mornings a week, very early, I hitchhiked over Teton Pass to Driggs, Idaho, where I was paid $2.30 an hour to help Alan Franklin, a graduate student from Humboldt State University, on a great gray owl study. This work did little to support my volunteer wolf efforts, but I loved it dearly. We were mapping nesting habitat, tiptoeing through dense forests peering up into the dark heavy boughs, not unlike those of my childhood pine stand, hooting the deep, booming *whoo-hoo-hoo* great gray courtship calls. Now and then one of the soft pewter-colored birds would answer with a penetrating echo of our call, and excited, with our hearts thumping, we would comb the area for a possible nest. Once I called and a huge female swooped down, her wing tips coming so close I could feel the air stir against the hollow of my cheek as she dove. Her talons grazed Bristol's back as she lifted and lighted just above our heads. Unknowingly, we'd been standing right below her nest.

Just before I started working on the project a nest had been accidentally felled by a forest crew and the female was killed. Franklin had taken the chicks, named Zeus and Zoe, and was hand-raising them. When they got old enough to hop and fly they were taken over to the property of Bruce and Molly Hampton, who ran a honey farm near Driggs, Idaho. The chicks perched in a stand of old Doug fir down below the honey house, and four mornings a week Alan and I would run the mousetrap lines we had set all over the county and deliver the harvest.

Although I haven't seen it documented in the literature, female great grays have a unique call to gather their young during the fledgling stage. It sounds something like *ooooowheeeeep . . . oooowheeeep . . . oooowheeeep,* on a rising note. We would do our best to imitate that call and the chicks would come hopping and flapping in. Later, as they grew, they would swoop down and in a flurry of wings, tipping and wobbling, land on your shoulder or head, their talons sometimes painfully gripping your arm or scalp, as they greedily snatched the dangling mouse from your fingers. We quickly learned to wear heavy caps and canvas jackets for our visits. Poor Molly and Bruce eventually had to calculate their comings and goings, timing a stooped run from their front door to the honey house or car to escape the birds, so watchful and ravenous were the owls, eager to swoop in for a possible meal.

Molly and Bruce spent long hours trying to teach the young owls hunting skills using mice and a fishing rod, but years later Bruce would tell me he doubted they were successful in teaching them survival skills. Both chicks were returned to the wild. One was later found with an unmendable broken leg and had to be euthanized; the other disappeared from the release site and no one knew how it ultimately fared. Still, I admire the hell out of Molly, Bruce, and Alan for their long hours of effort to give those fledglings a chance. All of us still dream, I'm sure, of the shadow of those wings darkening the sun as they alighted on our shoulders, their reaching across the chasm between creature and human for the sustenance that might bear them into the wild lives to which they were born. We fed them mice, they fed us dreams. Such is the nature of the wild's reciprocity.

I sometimes brought the extra mice from our trapline back to Bristol.

Dead mice, however, were deemed barely worthy by my proud partner. She much preferred supplementing our ramen diet with rabbits, which she was quite adept at catching in the meadow surrounding the tepee. However, she had an odd habit of leaving me the heads of her prizes. I would hitch back over Teton Pass late in the evening, often arriving at the tepee in the black of night. Bristol would run to the pasture's edge to meet me, leading the way back to the tepee through the tall wet grass, her ears bobbing in time to my flashlight beam. The first rabbit head I found was a young tawny brown, deposited just inside the door flap, dark eyes shining iridescent in the beam of my flashlight, and those soft, faintly pink ears stiff in the frigid night air. Bristol seemed slightly injured when I flung her gift out into the deep pasture grass, but in future days it would be replaced by other bunny heads. Always the head, only the head. I would halfheartedly admonish Bris, and she would peer up at me, incredulous that I wasn't more appreciative. She nonetheless was proud of her gifts, and never stopped her sweet offerings for my late night homecomings.

As it grew colder the nights were whittled down into a lean ritual. I heated up the nightly pot of creek water on my camp stove, poured out enough to bathe, and into the remainder went our noodles. As they boiled I raced through a cursory sponge bath, hopping and wiggling my shivering body into the old pair of my grandpa's white nubbly long underwear that I kept tucked under the pillow. With cold and fumbling fingers I ripped open the little flavor packet and dumped it into the pot. Clutching the pot's warmth in my lap, I slithered into the cold cotton of my bird-blessed bedding. As a young girl I had loved the idea of sleeping among flying ducks and geese, but as the autumn cold set in I longed to be enveloped in the down feathers rather than the winged images of those birds. I was facing Wyoming's "three-dog nights" and I had only one, who eagerly awaited the pot of warm noodles after I'd slurped down half. Once finished, Bristol climbed onto the cot, turned three perfect circles, and settled into a tawny ball that fit perfectly against my belly. So the nights passed. Now and then I wondered what I would do with no money and winter pressing close, no hope of wolves on the horizon, but I was young and trusted in the world, and had learned to wait. Sleep would come swiftly those nights, carried on the wings of ducks and geese and the hushed calls of owls.

Nine

❖ ❖ ❖

We must assume our existence as broadly as we in any way can; everything, even the unheard-of, must be possible in it. That is at bottom the only courage that is demanded of us: to have courage for the most strange, the most singular, and the most inexplicable that we may encounter.

RAINER MARIA RILKE

I RETURNED FROM my "owling" one day to find a note pinned to my te-pee. The note, from a friend, said I should call Bob and Anne Yarnall, who were looking for a house-sitter. I did, and they invited me down to meet them and see the house, located at the end of Fish Creek Road. My Maverick was having yet another fit of colic and wouldn't start, so Bristol and I set out to cover the five miles on foot, determined not to let the possibility of a warm house for the winter slip away.

I discovered Fish Creek Road is one of the most beautiful in the Tetons. It hugs the bottom edge of the mountains as though it had melted down the slopes and collected in a tar stream along their winding base. That evening it seemed an elegant, innocent road, threading its way beneath heavy boughs of Douglas fir and through the fall-tinted lemon leaves of aspen stands. The Tetons rise without warning from its flat shoulder, climbing some 14,000 feet. They are a young and a proud range, allowing no plump and dimpled foothills to prepare their way. So abrupt is the transition from valley floor to mountain that one can stand on certain sections of the road with one leg planted flat on the sleek pavement and the other at a forty-degree angle on the lower slopes of the Teton wall. The road hops over Fish Creek by way of an old wooden bridge under which magical birds called water ouzels weave their hivelike nests and the creek bubbles absentmindedly along the road and out across the valley with yellow warblers and song sparrows knitting their songs along its willow-lined banks.

That first evening as Bristol and I walked down Fish Creek Road I saw a porcupine, the first of many sightings. It was a bitterly cold fall evening, we were walking fast, and at first I couldn't make out what was shuffling along the shoulder of the road ahead of us. As we neared I realized it was an old porcupine. Porcupines are always old. They have that wizened, knowing look that makes one think they have learned all the secrets of the world in their slow, eternal living. I called to him in the fading evening light to send us luck, that we were on our way to an interview for a house-sitting position and badly needed a home.

The Yarnalls' house was a simple and fresh-looking A-frame house made mostly of glass, interrupted here and there by clean white walls. There was a blond wood table, four lodgepole chairs, a canvas-covered couch, a chocolate-colored pillow chair, a bookshelf, and a fireplace, all positioned on a soft mouse-brown carpet. The back of the house was hugged by an open stand of quaking aspen, then nearly leafless. A pine porch swing swayed peacefully over the weathered wood deck that looked eastward toward Fish Creek. A huge Douglas fir sheltered the northeast corner of the deck; the lowest branches, to my tree-scaling eye, looked to be just the right height for an easy swing mount.

The Yarnalls were a lovely couple from Philadelphia who, I'm sure, immediately and astutely read the symptoms of my penniless condition—my cheeks were flushed from the five-mile walk. Obviously I was carless and living in a tepee with winter settling in. I told them about my work on the wolf project and the owls and what I could about myself and then fell silent. Bristol lay at my feet waiting, sure and secure, already knowing that this would be our home.

We moved in a week later and thanks to the tremendous generosity of the Yarnalls lived there for nearly four years, until the house was sold. It was on Fish Creek Road that the possibility of The Wolf Fund began to germinate. The Yarnalls were my first "enablers," providing shelter, free of charge, for

Bristol and me. It was a kindness so great and far-reaching that I still have no words adequate to express my gratitude.

Through the early eighties, dodging avalanche shoots and spring floods, I wound my way home along Fish Creek Road to where it dead-ended five miles north of Wilson, Wyoming. The winters were long. The few of us who lived there in those years, burrowed in the slopes at its far north end, would endure the lovely but relentless pearl-painted winter skies, waiting and waiting until at last the repetitious gray gave way to the splintered pastel glory of spring mornings. They were wet and windy dawns, the skies torn with racing clouds and the horizon filled with a far-off dazzling light.

On those mornings I would climb the Doug fir, clinging to its thick branches and shivering against the wind. For some reason I felt nearer to spring perched high above the world. I could feel it coming close, moving across the bleak mountain snow in the new morning light like the long-winged flight of a migrating swan.

It was in spring that the porcupines made their mysterious migration to Fish Creek Road. They came down from the lodgepole pine perches, shedding their winter lethargy and shuffling across the packed-snow surface of the lower mountain slopes, winding their way through the tall forests of fir and spruce, clambering to the banks lining the road, virtual cliffs sliced by the huge plows. Here—daredevil porcupines!—they plunged their needled bodies, sliding and tumbling down the snow wall onto the matted brown grass sprinkled with tender shoots of new green and the salty rime that ran along the road. Every year they collected for a few weeks, just when spring began to lean on winter and the rising sun changed its cool, thin, slanting light to the warm, wine-colored rays that presaged that deep and secret thing about to happen.

Perched in my fir overlooking the deck, I would long for the arrival of the porcupines, as though they were the ones who escorted spring to the winter-chilled valley, swaying down the road, their great tails swishing the snow back farther and farther until it melted into the willows that edged the creek. I would often roam the hillsides near the house watching for porcupines nosing their way down the slopes. It was a brave but reckless lot of porcupines that came to beat back winter. Too often they rambled in front of impatient cars and were left silent carcasses along the roadside. Driving home those nights, I would sometimes count thirteen or fourteen porcupines lumbering along the grassy shoulder, their eye-shine an amber red in my headlights.

During my last spring on Fish Creek, while driving home one night, my headlights fell on a single carcass rolled in a quilled ball against a snowbank. The trees reached down the steep incline to the bank, their great boughs, still heavy with snow, shadowing the roadside. I slowed, and then, seeing the red slash of blood and scattered quills, continued onward. Dead porcupines were a familiar scene, but on that particular night the picture of the needled ball and streaked blood haunted me.

I rose early the next day and, still sluggish from troubled sleep, dressed and drove to work. Passing the carcass, I noticed the blood had dried to a dreary red, and a dream from the night before came flooding back. I had dreamt of an old man curled in a fetal position along the roadside. He had lived his whole life deep in the mountains. His eyes were alive and wise with age, and his leathered skin hung in fine creases and folds around the soft lines of his eyes and mouth. He was weak with hunger and cold.

As I drove home that evening a light snow began to fall. It covered the blood streak and dusted the back of the dead porcupine. That night I again dreamed of the old man, huddled by the road, his brittle hair matted and cold and his dark eyes silent. He called out in small moans and whistles. Awakening, I lay there in the dark hearing the moans echo in my head. I got up, built a fire, and curled down into the pillow chair with a mug of cocoa, trying in vain to shake the dream.

Exasperated, I finally decided to go get the carcass and give it a proper burial. I slung my down parka on over my nightgown, yanked my Sorel boots on to my bare feet, and stuffed an old rose-colored wool blanket into a box. Grabbing the box and a flashlight, I waded down through the spring slush and snow to the car. The road was lightly covered with fresh snow, muffling the tires as they skimmed down the road, quiet as owl flight. I parked in the middle of the road so that the headlights illuminated the snow-covered ball. Planning to use the blanket as a broom, I burrowed the toe of my left boot under the heavy quill lump in order to roll it into the box. At that moment the porcupine lifted its head and looked at me. The snow fell, the drifting flakes arcing against the night like a pearly meteor shower in the beam of headlights. The porcupine fixed me with its gaze. The silence seemed infinite.

I'm not sure how long I stood there, astonished, my flannel nightgown luffing in the breeze. Not knowing what else to do, I covered the porcupine with the thin wool blanket to avoid being slapped with quills and coaxed him into the box. His right foreleg, caked with blood, was held close to his body. I realized he couldn't get back up the snowbank. I carried the box with the blanketed porcupine back to the car and put it on the seat next to me, turned on the heat full blast, and sat there as the sun came up to think this all over.

The rich, not unpleasant, wheaty, ammonialike smell of the porcupine permeated the air. Knowing that porcupines are territorial, I didn't want to remove him from the terrain he knew best. I figured with his injured leg he couldn't scale the snowbank, so the best thing was to take him into the nearby lower forest slopes of Phillips Canyon where he might make it back into familiar habitat.

I found an uneaten sandwich from the day before on the seat, stuffed it into my pocket, grabbed the box, and went clambering up the snowbank. Stumbling over my nightgown and sinking up to my thighs every other step, I trudged up the slope hugging the box. After a hundred yards or so I stopped. My legs burned a bright wet red and the heavy snow packed and melted into my boots. Setting the box down under a large spruce tree, I began to ease the blanket out onto the snow. The porcupine's wizened little face peered out from the blanket. Its thin weave had settled down around the dark-tipped blond quills, which poked through the worn wool, giving the impression of a plump, rose-colored pincushion.

Breaking the frozen tuna sandwich into chunks, I spread it around him, then turned and started wading back down to the road. After a few steps I had one of those odd memory flashes, recalling the porcupine I had called to, almost on this very spot, on my first walk down Fish Creek Road to be interviewed by the Yarnalls. I looked around at the still-blanketed porcupine. He looked back at me, his clear dark eyes steady and calm. I returned to the spruce on my way home from work that evening. I had filled my pockets with carrots and walnuts. The sandwich was gone and my blanket lay there in a heap. No porcupine. I scattered the food across the snow and picked up the blanket, plucking the quills from the rosy wool as I headed back down the slope, once again reassured of the nature of wild reciprocity.

Ten

❖ ❖ ❖

Our most urgent social and political question [is]: how to live in right relationship. In learning to pay respectful attention to one another and plants and animals, we relearn the acts of empathy, and thus humility and compassion——ways of proceeding that grow more and more necessary as the world crowds in.

WILLIAM KITTRIDGE, *Places of the Wild*

I FONDLY REMEMBER my years living at the end of Fish Creek Road as the Dolittle years—because they were filled with coming to know so many different species of animals. During that time I worked on several wildlife films and a number of endangered species projects. Those years were filled with leaping, crawling, flying, swooping, browsing, charging, furtive, and whimsical creatures. From the reaches of Jasper National Park in Alberta where I watched bighorn sheep rams in bloody battle on the cliff edges of the Canadian Rocky Mountains to the humid, leaf-strewn deep-forest floors of the Santa Ana National Wildlife Refuge in southern Texas where chachalacas scuttled in quiet foraging, my life was completely, deliciously, happily submerged in the lives of animals. During those years I worked on whooping cranes, bald eagles, black-footed ferrets, water ouzels, mule deer, elk, and moose. If I hadn't loved the realm of creatures before, those years afforded me the leisure and opportunity to feel the pulse of life about me, as an aspen might experience the rich spectrum of sunlight bathing its branches and leaves.

Oddly, it was the wildlife fieldwork unrelated to wolves that I took on to support my "wolf habit" that supplied a critical foundation and training for the years ahead which would be focused solely on wolves. It was also during this period that I would be introduced to the political quagmire of endangered species recovery efforts—the ethical tangles, financial struggles, competing interests, the compromises inherent in research, and the heartbreak of losing precious animals that were members of species fast disappearing from the face of the earth. It was a time of moving from "the melancholy time of not knowing," as E. B. White describes it, to "the unbearable knowing and knowing."

One of my first wildlife projects in the West, after the owl work, was the Grays Lake whooping crane foster parent program. It introduced me to the tedium and tangles inherent in many endangered species efforts. The goal of the project was to establish a new whooping crane population by introducing the eggs of both wild and captive-born whooping cranes into the nests of wild sandhill cranes. The single population of whoopers in the United States, which migrates 2,400 miles twice a year between northern Canada's Wood Buffalo National Park to the Aransas National Wildlife Refuge in southern Texas, is highly vulnerable; any catastrophic event could wipe out the species. The hope was that the Grays Lake program could generate a second population of whooping cranes that would utilize the migration route and summering and wintering grounds of these particular sandhill cranes.

Behind so many endangered species stories are the heroic efforts of a person or persons who devote their lives with fierce singularity to the fate of that species. With chimps it is Jane Goodall, with mountain lions it is Maurice Hornocker, with gorillas it was Dian Fossey, and, in the early eighties, with cranes it was Rodrick Drewien. The Grays Lake project was the brainchild of this delightful man, a rosy-cheeked biologist with twinkling eyes, an easy laugh, and an irresistibly infectious passion for his birds. He had been watching sandhill cranes on Grays Lake for nearly twenty years when I joined the project for a short stint in the fall of 1982. I consider Drewien's influence on my thinking to have been substantial even though I worked with him for only a short time. His commitment to the birds, to the project, his essentially giving over his life to this quest deeply impressed me. He was one of the first people I encountered who personified one of my favorite Robert Frost lines: "My object in life is to unite my vocation and avocation as two eyes make one in sight."

Drewien had conceived, designed, and almost single-handedly procured funding for the whooping crane/sandhill crane (WC/SC) foster parent program. In the process he had become a skilled navigator of the political minefield of endangered species politics and state and federal jurisdictional battles. Somehow through his good humor, hard work, passion, and grit Drewien had managed to pull numerous competing entities, private and public, national and international, together to work toward a single goal—establishing a new migrating population of whooping cranes. Rod introduced me to the inner workings of international endangered species projects, particularly the compromises and challenges associated with a restoration effort that involved enormous amounts of intervention and risk. I began to appreciate that at the root of most endangered species rhetoric lies the questions of ethics: How far should man be willing to go to save a species? To what degree should we so-called stewards be willing to compromise the autonomy of individual animals in order to benefit the long-term survival of a species? (We are very uncomfortable when this question applies to humans, yet decisions are routinely, even casually, made with animals.) Where are the limits to manipulating one animal to favor the fortunes of another? In terms of ethics, what are the costs?

The WC/SC foster parent program, although imaginative and meticulous in design, met with many heartbreaking setbacks and frustrations. Survival of the introduced whooper eggs and the chicks they produced was constantly challenged by storms, predators, hunters, fences, power lines, poison, and disease. In addition to confronting the considerable biological challenges of introducing wild and captive-produced whooping crane eggs into the nests of wild sandhill cranes, Drewien was faced with the constant resistance of ranchers to the presence of an endangered species, the inability of hunters to distinguish a whooping crane from a snow goose (which could be legally shot) or a whooper juvenile from a sandhill adult, and simple bad luck.

The project had experienced a number of devastating blows in the months before I joined it in the fall of 1982. Misfortune had befallen the bird that showed the most promise of being the first wild-born whooper to breed— Whooper 75–1, a chick hatched in June of 1975. Drewien had nicknamed him "Miracles," a reference to the many difficult situations this bird got himself into and, against all odds, managed to get himself out of in the seven years of his life. In May of 1982, Rod found him entangled in a barbed-wire fence, dead.

The photograph Rod took of Miracles in the death clutches of that barbed wire is one of the most haunting images of man's collision with the wild I have ever seen. One three-toed claw, noosed by the upper two strands of the barbed wire, is held erect, the middle toe pointed to the sky, the other two bowing horizontally like a primitive cross, hailing the heavens to bear witness to this death. The bird's other leg, horribly mangled, is entangled in the lower two strands of the fence held against the bird's feathered breast. Its snowy white body, bloodied from a prolonged and merciless struggle with the fence, is suspended upside down, the wings inverted and slightly open, dangling above the long, slender neck, surrendered limp against the tender green of spring grasses. One cannot turn away from the image of the fallen angel clutched to the earth by man's fear, by our need to control, contain, regulate, and delineate with the tautness of our barbed fences cutting through the wild landscape of the West.

Unfortunately, the loss that year was not limited to the fall of Miracles. Two other promising birds were lost, another one to barbed wire and the third to disease. Both Miracles and Pancho had begun establishing and defending territories in the years preceding their deaths. In fact, in May of 1982, Miracles had begun gathering nesting material and was showing a distinct interest in a captive-born female that biologists had introduced into his territory. Only weeks later, with the nest uncompleted, the seven-year-old Miracles died. Autopsy results showed he had been in excellent health. Only three months after that the same four-stranded barbed-wire fate would befall Pancho, the other seven-year-old male. These stories revealed the other side of the endangered species story, the dark irrefutable reality that man's actions can inadvertently speed us toward the potential extinction of a species.

It was also through whooping cranes that I was introduced to the bitter irony of endangered species recovery efforts that require killing members of one species to assist another. During years of drought both the precious whooping crane eggs and the young chicks became primary targets for predators. A crash in the ground squirrel population was apparently driving coyotes and foxes deeper into the marshlands, where sandhills nest, in search of food. The Grays Lake staff felt they were facing an epidemic and that nothing short of major predator control efforts would suppress it. Thus, in order to protect the rare whooping crane eggs and chicks, nearly all the tools of the predator wars were deployed against these animals that might threaten the cranes—M-44s (or "coyote getters," which pump cyanide into the mouth of any animal tugging a scented device), traps, helicopter hunting. Coyotes and foxes were the main focus. Although they were never the target of control efforts, Drewien suspected golden eagles were part of the problem, and even American crows and ravens were implicated in egg destruction. These actions demand that we face questions like "To what lengths are we willing to go to protect species that are endangered from those that are not?" The maze of ethics becomes very complicated in the face of the potential loss of an entire species.

Predator control was only one facet of the project that forced me to examine some of these difficult moral issues. The WC/SC foster parent program unquestionably involved a certain amount of disruption and invasion of the lives of its subjects. In the case of the cranes the invasiveness was minimal: small telemetry radio transmitters were attached to the ankles of the cranes when they were young, after which the birds were monitored while on the ground and tracked from the air during migration.

My job was to monitor flight activity in anticipation of migration. The cranes would climb up into the clouds, riding thermals in winged spirals, higher and higher, testing the fronts. Most often they would descend back down in comical parachuting style, their wings spread and legs swinging, tipping to and fro in the gusts until they lit in a field among the raucous cry of the flocks on the ground.

Radio tracking, or telemetry, utilizes electronic equipment attached to an animal or bird, either a collar, harness, leg brand, or surgical implant that emits an inaudible radio signal to be picked up by the researcher's antenna. The signal is used to locate an individual animal and can relay information about whether it is bedded or moving, in which direction and how quickly. Telemetry also makes animals or birds observable at night or when they are in cover.

The radio transmitters helped considerably in keeping track of individual birds, but there were always the inherent compromises. Sometimes the transmitters had to be replaced, which meant recapturing the bird. Sometimes the birds were flushed from nests or stressed because researchers got too close. I was troubled by the feeling that these wild creatures were somehow lessened by their manipulation by humans. As with the captive wolves, I considered it a great privilege to watch these magnificent birds, yet at times the contradictions were chaffing.

I couldn't escape the nagging sense that the manipulation represented by the telemetry equipment might reveal a troubling assumption—that our domination of these creatures was complete and irrefutable. Our right to adorn them with tags or collars, antennas, and radios was not questioned because we were there to "help." Yet these birds, like so many animals that were the subject of wildlife research, were very vulnerable to our hubris.

Although the project met with marginal success, due to bad luck rather than bad science, it was an inspired plan that in spite of its manipulation of other species was justified, in my opinion, by the imminent danger of losing whooping cranes from the planet. Using telemetry gear that first time made me deeply aware of the way in which scientists must invade the lives of their study subjects and yet remain humble, as I believe Rod Drewien was, and aware of the autonomy and rights of each single creature over which we presume the right to wield such power.

The crane work was followed by several other endangered species projects that only seemed to deepen my conflict over the strain between research intervention and respect for animal dignity and autonomy. In 1984 I found myself returning to the early mantra of my life—counting deer. This time, however, I was paid to do it, hired as a wildlife biologist on a study to monitor and map mule deer use of winter habitat in Jackson Hole.

Development pressures were beginning to build in Jackson Hole in the early eighties. Ninety-seven percent of the valley is public land; unfortunately, however, the remaining 3 percent of private land includes much of the critical winter habitat for wildlife. East and West Gros Ventre Buttes and Boyles Hill rise like the rounded backs of great sleeping dragons scattered in repose across the flat floor of the valley. Some of the buttes are substantial geologic features of the valley, measuring ten or fifteen miles in circumference at their base. Their exposed hillsides provide forage for several species of ungulates because snow depth is minimal on their windswept slopes, providing browse for foraging deer and occasional moose or elk. The study I worked on was commissioned by the real estate developer of East Gros Ventre Butte in a laudable attempt to minimize impact on resident mule deer populations.

The work was concentrated in the depths of winter, and because the deer were most active in early morning it demanded a predawn rising when it was often ten or twenty below zero. Because the Maverick couldn't make it up the hill where the A-frame was perched, I had to park it down below on the shoulder of Fish Creek Road, where there was no way to plug in a battery warmer. This meant that every morning I had to face the inevitable battle to get it started, a ritual which involved much cursing, ether, a spare car battery, and oft-used jumper cables. Once that ordeal was over my frustration was usually soothed by a mug of hot cocoa from the thermos kept by my side in the car, topped off with a handful of miniature "jet-puffed" marshmallows— a fistful for the cocoa, a fistful for Bris, who sat in the back curled on the rose wool porcupine blanket. Her alert readiness for an adventure, any adventure, always raised my spirits. Counting deer, if only from her backseat perch, her head propped out the open window, scenting the frigid air, qualified in her mind as one of the better in-car outings.

Once I succeeded in coaxing the car to life I would start down the silent and unplowed depths of Fish Creek Road. I was almost always the first to "break trail," the muffled motion of the tires through the deep snow giving the feeling of entering a secret world. The frosted windows added to the sense of furtiveness. I had to constantly scrape the inside of the windshield to maintain a cleared portal through which to see the road. The small scraps of frost from the scraper would gather on my lap like fresh flakes of coconut as I made my way into the village of Wilson. From there I turned east and drove to the starting point at the base of East Gros Ventre Butte and began the morning count. My job was to scan the buttes with spotting scope and binoculars, to locate the deer, use the telemetry antenna to identify any collared animals, and map their location and activity.

The truth is I hated the cold—the heater, let alone the defroster, barely worked in that damned car—but I loved the work. The dawn would light the east-facing slopes like a misty corner of heaven, the swirls of fresh snow and morning fog against the hard blue dawn sky creating an ethereal landscape like I imagined Avalon to be.

In many instances mule deer are quite difficult to see in winter habitat; curled in the shadow of trees or obscured by rock ledges, they are remarkably camouflaged in the mouse brown mottling of snow and a brush-pocked slope. The deer, often still bedded in their hollowed earthen nests, would emerge out of the blankness of the slopes only after patient study. I remembered how Stephen Alexander taught me to look for wildlife when I was a young girl. He would say, "Look for the irregular, let your eyes know the slope or the tree or the swamp. Watch for the interrupted line, the wisp of movement, the unusual angle—*there!* will be the animal." It was like solving an eye puzzle, and the prize was discovering a live animal. As I became more familiar with each group of deer and their habits I began to feel their presence before I would find them with the scope or binoculars. If the snow was fresh, tracks could expedite the searching. But the scanning of a seemingly barren hillside, complicated by swells and snowdrifts, became something of a meditation—illuminated only by a flickering ear or the stomp of a foreleg.

It was both mysterious and mundane, the shivering, the aching and numb toes and fingers, the fogged-up car and scope and binoculars. And then there was the experience of finding the near-invisible deer, delicate and limber, the long-legged lithe movement across rugged terrain, silent survival unfolding on the mottled slope. I loved how the morning traffic would start on the roads that snuggled against the base of the buttes, the awakening of a town, the morning drivers hurrying to work, sipping their coffee from their thermos cups, listening to the radio weather forecast in the hard-edged cold, their steaming exhaust clouding the air, oblivious to the tender creatures a half mile up the slope from where they idled at a stoplight. The deer moved silently above the town on the buttes, their tracks a woven decorative braid across the lower slopes like a garland across a Christmas tree, the quiet creature counterpoint to the industrious workday start of a bustling resort town.

Jackson Hole's deer were both choked and fed by civilization. Not only did many well-meaning but misguided homeowners feed them, luring them into places where they were vulnerable to traffic and dogs, but many of the deer wore the adornment of our science in the form of radio collars and ear tags. Some twenty-five deer had been collared and tagged at the beginning of the study into which I had stepped when it was nearly three years under way.

The information gathered was extremely valuable in understanding how the deer utilized their habitat (of particular interest were the shifts in usage when development occurred), but I was keenly aware of the compromises that went along with the use of telemetry equipment.

As I became more familiar with the individual deer, the experience began to again force an examination of my feelings about the use of telemetry in wildlife work. The heavy black collars decorated with blue stripes or gaudy yellow squares, the ghastly-colored ear tags on the slender beautiful ears burdened the deer in ways that went far beyond the weight of the equipment itself. As with the whooping crane project, I believed the ends of the work were noble, but that the means included a level of intrusion—capturing, marking, tracking, and monitoring—that go largely unexamined in wildlife work. There are ways to evaluate the direct impact of using telemetry techniques on animals—looking at injuries in traps, wounds from malfitting collars, etc.— but there is no protocol for, and very little interest in, answering the basic question: Is the information worth the invasion of a wild creature's life?

Most ethical wildlife research comes down to a question of maintaining humility in the face of today's technological power. Because we can collar an animal does not mean that we should. The question that every researcher must ask is, Do the ends justify the means? In that calculation, the difficult issue of each individual animal's autonomy and dignity should be considered. Beyond the scrutiny of animal rights groups and a smattering of ethical scientists who, risking the scorn of their peers, have challenged our assumptions about the use of collars, implants, ear tags, and such, there is no accepted protocol that ensures that these issues are considered in evaluating wildlife research.

Eleven

◇ ◇ ◇

But environmentalism, in its deepest sense, is not about environment. It is not about things but relationships, not about beings but Being, not about world but the inseparability of self and circumstance.

NEIL EVERNDEN, *The Natural Alien*

A T TIMES IT was quite a juggling act, fulfilling the requirements of the wildlife jobs that actually paid my living expenses while spending the majority of my "leisure" hours on wolf-related pursuits. Although I'm not sure I realized it at the time, those years of weaving together my vocation and avocation created a patchwork of apprenticeships during which various teachers took me under their wing, generously and patiently teaching me everything from the language and history to the personalities, internal politics, and pressure points of undertaking a project like Yellowstone wolf recovery.

During this time, in the early eighties, I accompanied John Weaver and his wife, Terry, to a gathering of biologists from Canada and the States at a rustic camp on the north fork of the Flathead River in Montana, just a few miles from the Canadian border. The three-day seminar focused on the issues surrounding wolves and bears in the northern Rockies, and the meetings offered a marvelous mixture of information exchange, collegial discussion, and planning, mentoring, music, and beer drinking. The presentations were given in a dusty log lodge with cement floors and rickety folding chairs. Black garbage bags were employed as makeshift window shades during slide presentations, the beam of the projector cutting through the kaleidoscope of dust particles that seemed permanently suspended in the room to cast a grainy graphic on the screen. The sheer funkiness and informality went a long way to defuse the competition and sniping that too often divide the scientific ranks of biologists who specialize in predators. At that meeting John made a point of introducing me to Dr. L. David Mech, the internationally known wolf biologist from Minnesota, which was at that time the only one of the lower forty-eight states that had a thriving wolf population.

Mech, who probably has spent more time among wolves and studying wolves than anyone in the world, had for a long time been one of my heroes. He was a study in energy and intellect; his intense brown eyes focused like a wolf alerting when he talked with a student. Outfitted in a slightly disheveled assemblage of plaid shirt, work pants, and dusty walking boots, he had an easy manner and ready humor that disarmed the intensity of his laser-beam focus. Despite his status as a legend, he put the legion of graduate students that followed him around at ease by showing genuine interest in their studies and research designs. They trailed him like a clutch of adoring ducklings, all patiently waiting their turn to discuss their project with him. Like Weaver, Mech has made the training and mentoring of young people a major part of his life's work, and he went out of his way to listen to and encourage nearly every one of the students he met.

He was extremely interested in the effort to restore wolves to Yellowstone, and was one of the few people in the world who had the expertise and experience with wild wolves to be able to guide the development of a technical blueprint for reintroduction. He was extremely generous in answering the hundreds of questions I had about biological approaches, and took time to ask about my work and made numerous helpful suggestions. That meeting marked the beginning of a long, cherished friendship that would play a critical role in my work over the next decade.

During one of our conversations in Montana about the political obstacles to wolf reintroduction, Mech had suggested I look into the logistics of bringing an exhibit, titled *Wolves and Humans: Competition, Coexistence, and Conflict,* to Yellowstone. He had been a consultant on its development by the Science Museum of Minnesota. It had been extremely well received in Minnesota, and

Dave thought the museum's staff was just in the process of booking its traveling venues. He gave me the name of the exhibit's developer, Kurt Hadland.

When I returned to Wyoming I tracked Hadland down through the museum. He sent me a comprehensive information packet and all the venue specifications and requirements for housing and hosting the exhibit. The exhibit's goal was to translate the long history of man's relationship with wolves into a three-dimensional story. The result was a sort of physical echoing of Barry Lopez's groundbreaking book *Of Wolves and Men,* which had provided important source material for a number of the displays. As luck would have it, I had hosted Lopez for a speaking engagement in Jackson the year before, so I called him and he told me quite a bit about the exhibit and its history.

One of the truly remarkable aspects of the exhibit was that it used the power of the wolf's mythological role throughout history to examine how we relate to the animal today. Too often science is isolated from myth; both Hadland's and Lopez's genius was in seeing that each dimension deeply informs the other, and that allowing the imagination of the viewer or reader to range between the scientific and the mythical helped create an intimacy with the real animal. The exhibit explored myth and fable, biology and ecology, and the social and political dimensions of issues such as wolves' predation on livestock, purported attacks on humans, etc. Its primary goal was to penetrate and integrate the superficial dichotomy between what wolves have been to humans culturally and what their presence could mean today, biologically. Mech's intuition was astute—the exhibit could be a perfect vehicle for gently forwarding the discussion of Yellowstone wolf recovery.

With Hadland's designs in hand, I first approached officials at Yellowstone, who expressed cautious optimism about the prospects—if the funding could be arranged. I then contacted Defenders of Wildlife, one of the national conservation groups most active on wolf recovery, and asked them if they would act as an umbrella organization for the project if I wrote the necessary grant proposals. Defenders and Yellowstone agreed to participate. After over a year of haggling and rewriting and rebudgeting, the proposals were successful. By then, however, Defenders was undergoing a massive reorganization of their D.C. offices and some important details fell through the cracks. A couple of crucial contracts got caught in red tape and were stalled on someone's desk, unsigned. Officials at Yellowstone were frustrated and ultimately fed up; at the eleventh hour they called off the exhibit. When I got the conference call from Bob Barbee, then superintendent of Yellowstone, and John Varley, chief of research, to inform me of the decision, I was stunned, then belligerent. I outright refused to believe they could cancel the whole thing. I wheedled and pleaded, and then just outright refused to accept their decision. "You CAN'T call it off," I declared, "it's too important." They were amused, even sympathetic, but their decision was unchanged. I was heartbroken. I had worked for over a year and a half to organize the exhibit's venue and a number of associated outreach programs, and now all that effort looked to be for naught.

Next door to me on Fish Creek Road lived Dottie Smith, a former Washington lobbyist and seasoned grassroots organizer. She was a dear friend, and well aware of how much I had invested in getting the exhibit to Yellowstone. By chance she stopped by just after I hung up the phone with the Yellowstone administrators. Utterly dejected and resigned, I told her what had happened. Dottie was incredulous, but undaunted. She said, "Renée, don't quit. They're bureaucrats, they always respond to pressure." Dottie argued that since the exhibit already existed and the hall in Yellowstone was empty and waiting, surely some unsigned contracts and dangling financial commitments weren't sufficient reason to abandon the project. That afternoon we started a phone campaign. Mardy Murie, an internationally known conservationist and Dottie's close friend (she had also helped edit the *Wolves and Humans* exhibit proposals earlier that year), soon joined the fight.

Coached by two veteran lobbyists, I had my first lesson in grassroots persuasion. The goal was twofold: to get Defenders back on track and to reverse Yellowstone's decision. Bristol added her wisdom to the strategy by initiating a game of tug-of-war with one of the rolled-up proposals I'd thrown in the garbage in disgust—her message: grab hold of what you want, don't let go, and shake the hell out of it, which is essentially what we did. I called every conservationist I knew, begging them to call every conservationist *they* knew, and soon the Yellowstone Park hierarchy was being bombarded. Mardy was on the phone with her contacts, who were undoubtedly significant, and soon Washington, D.C., heavyweights started calling Yellowstone. Much to my astonishment, within two days Alan Smith, the acting director of Defenders, was flying to Yellowstone to resurrect the deal, and Yellowstone had tentatively agreed to reconsider. Alan Smith and Dan Smith, the program director for Defenders, and Bob Barbee, John Varley, and I all met in Yellowstone early the next week. The necessary paperwork was completed and the exhibit was on its way less than a month later.

The Park Service hired me to coordinate the exhibit while it was in Yellowstone, and I in turn urged them to hire my old friend Timm Kaminski, who could bring his valuable field knowledge to the array of exhibit programs. Due to a remarkable spell of good luck and some hard work on the part of Barbee and Varley, every key decision maker on wolves—all the way up to the secretary of the interior—would visit Yellowstone that summer, and every single one of them would tour the wolf exhibit. In my grant proposal I estimated that 30,000 people would visit the exhibit. The park hierarchy had feared I was exaggerating, seeing everything through the lens of my own enthusiasm, but to everyone's surprise and delight, 215,000 people went through that summer in Yellowstone.

Once the exhibit was up, running, and proclaimed a success, my mind turned back to the wolves themselves. My views on politics and decision making had matured, and were about to turn another corner that summer. In the process of writing the proposals and fighting for the resurrection of the exhibit, I had learned a great deal. I had also become quite fond of both Bob Barbee and John Varley. They had always been honest and encouraging, and in the coming years they would become indispensable allies in navigating federal bureaucracies and surviving western politics. It was a gesture of kindness and faith when Barbee called me over to his side at an inauguration party for the new Park Service director, William Penn Mott. I'm not sure what Bob had in mind when he introduced me to his brand-new boss, but he undoubtedly knew that I had only one thing on *my* mind.

When we were introduced, I asked Mr. Mott what his goals were as director of the Park Service. He talked about infrastructures, personnel morale, biological integrity, visitor engagement, and a passionate wish to have U.S. national parks be an example for international efforts. He surprised me by generously asking me what my goals were as a freshly hired Park Service employee. I explained I had only one goal, one that he might share, given the priorities he had just listed. I demonstrated how the wolf project in Yellowstone directly related to several of his personal goals. He astutely sensed that my involvement in the project was both personal and passionate, and asked why I cared so much about it. I contemplated enumerating all the ecological and ethical arguments, my customary and politically correct answer. Instead I told him a different truth—I told him the story of Natasha, a disclosure that surprised even me, for rarely did I invoke her memory in a professional encounter.

At the end of our conversation I pointed out how his personal involvement, not just his professional endorsement, could make a difference in this particular project. Mr. Mott was both open and curious. He asked a lot of questions about the prospects for reintroduction, and in the next few days of his stay in Yellowstone he asked a lot more of Bob Barbee and John Varley. He toured the exhibit and asked more. He left Yellowstone that spring a committed believer in wolf reintroduction. Much to the astonishment of us all, in the next five years he would become the single most important Washington, D.C., champion of wolves, running interference for almost every political initiative and undertaking several of his own.

Mott's interest in wolves was, of course, the result of conversations with many people. What I felt was effective in my discussion with him was not that I persuaded him to do something, but rather that I showed him how the wolf project offered him an opportunity to *personally* make a difference. What I learned in this experience is that most people want to do the right thing. They want to make the world a better place, whether they are director of the National Park Service or the head of the maintenance department. Sometimes it's just a matter of suggesting an avenue. Too often conservationists believe that the only effective method of engaging key decision makers is bludgeoning pressure or shaming exposure. We forget that people respond to people. Personal contact and a simple conversation can be more effective than grandstanding or political roughhousing.

In looking back at the events that were pivotal in the evolution of the recovery effort, I am often stunned at how trivial some of the actual incidents seemed at the time—how key decisions were just part of the rough-hewn unfolding of life's events, but were driven by synchronicities or coincidences that in retrospect seem almost eerie—how some decisions teetered on the edge of insignificance and yet years later, with the clarity of hindsight, were revealed to be pivotal. Dottie's visit following that phone call and her urging me to fight the decision to cancel the exhibit led to my making some calls rather than giving up. Those calls, which led to other calls, led to the exhibit going forward, which significantly contributed to the recruitment of Mott to the cause, which I'm sure changed the course of wolf recovery. One thing I know for certain is that the wheel of fate turned in the direction it did at the pace it did because people cared. Dottie cared. Mardy cared. Bob Barbee and John Varley cared. Even in the midst of organizational trauma, when they were crushed by other issues, the people at Defenders cared enough to put the effort into resurrecting the exhibit deal. It was undoubtedly the little fights that counted, the small gestures, the simple truths, those added bits of effort that were pivotal.

The other dimension was also key: many of these people took it personally. My conversation with Mott was, I'm sure, one of many he had on the topic of wolf recovery, but our discussion was probably the most personal, because the issue was a very personal one to me. Nearly three years later when we met again at a tea at Yale, planted in the overstuffed chairs in one of the formal sitting rooms, Mr. Mott recalled our conversation at the inaugural party and asked if I had ever heard more about Natasha. I was astonished that he remembered. He told me he had responded strongly to my story about her. The point of all this is that the simple act of telling someone that you care, why you care, why they too might care, can cause mountains to move. Wordsworth wrote in a compelling poem, "What you have loved, others will love, and you will teach them how." We should never be afraid to simply speak of what we love, from the place in us which has loved. It can make a difference.

Twelve

❖ ❖ ❖

Living is a form of not being sure, not knowing what next or how. The moment you know how, you begin to die a little. The artist never entirely knows. We guess. We may be wrong, but we take leap after leap in the dark.

AGNES DE MILLE

M Y HOPES HAD soared the fall before with the success of the wolf exhibit and the enthusiasm it generated within governmental ranks, only to crash when the flickerings of action were soundly doused by several powerful western senators and the unsurprising nonaction of Frank Dunkle, Reagan's appointee for director of the U.S. Fish and Wildlife Service, the principal agency in charge of restoring wolves. The wolf recovery plan sat dormant in Washington, with the aides of several western senators poised to pounce if it emitted any signs of life.

When the exhibit closed and was sent on to the next venue, my obligations to Yellowstone were fulfilled and I eagerly returned to the Tetons. The year before I had moved from Fish Creek Road into a cabin in Moose with Jack Turner. Turner—philosopher/mountain climber/photographer/writer/radical—was both my lover and intellectual mentor, and our conversations, which ranged from recitations of Neruda to debates on democracy, influenced my ideas and future in profound ways. In spite of its habit of burrowing into winter like a hibernating grizzly, our tiny log cabin on the Snake River was an enchanted home where in the predawn light bald eagles chortling their mating calls would awaken us, and at night the river would lull us to sleep. In truth, Turner was my best friend. I couldn't wait to wake up in the morning so we could start talking, and I hated having to go to sleep because we would have to stop talking.

We had a tough winter that year, temperatures plummeted to thirty degrees below zero (some nights even fifty below) and stayed there for weeks. Nothing moved. Snow was piled to the roof, covering almost every window. To go in and out of the front door of our little cabin one had to descend into a virtual tunnel, as though entering an igloo, which made for short sunless days and long frigid nights. I'm sure the cabin fever created some exasperation, and even though it was a very happy time for me personally, professionally (if you could call the wolf work a profession) I was feeling a sense of impotence and frustration over the wolf project's apparent paralysis. I had been asked to work as a consultant on a number of wolf-related projects, but none of them paid well or held much hope for really changing the political tide, so I approached them with little excitement. The cumulative pressures of teetering on the edge of poverty, stress, and shattered optimism were taking their toll.

In addition, earlier that fall I had made a trip back to my father's home in Michigan to visit him and my grandmother. Upon returning from her usual evening mile-long walk, she had come in the house and handed me a beautiful bouquet of wildflowers. "For you, Renéesha" were her last words. She turned, took two steps, and fell down with a massive stroke. She died shortly after. It was a merciful, swift death, which is what she would have wanted, but the grieving of it, of course, wasn't. Part of my great sadness was that I would never get to bring her back to the mountains of Yellowstone to see the wolves "yump and yump."

In spite of the efforts of so many people for so many years, there had been little progress toward seeing wolves on the ground. The stalemate was in part due to the stagnation and bureaucratic inertia inherent in large, politically influenced organizations. Government agencies are structured to maintain the status quo, especially when it comes to controversial initiatives. By then I'd also lost my hope for dramatic or innovative action from any of the national conservation groups. These organizations, particularly those based in D.C., have a complex relationship with the government agencies they purport to watchdog. Their willingness to act or use their resources on an issue is largely determined by measuring the amount of "political capital" it will "cost," how much membership engagement it might drain or generate, and the perceived advantages and risks associated with the different methods of cajoling, urging, or shaming action from a politician or agency. Although there were some shining examples—individuals within the large national organizations who valiantly worked to engage their group in the frontline battles—the controversy around wolves was basically deemed too costly by most of the "Big Ten" conservation groups, and few really entered the fray with the exception of Defenders of Wildlife (DOW) and, later, the National Wildlife Federation.

By the winter of 1985 I realized that perhaps I'd had my nose up against the glass a little too long. My vision was fogged and I needed some outside perspective. Nudged by the notion that collective thinking is a way to break through the brain-blocks, I began a series of conversations with my friends, family, mentors, and heroes about what to do next to move the project forward. Many of the people I chose to talk with had in their own lives and professions defied convention, and had in business, art, or activism accomplished great things against the worst of odds. I alternately called them the "conception conversations," or, if feeling more honest and fretful about how lofty my goal was, the "chimera conversations." In the end a chimera was indeed conceived out of the fertile fantasy generated in those discussions. The talks were not usually prestructured but generally followed the theme of presenting the history, the players, and the obstacles, then asking the person how *they* would organize a strategy to reach the goal of reintroducing wolves.

I talked to conservationists like Mardy Murie and Peter Matthiessen, businessmen like Yvon Chouinard, the founder of Patagonia, and Wally Dayton, a visionary Minnesota businessman and conservationist, and biologists like Dave Mech and John Weaver. I roamed and listened to the minds and hearts and imaginations of lawyers, biologists, artists, activists, friends, and family. What came of those talks was a vision fertilized by many. If one looked too hard, the notion dissolved into one definition of a chimera: "an impossible or foolish fantasy." But if you looked at it out of the corner of your eye, with a broadened gaze, as you would look for an animal in complicated habitat, allowing traces of your imagination to enchant your vision, you would see another aspect of the chimera—the fire-breathing creature with the head of a lion, the body of a goat, and the tail of a serpent—in retrospect a rather apt description of the organization that was born of those conversations, The Wolf Fund.

From the stew of ideas of so many disparate minds emerged a rather practical common recommendation: create a small, focused organization with a single goal, an organization that could take risks the large groups couldn't, or wouldn't, because of their fear of losing ground on one issue if they became too strident on another. A novel element that also emerged was the idea of a sunset clause for the organization: it would voluntarily shut down when the goal was accomplished. This would function to keep The Wolf Fund focused, deliberate, and unhindered by becoming more concerned with its long-term survival than accomplishing a specific goal. The sunset clause also provided a bearable job description for me because it meant the task was finite and I could look forward to a finish line and a promise fulfilled.

I reluctantly admit I am a born organizer: bossy, opinionated, and determined. As a child I organized parades around our block, circuses, revolts against my mother's tuna fish casserole, meetings for the twelve-year-old survivors of catechism. It seemed a natural step to create an organization, but of course it would be an odd organization whose development, like an aberrant infant's, matched no other's.

By that time I had poured five years into the wolf project and seen very little progress. I had worked or volunteered for nearly every entity involved—private, nonprofit, and federal—but most of the work was intermittent, low-paying if there was any pay at all, and the fruits of my efforts, and so many other people's, were often abruptly swept away by the ever-shifting political winds.

In retrospect, the notion of starting an organization at that time was absurd. First, I was flat broke, and second, I was teetering on the edge of a decision to return to graduate school. I had been accepted to the master's program at Yale University's School of Forestry and Environmental Studies the year before and had deferred admission for twelve months in order to complete my commitment to the wolf exhibit. I had no money to go to school, no money to start an organization; in truth I had no real idea how I would pull any of it off. This was the beginning of learning what it means to be enabled. I've always loved the word "enable"—to provide with the means, knowledge, or opportunity; to make possible; to give capacity. I've come to believe that to "enable" is one of the great achievements in living and loving. And being enabled, like being loved, is one of the marvels of the world's benevolence. It is to be given wings.

I will always be indebted to Turner for his kindness and forbearance during that time. I was a waif filled with a passionate dream, but without the means or direction to realize it. He helped me articulate the form of The Wolf Fund, and then in a goodness that reaches far beyond words, he helped me in every conceivable way to give flight to the vision. He, in short, was the first enabler of The Wolf Fund.

Although I'm sure I wasn't completely aware of it at the time, I began to see the possibility of creating an organization as an opportunity to experiment with merging my often warring creative and organizational impulses. I'd witnessed the dysfunction of nonprofit conservation groups for so long that I had an idea conservation could be approached in a different way, but I had no real idea what it took to start or run an organization. I wasn't even sure what the organization should be, although I had a very clear idea of what it shouldn't be. It shouldn't perpetuate the sexism, the elitism, the competitive, mean-spirited backbiting I had seen all too often in overworked, underpaid non-profit staffs. The chimera conversations had produced a vision that emerged like a collage of colorful and wild images; I instinctively knew what I wanted to create, I just wasn't sure how to go about doing it.

I had glimpsed models over the years that hinted at the possibility of doing something differently. I'd worked at the Teton Science School running a lecture and workshop program for a short period in the early eighties. During the first part of my time at the science school there was a short period when the whole staff was composed of women. Colleen Cabot was then director, and for a short, sweet period there was essentially an abandonment of the old models of hierarchy. Colleen managed in a spherical form, with her guidance radiating from the center and the rest of the staff, like so many electrons, orbiting around her, magnetized in a certain order by her charismatic leadership and direction. Sadly, it all ended rather abruptly when a man with traditional hierarchical tendencies joined the staff. In spite of a lot of rhetoric about team playing and credit sharing, his authoritarian style quickly crushed Colleen's intuitive, democratic approach; the gentle utopian environment evaporated and was replaced by the more typical, competitive atmosphere. That experience made me realize how difficult it is to live a vision; how, as T. S. Eliot put

it, "Between the idea/And the reality/Between the motion/And the act/Falls
the shadow."

Nonetheless, The Wolf Fund was born of visions. What it became, of
course, was something less than those visions, but still I think it helped in its
own faltering way to carve a new model for what was possible. It was the summer of 1986. Two weeks before I was to leave for Yale, Mardy Murie, who had
lobbied for the wolf exhibit, and who with her husband Olaus had started the
Wilderness Society, offered to host the first fund-raising event, an intimate
dinner, to jump-start The Wolf Fund. Another neighbor, Frank Craighead,
the renowned grizzly bear biologist, and his sons Lance and Charlie had agreed
to "parent" my fledgling project under their existing nonprofit until I formed
a board and was granted nonprofit status of my own. About fourteen people
attended the dinner, among them Yvon and Melinda Chouinard, Tom and
Sibyl Wiancko, and Gertrude Brennan, all of whom would become guardian
angels of the project. We sat together that summer evening in Mardy's log
cabin living room in Moose, Wyoming, and I explained my nascent dream.

I talked about my work with the wolf project over the preceding five
years—the slide and tape shows, the endless meetings, the wolf exhibit, and
the changing political climate. The ecological arguments for restoring wolves
were irrefutable; the objections and political obstacles we faced were really the
issues. The tough reality was that the project was stalled. I expressed my belief
that we could overcome the problems if we took a slightly different approach.
I had a notion of creating a "SWAT team" that could work the edges and holes,
rather than the center charge. We would play herding dog, heralding horn,
and hell-raiser all at once.

The key was to try to figure out what every existing entity did best and
then get them to do it on the Yellowstone wolf effort, simultaneously attempting to minimize the replication of effort and infighting that unfortunately undermines so much good conservation work. We needed to mobilize
resources, get the grassroots organizations to do grassroots work, and the na-
tionals to do the lobbying at which they were so skilled. We needed to understand the opposition better by really listening to their concerns. Although
many of my fellow conservationists would call that accommodation, I called
it compassion. I really wanted to obliterate the "us against them" model by
creating policy that could disarm the objections by recognizing human concerns rather than enemy positions. I also believed we needed a much more

personal approach with friendly politicians. I had a notion that we could escape the "detect and squash" radar of the western politicians if we began a campaign to involve the national public using the avenues of free media to really engage a broader political constituency in the effort.

I also told the small dinner audience that I wanted to create an organization that would reach out to children and make them part of a project in which they could see that they had made a difference. And as long as we were starting an organization, I emphasized that the process was as important as the goal and I wanted no membership fee; I wanted everyone and anyone to be able to get our materials or use us as a resource regardless of ability to pay. Africa had taught me how poverty can directly undermine democracy. I can't imagine what those poor dinner guests must have thought—I was throwing out ideas like ticker tape.

It was all only a vision—I didn't have a cent to make it happen. I handed out a proposal with a number of projects outlined. I planned to try to work ten to fifteen hours a week to get them under way while at Yale, if I went to Yale. I said I was planting a seed and didn't know how fertile the soil would be, whether there would be sufficient rain to nurture it, or whether it would ultimately bear fruit. I just described my hope. I would have to wait to see whether any of the participants shared it.

Once the dinner event was over I was still faced with the decision about going to Yale, but leaving wasn't quite that simple. Even though I was better off than in the days of tepee living and ramen noodles, I literally didn't have enough money to make the trip from Wyoming to New Haven, nor did I have the first and last months' rent deposit for an apartment there, even though Yale had provided me with scholarships and loans that covered the tuition. I was unsure whether this new organization should be planted in the East, where the media and politics were centered, or the West, where the wolves would one day return. Probably most significantly, I was deeply ambivalent about leaving Turner. He was certain that it would mean the end of our relationship. I refused to believe it, but he was right. I still think of his kindness and selflessness—in offering to loan me his computer and launch me on a new life that he had enabled and empowered but knew he would not share.

One night about a week before I was to leave, if I was to leave, Turner and I went to a dinner at Gerry and Imagine Spence's. Turner had been doing some work with Gerry, and although he denies ever having asked Gerry to help in any way, that night Gerry drew me away from the other guests. As we stood outside under a starry sky, Gerry put his hand on my shoulder and said, "Young lady, Imagine and I think you should go to Yale, we want to help you do that. This is a gift, not a loan. We wish you luck."

He handed me a check that allowed me to drive across the country, pay the rent, and buy the first semester's books to begin graduate work at Yale. I was flabbergasted. It was a kindness both direct and empowering, and to this day I am deeply grateful. I think what made this gesture so profoundly moving is that it was unbidden, and unconditional. No "If you do this, we'll do that," just "Go forth, do well. We believe in you."

And so it was that this fierce little organization called The Wolf Fund was born and took up residence for the first years of its life not in Moose, Wyoming, but in New Haven, Connecticut. It was conceived through the generosity of many people, and like a child with a secure extended family, it flourished because it was rooted in the fertile soil of diverse ideas.

Thirteen

❖ ❖ ❖

Deep night. I cannot sleep.
I get up and sing softly to my lute.
Moonlight glows in the gauze curtains.
I open my nightgown, and let
the fresh night air bathe my body.
A lonely wild goose cries out
in the distant meadow.
A night bird flies calling through the trees.
I come and go without rest.
What do I gain by it?
My mind is distracted by worries
That will never cease.
My heart is all bruised
By the troubled ghosts who haunt it.

YUAN CHI, "Deep Night"
TRANSLATED BY KENNETH REXROTH

A FEW DAYS before I was to leave for Yale I attended a concert by Leo Kottke. Some friends had given me a ticket, and although I had been in the field all day, blistering hot hours of hiking and hurry, I felt obliged to appear. Sitting at a small table, sun-wearied and waiting for my friends to arrive, I sort of nodded off to the lulling chords of Kottke's sublime fingerpicking. It would be in that particular state, sound asleep with my face buried in the wrinkles of a cocktail napkin, undoubtedly drooling, that my future husband, Tom Rush (TR), would notice me.

Rush knew who I was because we had been fleetingly introduced at a restaurant earlier that day by a mutual friend. As a favor to the friend I had agreed to take this virtual stranger and his son, Ben, out to see wildlife later in the week. When they joined me a few days later for a field excursion, we had to stop at their room to pick up a pair of forgotten binoculars. Tom picked up a guitar and started doodling. Unaware of Rush's musical expertise, I commented to Ben, "Hey, your dad's a pretty good guitar player, you guys should have heard Leo Kottke the other night." In a gallant show of reserve Rush never mentioned seeing me asleep at the concert or the fact that he was also a performer with over sixteen albums to his name.

I set off shortly after that for Yale in a steamy August heat wave. I had by that time traded the Maverick in for a used Suburu, once silver but by then tarnished, fittingly named the Bulimic Bullet for its habit of ejecting all sorts of vital fluids at inopportune times—radiator coolant, oil, brake fluid, windshield wash. It didn't matter as long as it was wet and there was a hose to burst and I was in a hurry. This car just preferred to run dry, or, more honestly, to not run at all. It broke down three times en route to New Haven from Moose, once halfway up the Powder River Pass, which cuts through the Bighorn Mountains of Wyoming at about 9,600 feet. I somehow managed to get it turned around using a series of rock wedges and logs and pushing, and then coasted the whole way back down the pass, without power, taking perilous turns at a bit of a clip to make the next rise. Remarkably, I made it to a run-down gas station at the bottom of the pass in Ten Sleep, Wyoming. After much begging and pleading I persuaded a cranky old mechanic to stay late to fix the car. It cost me a few six-packs and listening to hours of antiwolf ranting, which I endured in uncharacteristic silence, but by midnight the car ran and I was on my way, both of us freshly hydrated.

The second Bullet belch was the next day on Interstate 90, not far outside Rapid City, South Dakota, a town with which I was far more familiar than I wished thanks to the time my Maverick had broken down while bringing my grandmother across the country. This time the Suburu quit on a scalding afternoon in the midst of the annual Sturgis, South Dakota, motorcycle rally. Motorcycle gangs covered the highway like marching black ants, most of them probably doctors and lawyers in their black leather getup for the weekend, but I was nonetheless terrified by the sheer numbers of greased-back, leather-slicked bikers. I did what any intelligent, self-sufficient woman would do under the circumstances—crawled up on the roof of the Suburu (as if getting off the ground would help) and cried. Some nice old man in a sky blue Dodge Dart rescued me, and after another tow truck and gas station ordeal, and the replacement of some pump, I was once again Yale-bound. The finale to this wretched wreck's shenanigans was outside Chicago somewhere, but by then I had joined AAA; a phone call and tow truck made the engine trouble seem like a mere diversion.

Against all odds I arrived safely in New Haven, but after less than a week of enduring the frenzy of the East Coast I was ready to abandon the plan of graduate study and head home to Turner and Bristol. It was exactly then, in the gleaming afternoon sun, locked and parked ten feet from the Yale Forestry School door, that my car with all my worldly possessions (except of course my dog, who never considered herself a possession) was stolen.

Mostly it was my bird books, binoculars, spotting scope, tent, and backpacking gear that I mourned. In truth, I hated that car. Anyone stupid enough to take it deserved it. The police found it a few days later, abandoned in a pool of radiator fluid, the body stripped and totaled. The incident not only eliminated my belongings but also eliminated my choices. I didn't have a car, let alone enough money to leave New Haven. I had used every penny to pay first and last months' rent on an apartment and I was trapped. My reaction to this new development was to stop sleeping, as though sleepless delirium might reveal a solution unavailable to the conscious mind. I don't mean I had a difficult time sleeping; I mean I altogether stopped. In retrospect it was an interesting way to come to know a place, interminable late night pacing of that city, like a caged creature with no escape. The ivy brick buildings became chain link and the beautiful cobbled streets dissolved into pocked cement. For those who love cities it is difficult to comprehend the reaction of a rural person to the onslaught of the urban, but it is not unlike that of a feral creature to sudden captivity.

I was sure I would never survive the grinding, grating, gritty, endless noise, the blinking neon and slicing sirens, the throbbing August heat and hell of sun-melted pavement and treeless ghettos. I admit my innocence of cities; although I had visited them, plenty of them, I never fathomed what it was to live in one. It was the first time in my life that I felt the flailing sense of mankind falling into an endless darkness, away, away from the brilliant light of the world.

Carless, I would hitchhike down to Long Island Sound to gulp in the light, the only place where I was able to find an open sky at sunset absent of man's scrawling. I would watch the seabirds fly in long lines or pairs, dipping and swooping and circling each other, calling out their mournful cries. They charged and receded and I would recognize, for a moment, that all life was made of this coming and going, the giving and giving up, the longing and leaving and relentless aching and aching. The hazy blue sea splashed with frothing white crests, and long, low-slung clouds stretched into the water's distance. There was no horizon—sea became sky and sky fell to sea and the birds rose up from the swells as though the foam and froth collected into light white feathers and took flight. Flying low, their wings long and tapered, the birds sliced through the blue until they blended with the waves and the sky, and I wondered if there had been birds at all.

It was a long leap from Moose to New Haven, and like my favorite childhood hero, Lassie, I desperately wanted to find my way home. I was such a long way from the cool nights of my tepee and the comforting flannel of ducks and geese and the winged sleep of faith. Sometimes at dawn after endless nights of wakefulness, terribly homesick and heartsick for Turner and Bristol and the solace of western space, I would sit at my inner-city window and howl in an admittedly odd search for comfort. The neighborhood dogs would respond to my howls of cold despair, delivering a few fleeting moments of calm in their responding calls of recognition. It was as if we each asked of the other, How is it we have come to this? It was during this period that the poet Mary Tall Mountain, who had somehow heard of my work on wolves, sent me her poem "The Last Wolf." It was forwarded to my Yale address from Moose.

> *The last wolf hurried toward me*
> *through the ruined city*
> *and I heard his baying echoes*
> *down the steep smashed warrens*
> *of Montgomery Street and past*
> *the few ruby-crowned highrises*
> *left standing*
> *their lighted elevators useless*
>
> *Passing the flickering red and green*
> *of traffic signals*
> *baying his way eastward*
> *in the mystery of his wild loping gait*
> *closer the sound in the deadly night*
> *through clutter and rubble of quiet blocks*
> *I heard his voice ascending the hill*
> *and at last his low whine as he came*
> *floor by empty floor to the room*

where I sat
in my narrow bed looking west, waiting
I heard him snuffle at the door and
I watched

He trotted across the floor
he laid his long gray muzzle
on the spare white spread
and his eyes burned yellow
his small dotted eyebrows quivered

Yes, I said.
I know what they have done.

Turner had been right. Ultimately the distance and difference of separate lives led to the end of our relationship. We stayed in close touch and remained dear friends. It also was during this period that Tom Rush tracked me down at Yale. He called to see how I had fared on the journey and adjustment to city life. My response was, I'm sure, anything but brave, and somehow in my delirium I confessed my desperate homesickness and sleeplessness to this almost total stranger. Not long after our phone conversation I received a small package in the mail with a note thanking me for the wildlife tour in Jackson Hole and welcoming me to the East Coast. In the package was a cassette of Leo Kottke's instrumentals, signed "For your sleeping pleasure. Best wishes, Tom Rush." It did make me laugh, providing a small ray of light in a dark time.

So the fates kept me at Yale and somehow I survived that first adjustment from mountains to metropolitan mayhem, gently facilitated by a lovely man and his guitar, with whom over the next several years I would fall deeply in love. Rush not only became my husband nearly ten years later, he became my most important partner and adviser in creating The Wolf Fund, and ultimately one of its greatest champions.

In spite of the demands of graduate school and my difficulty in adjusting to a city, The Wolf Fund remained my central passion, like a lingering star in a dark dawn. I still believed that fulfilling my promise to Natasha was the central calling of my life. Mardy Murie's fund-raising dinner had generated enough money for me to work part-time on building the infrastructure of

The Wolf Fund the first year I was at Yale. I spent much of my time, when I wasn't studying or racing to get a paper in, learning to navigate the complexities of the New York and D.C. political and philanthropic worlds. I learned how to lobby decision makers and prod conservation groups and became familiar with the terrain of foundations and the media. During that time I would meet many of the people who became guides and advisers to The Wolf Fund—George Schaller, Michael Bean, Ted Turner, Ted Williams, Robert Redford, and many more.

I would also encounter William Penn Mott twice more at Yale events, each meeting leading to a personal conversation about Yellowstone wolves. The second time I saw him at Yale, which would be the last time before his death, he brought me a campaignlike button that had been produced as part of a wolf education initiative within the Park Service which he had spearheaded. He was very proud of his own little version of wolf kitsch. It boasts the front-on face of a wolf with raised yellow eyes which, when switched on, become blinking yellow beacons that light up like distant stars, twinkling not unlike the proud blue eyes of this old gentleman when he handed it to me with a wink.

Peter Matthiessen, a friend from my days of coordinating a speakers' program at The Teton Science School in 1983 and 1984, was one of my writing teachers at Yale and had a powerful influence in defining The Wolf Fund. Through the example of his work and passionate advocacy of wildlife and native cultures he would profoundly affect my approach in establishing the tone of this new organization. Matthiessen had just finished a book called *Men's Lives,* a powerful and moving portrait of the waning, three-hundred-year-old commercial fishing culture of Long Island. Although his course was a writing seminar, class discussion would invariably turn to the topics of conservation and advocacy which Matthiessen's book propounded. I was keenly interested in this approach because the commercial fishing culture, although older, parallels the culture of ranchers in the West, defined by similar prejudices and fierce independence; both are industries beleaguered by the force of changing values. Although, like ranchers, commercial fishermen evoke mixed sentiments among the ranks of conservationists, Matthiessen's work defined an approach that focused on the people, rather than the industry. His compassion was derived from a stubborn fairness and respect for those carving a living from the land or the sea. He spoke often of the grace and humanity of these people, of the harshness of their lives and the danger of their work.

I was deeply moved by his compassion and his attention to the people and their union with the natural world, even though commercial fishing is judged by many to be exploitative and environmentally abusive. Matthiessen didn't back down from this dichotomy. Instead he tried to push through it, to carve a bigger view that honored people and traditions in the quest for resolution of environmental conflicts. His unwillingness to stoop to the simple "us against them" models so ubiquitous in most conservation battles was extremely influential on my thinking about how we would approach the ranching industry, and ultimately helped shape The Wolf Fund's whole approach to working with opponents of wolf recovery.

By 1987 The Wolf Fund had a more established presence and a small board, and we were facing the step of defining the organization publicly through a brochure, newsletter, press packet, and business cards. Although to many this may seem like a small mechanical element, it was not. In the end, the materials that represented The Wolf Fund became a fundamental component of its success.

I still had only the bare outline of an idea, a vision, a few theories. One theory was that the way to reach the public and engage them in the effort to restore wolves to Yellowstone was through art. I believed that art could reconnect the cauterized tendrils that bound man to his relationship with wild animals. That relationship unquestionably exists; it just goes unrecognized or unrealized, submerged in the frenzy of industrial society. I felt we needed to reawaken what people already knew. At the root of our response to art is the experience of recognition—to see, read, hear, feel what we already know. To offer the familiar through the prism of our own experience is not repetition, but rather affirmation.

The most obvious means of expressing this theory was through the physical materials—brochures, newsletters, press packets, etc.—that represented the organization. They needed to reflect the integrity and consciousness of both our goals and the creature they represented. We needed art to reach far enough to reconnect the public to what I believed they already knew and felt not just about wolves but about animals in general. I believed that the drama of art representing the power of something passionate, a drama that works through the power of image and language, could, like fine dance, music, or painting, take a reader or participant into the place of our true human wisdom.

It was a grandiose theory that began with a mundane search. I went through hundreds and hundreds of environmental newsletters. Combing the shelves of Yale's libraries, my friends' environmental solicitations, and the announcement boards all over the college, I finally came across one piece, a small single-page brochure from the Connecticut Nature Conservancy that was dazzling. It was simple, elegant, and striking. I knew I had found my designers the minute I saw it. Through the conservancy I tracked down the designers, Jeff and Adrienne Pollard, a husband-and-wife team who lived in East Hartland, Connecticut.

As the wolf angels would have it, Jeff and Adrienne had just returned from a three-week trip in the Wind River Mountains of Wyoming, and together had vowed that they would somehow give something back to this place, to the landscape with which they had fallen in love. By the end of our first conversation we had a meeting scheduled, and by the end of that meeting I had two of the most important collaborators, and eventually dearest friends, that I would have the honor to work alongside for the next ten years.

It began with a prototype for a newsletter which we intended to send out only once a year. We had a burgeoning mailing list garnered from the baskets of mail we'd received in response to an article on our work in *Parade* magazine. I realize it is absurd to mention "revolution" and newsletters in the same breath, but so fine was the work, so unusual was the layout and design, and the sprinkling of words and poems and images and space, that the public did seem to take notice.

By this time I had a bright young Yale student, Nicholas Lapham, working with me. Although Nicholas would later become The Wolf Fund's first full-time employee, his first assignment as an intern was editing and coordinating the production of the newsletter. Another Yale intern, Jenny Wood, helped organize a roster of individuals and foundations that would be likely supporters of our projects. That year we showed the newsletter prototype to Patagonia, the outdoor gear company, and a catalog company in Idaho called Coldwater Creek and they both agreed to underwrite the development and printing. Then, in a stroke of true luck, largely engineered by the Pollards, people from Simpson Paper saw the newsletter and approached us asking to donate recycled paper for the project. Because of the design they were so enthusiastic that not only did they do the first run of 10,000 for us, but they also produced another 40,000 for their own promotional purposes. We were ecstatic. Only a few years after its inception The Wolf Fund was borne into public view on the wings of artists and angels.

A remarkable thing occurred in response to that first newsletter. People actually read it. They didn't throw it away, they gave it to friends who gave it to friends who gave it to friends. Suddenly foundations, donors, reporters were all calling us to find out more about the issue and The Wolf Fund. We desperately needed money because, aside from my Murie dinner participants, we had absolutely no benefactors to pave the way, and no ability to hire a professional fund-raiser to get things started.

Media interest was key because it was the means through which we could engage the broadest public in the battle. We couldn't pay for frequent bulk mailings, ad campaigns, or sophisticated lobbying efforts, so we turned to the media, believing it was the best way to educate the public for free. Soon we had major foundation funding, a story in *Time* magazine, and spots on the nightly news. America loves a good story, and the saga of the wolf—first the eradication and now possibly the reintroduction of a charismatic creature— was a great one. Public checks started trickling in, and a staff was hired.

An even greater phenomenon followed the newsletter, and though it is more difficult to define or quantify, I think it was key to the ultimate success of restoring wolves to Yellowstone. A shift took place, and not just in terms of public interest in The Wolf Fund. The public's imagination had been ignited and there was a new curiosity, a new approach to "seeing" the topic. Certainly, our little newsletter was just one dimension in what had been simmering for a long while, but I have to think that our unusual approach in lectures, press interviews, and publications also helped nudge the issue in a new direction. The language changed. People began to talk about the issue in a more expansive context. The debate was no longer defined by words like "management strategy" and "control plan." People were talking about the wild, about our bond with animals, our legacy in Yellowstone, and the importance of symbols. Imagination was at play.

Galileo said, "You cannot teach a person something he does not already know, you can only bring what he does know to his awareness." I believe the materials that grew out of our collaboration with the Pollards "worked" because they were distilled from art, and reconnected people with something they already knew, that they recognized, that was familiar—the history of our profound union with animals, a history in which the wolf's shadow moves silently but potently alongside our own.

What made this piece stand out was content not often seen in the environmental newsletters of the day. (Since then the Pollards' influence has spread; they should feel sincerely flattered by the many imitations.) There were photographs, old woodcuts and engravings, quotes from John James Audubon, Francis Parkman, and Robinson Jeffers, Jeff and Adrienne's stunning graphics, and an entire page dedicated to the letters, poems, and artwork sent in by children. This newsletter was not just a vehicle for information, it was a thing of beauty in and of itself, and that beauty made the reader *want* to read it. That beauty reconnected people to what they sensed, what they intuited. The response this newsletter generated, the curiosity and sense of empowerment and connection, was going to give us a fighting chance.

Fourteen

We live in an age of science and abundance.
But we are surrounded by loss.

CHARLES BERGMAN, *Wild Echoes*

B Y SOME MIRACLE I had returned to New Haven after a summer in Moose, and once again I was terribly homesick for the space and spectacle of the Tetons. New England, in spite of its storybook charm, more than any region in the country, represented "the controlled." The meticulous New England houses with their predictable, perfectly paned and partitioned windows made me feel confined. No matter the actual size, those windows all seemed small (of course for good reason—New England winters must be shuttered out and large panes of glass weren't available in the 1800s), and for some completely unreasonable reason those tiny gridlocked squares irritated me. I often think those paned windows were the precursors of the notion of planned subdivisions—perhaps because they so clearly represented the compartmentalizing of space, viewable space, as if to gulp in the expanse of a view from the spread of glass would be impolite, even rude. In New England, landscape, like evening cocktails, must be properly sipped lest the soul take flight in the unruly scenery. It is a land of refined lawns defined by polite borders, immaculate picket fences, and picturesque stone walls. Even the profusion of neat-cornered flower beds allowed only pedigreed blossoms with carefully coordinated colors. Although beautiful, the landscape of New England seems so restrained and genteel, except where the ocean licks indifferently at her shores. There she abandons her primness to be ravaged by the ocean, there the birds are raucous, there her shores rise like a disheveled nymph, flushed and beautiful from the passionate caress of the sea.

And so it was in my second year at Yale that, to survive the oppression of the city, I would move to Connecticut's shore to a huge drafty summer house rented cheaply for the winter, on a rock promontory northeast of New Haven. The bluefish ran in quicksilver streaks below the surface of the sea and the birds called out in a hungry chorus from the wind-tumbled wild horizon of their flight. The house was large and white with gauzy curtains that billowed in lush folds and nubbly white bedspreads that grazed the polished floorboards with the softness of their perfect fringes. The sea rocked the house to sleep at night, lapping at the wall of rosy granite that was its foundation. It was the only wild to be found in New Haven's shadow, and I settled there with a homesick thirst.

I lived on a point that for reasons of protecting the innocent I will call Cozy Concord Circle. The houses on Cozy Concord Circle were crowded, but politely, out on a rocky pink point, shoulder to shoulder like straight-backed debutantes. The lawns were fastidiously groomed, the flower beds perfectly appointed. Each house stood immaculate, a testament to the neighborhood's code of conduct. There was one rogue house on Cozy Concord Circle, low-slung with large plate-glass windows and weathered brown shingles. It had shouldered out a few hundred feet on each side of it. Instead of a lawn a dense thicket grew, tangled and tempting, from the house's edges. The house's mistress had cut little paths through it like a maze through mystery. There were tresses and arches and thorny rose twines. In front of that house the rocks reached beyond the thicket in a tumbling and unruly chaos to where the soft pink of the granite darkened to a mossy green under the constant nuzzling of the sea.

A neighbor to the east was a man I will call Bill Jones. He had a black cat, a big fierce creature who batted dogs and snarled at people. Jones was always whining about something: the lawn not properly mowed, the bushes not properly trimmed, the cars crowding too close to his house during a party, the noise too late, the noise too early, the weather too cold, the raccoons in his garbage. Except in Manhattan, which seems a continent all its own, upper-crust people in America, when pressed together, whine. Somehow in Europe and elsewhere our social nature, our primate past, has created systems of enduring—even wanting—close contact; but here, especially in affluent suburbs, snarling and pecking behavior surfaces like mold on old bread.

It was during this second round of adjustment that I had the unfortunate opportunity to experience some of this behavior at close quarters. It all began with a fascination I had developed for foxes—well, maybe it was an obsession with foxes—more accurately, for a particular fox. A half mile down the road, a small nature preserve stretched out in disheveled, ungroomed, profusion, providing a rare haven from the ordered primness of Cozy Concord Circle. Bristol and I often walked there, and one day we found fox tracks. The tracks, the spore of a wild predator, made me inexplicably happy. After that we looked almost daily for the tracks. I began to fixate on seeing the fox, finding the fox, knowing the fox.

Apart from my propensity for finding my way via the guidance of wild canids, I think there were some residual ripples, like the rings of a skipping stone, from my childhood love of Antoine de Saint-Exupéry's *The Little Prince*. My favorite part of the book was undoubtedly the prince's encounter with a wee fox. The story's fox is quite a whimsical and wise creature who insists that before he can befriend the prince he, the fox, must be tamed. Tamed, as the fox explains it, is "to establish ties." The prince wants to know why he should tame the fox. After all, he was nothing more than a fox, like a hundred thousand other foxes. In the story the fox solemnly teaches the prince that after the boy has tamed the fox they will need each other, that they for one another will be unique in all the world, and that through the taming each will see the world in a different light, for one only understands the things that one tames. In my interpretive lexicon, taming is not analogous to "making domestic." Taming can be coming to know, recognizing the habits and idiosyncrasies of a creature—it is recognizing the individuality of something. In this way I felt I had "tamed" Natasha, and she, me.

I love the notion of the wild creature teaching the child: this is how one comes to see the world and truly understand it—through relationship, with foxes, roses, lovers, even the twinkly stars. The little prince's relationship with his fox and the way the fox taught him about the true nature of relationship echoed my own experience with animals. For me there is great truth in this wisdom, that animals are our interpreters, our link to seeing into the wild world; but we must come to know them, come to understand their ways and needs and personalities. In the end, after the prince learns patience and the particulars of place, because he has undertaken the task of "taming the fox" the fox imparts a final wisdom to his new friend as he is about to depart. "Only with the heart can one see rightly; what is essential is invisible to the eye."

Perhaps it was part of my teaching that this wry New England fox was invisible to me. I looked and looked, covering every trail and hedge and swamp, but he did not reveal himself. I started researching and reading about foxes. I particularly loved the stories of well-adapted city foxes that had developed the cunning habit of rolling over on their backs and flailing their legs around when cats came near. Apparently this kind of fox behavior provokes the curiosity of house cats, who come in closer to investigate, and when they do, the fox in one graceful, whipping motion goes from its flat-on-its-back paw-flapping reverie into a marvelous pounce. Feline is then outfoxed and, well, you know the rest.

The fox is to easterners what the coyote is to most westerners. They abandon their wild habitats to invade our world, defying our boundaries, reminding us that the wild still does lap at our doors. Try as I might, I never saw the Connecticut fox. My brother and sister-in-law, house-sitting for me once, saw it dragging a raccoon nearly larger than itself across the road; neighbors claimed sightings. I only saw his tracks, which made me long more for the fox. I began to roam as a mantra for seeking the fox, leaning toward all the quiet places, walking the trails, looking everywhere for some silent sign.

I was away back in Wyoming, when at last the fox came to visit my house on Cozy Concord Circle. It was waiting quietly near the house, curled in a small ball looking out through the yellow forsythia bushes separating our yard from Bill Jones's. Unfortunately Jones spotted it and immediately called the police. He told them there was a rabid fox in the neighbor's yard. According to the 911 dispatcher, he screeched in a kind of panicked terror about the fox. The dispatcher described it to me later, explaining that Jones was very convincing. The police came with lights flashing and sirens wailing.

When the squalling police car pulled up, the fox ran out of the bushes and across Cozy Concord Circle to the thicket of the brown-shingled house. The police chased it and then shot at it in the thicket. The owner of the house emerged, screaming at the police, but they kept shooting. She told me the story in breathless recollection. (Her husband reprimanded her when he heard the story; he said she oughtn't scream at people with loaded guns.) She demanded that the police get off her land. They yelled back that there was a rabid fox and they must kill it. She wanted to know how they knew it was rabid. They looked puzzled and said Bill Jones had told them so. She screamed at them to leave. They didn't. They herded the injured fox out of the thicket, out onto the rocky point in front of her house where the granite is the most tender pink. They caught the wounded fox with a noose. And in front of the woman, for spite, for might, who knows why, they put their guns aside and beat the fox to death on the granite where the pink fades to deep green and the sea licks up toward the thicket. There was only a bloodstain left when I returned.

Not long after, I left that place. Something about the brutality of the fox's death left me full of despair and anxiety. I could barely let Bristol out of my sight. I'm not sure why I felt so clingy, except that I was terribly homesick for Wyoming, and Bristol was my only tie to a life and an identity that seemed far away. We moved from the shore into a lovely house owned by some artist friends in the wooded hills of western Connecticut where I had promised to house-sit for a few months. Even though the setting was more rural, unfamiliar animals were still treated with undue suspicion, as I was about to find out.

On our first day there I set up a run outside for Bristol, thinking it would be too hot to leave her in the car, and too disorienting to leave her locked in a strange new house. Off I went to run some Friday afternoon errands. I returned just before 5 P.M. to find Bristol gone. I pounded on the doors of all the neighbors scattered on the forested hill, and indeed one had seen her and admitted having called the dog warden because she had found the presence of a stray dog a bit frightening.

I should first admit that Bristol did not like being left behind or locked in when she wished to be out and was a virtual Houdini at finding ways out of a pen, a run, a locked room, or a collar. I admired her ingenuity. Once when my brother and sister-in-law were house-sitting for me she was left in a small sunroom and decided she didn't like it, figured out the door latch, and opened it and left, the door slamming behind her.

After some panic they found her, and the next time they had to leave her they wrapped a heavy chain through a window around the sunroom door-jamb and padlocked it. Because it was a heavy chain the linkage was bulky and they couldn't get it totally tight. If you could manage to unlock the latch the door would open slightly—maybe three inches. Before leaving, my brother measured the opening, making sure that even if Bristol unlocked the latch she couldn't possibly get through the door. They left her with her favorite plastic toy, which ironically looked like a yellow fox. There were cement steps outside the door only wide enough to meet the opening and a four-foot drop on either side. Bristol was not only able to open the latch and squeeze her seventy-five-pound body out the three-inch crack and down the four feet, but she took her fox with her!

When I returned to the artists' home late that afternoon and found Bristol missing I should not have been surprised, but I was nonetheless panicked knowing that she was completely unfamiliar with the area and I didn't have a clue where to begin searching. I immediately called the dog pound, which was closed, and then the sheriff's department, which said there was nothing they could do, but after a fit of hysteria and a lot of pleading I learned the name of the dog warden from the on-duty 911 attendant. I then called information for every township and county until I found him. He was more than a little irritated at my after-hours interruption. Over the din of the ball game and the pop of beer cans opening he finally confirmed that they had picked up my dog, but said they would not be open until the following Monday and I could get her then. I tried to explain that her middle name was Houdini and that she would try to escape and could injure herself and couldn't I get her right away and save them the lawsuits, etc. He hung up on me. I called back. He hung up again. I was very unhappy.

I set out to find the dog pound—after all, I'd had some experience at such places. I didn't know my way around the area at all, and quickly learned that most shop owners, gas station attendants, and waitresses have no idea where their county dog pound is located. After wandering around endless back roads I finally found a patrol cop, waved him down, and got good directions to the pound on a street I will call Wilbur Marsh Way. By then it was pitch dark.

I found the street and the pound, which was set back from the road a hundred feet, but all the dogs were locked inside. I howled and Bristol immediately answered; her howls amid the frenzied barking and howling of all the dogs brought back memories of Thunder and the ponderosa pines. I admit I may have been just a little bit hysterical, but at that point there was no turning back. Bristol had never been kept behind a fence or in a cold cement room in her life, and as far as I was concerned she wasn't going to start in some hellhole Connecticut animal prison. The whole compound was surrounded by two twelve-foot chain-link fences with open wire tops, both gated and double-padlocked. Inside the double fences lay the building itself—an office connected to a kennel with numerous six-foot chain-link dog runs that opened through little doors into individual cages inside. The doors were all covered with plywood, blocking the dogs from going outside.

The first challenge was getting into the enclosure. I went up and over the outer compound fences with relative ease, ripping up my wrists pretty good on the top wires, but my fury easily obliterated any pain. The next challenge was finding Bristol's run; even in my state of mania, I realized crawling into a mad Akita's face was probably not a good idea. More howling. I found the run I thought was hers, went up over the six-foot fence, and found to my joy that the plywood keeping her inside was loose. With a little bit of nudging it slid to one side. Bristol was of course overjoyed, and after a raucous reunion agreed that we should get out of that awful place. It was very dark inside and the other dogs were now howling like crazy, but by some grace there were no neighbors and no one drove by. At about this moment I realized that what I was doing was called breaking and entering. I'm not at heart much of a criminal, but there is little that I would not do for that dog.

As I had a little experience with B&E, in the lucid clarity of that moment I decided the sensible thing to do was to take care not to leave fingerprints. When the adrenaline's pumping one's priorities can become a bit fuddled. I took off my T-shirt and executed the rest of our escape from the darkened kennel topless, with my hands wrapped in the T-shirt. I knew I couldn't get Bristol over the six-foot fence outside the plywood door without giving her a running start, so that meant we had to get out of the building through the inside.

The gate to her kennel was of course latched, so my only alternative was to scale the gate, climb into the rafters, and swing down into the main corridor (not leaving any fingerprints of course), which I did. I unlocked Bristol's door and we made it into the corridor between all the cages. The other dogs found the commotion very exciting and I took their enthusiastic chorus as cheering us on. In spite of the clamor Bristol was dead calm, as though she'd done this a thousand times. I wanted badly to swing open all the gates, but I knew there was no getaway pony, no pines, and still formidable barriers ahead. My jeans pockets were always stuffed full of dog cookies, and I gave everyone a treat and then opened the door to the outside yard. The door had a slide bolt on the inside, so I had to let Bris out the door, relatch it from the inside, latch Bristol's gate and climb back into the rafters, rescale the gate into the run, shimmy through the plywood door again and back over the six-foot fence into the yard where Bristol patiently waited.

Only two twelve-foot chain-link fences to go. I tried in vain to stack some wire dog crates (no fingerprints and still topless) in order that Bristol might climb on them to scale the first fence. I'd seen her go up seven-foot fences, but after reexamining the twelve-foot chain-link wall I decided the exposed wires at the top were just too dangerous. So we began to pace the perimeter of the fence. I was overjoyed to find a place in the far back corner under a lot of piled junk where the two fences actually joined, making a single barrier. The grass was deep in this area, but after kicking and digging at the bottom, I found a place where the fence was slightly loose. I went up and over the fence several times more, trying to find a way to prop the fence bottom up enough. Finally I found a log with which I could stretch about five inches of clearance. I looked at Bris, she agreed it was tighter than most escapes, but what the hell, and to my astonishment with one call she flattened out and shimmied all seventy-five pounds under the five inches. We were out!! I carefully replaced the log where I'd found it—leave no trace—put my T-shirt back on, and let out one irrepressible whoop.

We sprinted to the car parked under a tree down the road. Somehow I found our way on those damn winding little New England roads, too charming for their own good, back to the artists' house. Once we got there my hands started shaking. Tom was on tour in Australia, so I called Turner, who was still my best friend, in Wyoming, figuring he could call Gerry Spence if this really got bad. I woke him up (he typically goes to bed by nine) and confessed my crime. He gently suggested it might be premature to call in a criminal lawyer like Gerry Spence, since I hadn't even been caught yet; but finding the drama irresistible, he commanded in a urgent voice, "Askins, you've got to get out of there!" I said, "I just got here." He said, "Look, they're going to be pissed, and they're going to come find you, so you need to get out of there for a few days."

So I did. I piled Bristol in the car and went to visit some friends on the other side of the state for the weekend. I arrived at their house at about three in the morning with donuts, coffee, and my wrists still bleeding pretty badly. My friends couldn't stop laughing, but they kindly cleaned up my wrists with Betadine and bandaged them, and just as the sun was coming up tucked me into a warm little bed with Bristol curled against my belly.

When I woke up they had already conceived a plan. I would show up at the Wilbur Marsh dog pound on Monday morning demanding my dog. I regret I didn't have the nerve to pull that off. Instead I stayed on the lam. I returned to the artists' house five days later thinking the dog wardens would probably have forgotten all about my dog by then. But not long after we returned the animal warden's truck pulled into the drive.

Uncharacteristically, Bristol barked and growled. Characteristically, I hid. They pounded at the door for about twenty minutes. Realizing that they weren't going to go away, I finally decided to face them. I went to the door yawning and feigning having just been awakened from a deep slumber. I left Bristol inside and faced the two officers alone.

The big beer-bellied one said, "Are you Renée Askins?" I said, "I am." He said, "Ma'am, I believe we picked up your dog last Friday." Yawning, I said, "I believe you did." He said, "Ma'am, I believe you spoke with me on the phone." I said, "I believe I did. That is, until you hung up on me." He ignored my insolence. "Ma'am, do you have your dog?" Growls from inside the door. "Yes, sir, I do." "Ma'am, would you mind telling us how you got your dog?" I had thought about that potential question for about five days by then. I am a truly lousy liar so I knew I had to say something truthful, but perhaps not completely revealing. So I responded, "I found her just off Wilbur Marsh Way." "You found her on Wilbur Marsh Way!" the warden blurted back. "Well, just off the road," I corrected. "Escaped the pound like I said she would." "Escaped!" An incredulous outburst. "Ma'am, there's a six-foot dog run and two twelve-foot chain-link fences." I looked straight into his beady little eyes, plugged into his fat-swollen face. "Really?" Tugging my sleeves down over my bandaged wrists a bit more, I said, "I told you on the phone her middle name was Houdini. She's an amazing dog. You're lucky she wasn't hurt because I would have sued you." Before he could respond to that little piece of audacity I asked, "Did she damage anything in her escape?" "No, ma'am, there wasn't one sign of how she got out except she had moved her kennel door to one side. That's the puzzling thing about it—not one sign." The silence waited there between us. Not knowing whether to arrest me or apologize to me, the two men seemed stymied. The silence bore down like the high-noon sun. I waited. Finally, my interrogator broke. With an exasperated curse, he turned and left; the other followed, shaking his head and muttering something about Houdini and twelve-foot fences.

Fifteen

❖❖❖

To live within limits, to want one thing, or a very few things, very much and love them dearly, cling to them, survey them from every angle, become one with them—that is what makes the poet, the artist, the human being.

JOHANN WOLFGANG VON GOETHE

I T WAS MY habit every few years to try to visit an area where wild wolves still roamed. It was a way of recharging and revitalizing my wolf work, remembering why it was important and perhaps most of all to keep some thread of connection with the reality, rather than the idea, of wolves. Sometimes it was northern Montana or Alaska, but in 1989 it was northern Minnesota. Dave Mech had arranged for me to do several lectures and, as an added benefit, offered to take me out in the field for a few days. One of the remarkable mysteries about Dave is that somehow in the midst of his research and writing he finds the time to mentor and shepherd so many young people into careers working with wolves. If one surveys the wolf recovery efforts across the United States invariably in every major project—Mexican wolves, Alaskan wolves, Yellowstone wolves—a student who has been trained or mentored by Mech will turn up.

Off I went to northern Minnesota for my annual "hit" of real wolf country. The first night I was there I gave a lecture in Ely at a small community college and returned to Mech's research lab, a snug log building built on the shores of Birch Lake in the Superior National Forest. Dave's master's and Ph.D.

students all bunked there in a cozy chaos of research gear, industrial-size peanut butter jars, and coffee cans. The walls were covered with maps adorned with shadings delineating pack territories, each filled with rainbow-colored pins marking different sightings. There was a big fireplace, and beat-up furniture strewn with research papers and half-read novels. Old defunct telemetry collars in different states of repair were scattered across tables. One could feel the richness of lives informed by science and animals merged in this half dormitory, half research facility. Dave had a telemetry study going on with white-tailed deer at the time and the crew had set up a net-capture site right outside the research lab. As part of the study they were trying out a new design of telemetry collar and were eager to catch a deer that night. The typical brutal cold of Ely in February, about forty below, had taken hold when I staggered into the lab after my lecture, exhausted by the flight from Jackson and a rough week in Wyoming. I barely said hello to the students hanging out near the fireplace and fell into an icy sleeping bag on one of the bunks in a chilly room adjoining the living room.

Among the ranks of young wildlife biologists there is a certain code of behavior that is fundamental to one's stature in the profession. One dimension of that code is a willingness to forgo sleep in order to observe interesting animal behavior, or at the very least the possession of an intuitive responsiveness that when wild animals are near one alerts to them with a sort of sixth sense. My awareness of this fundamental trait reached as far back as my apprenticeship with Stephen Alexander when we would have to sit long, silent hours waiting for a trap to be triggered or a fish to bite.

I made quite an impression in Minnesota that winter when sometime well after midnight a deer wandered into the capture site, a net was triggered, and the deer subdued. Because of the cold and concern over the deer's exposure under anesthesia the crew decided to move the anesthetized deer into the living room to process it—biological jargon for taking blood, affixing ear tags, fitting the collar, etc. Apparently the deer came out of the anesthesia prematurely and managed to rise and began stumbling around, crashing into chairs and tables, leaping over the couch. The students were grabbing at it while trying to avoid the substantial blows of its cloven hooves, everyone yelling and trying to subdue it. Only a few feet away in the next room, I managed the dubious distinction of sleeping through the whole thing. If I had been awake I probably would have protested man's manipulation of that poor creature—

and she would have thanked me by breaking my arm—but as it was my philosophy went unargued and instead I was subjected to merciless teasing for days.

The next morning we all awoke early, I at least shamefully well rested, and went out to help a student unload a wolf carcass (killed by a car) from the freezer in a nearby shed. I'm not sure what the point of the freezer was, given that it was still nearly forty below, but I helped haul the wolf out of its depths. As we swung the stiff carcass of the animal into the back of a pickup truck for shipment to another lab, a nearby pack of wolves started howling. This was a thrill for me, who lived far removed from wild wolves, and I was struck by the strange juxtaposition of the mystical and mundane one encounters in scientific research. The road-killed wolf lay stiff and inert, its tongue frozen in an unbecoming droop from its mouth on the corrugated dirty bed of the pickup, while the frigid air filled with the mysterious and beautiful howls of its living brethren. Somewhere near, a disoriented doe roamed, newly fitted with a radio collar, her ears pricked to attention by the morning's serenade.

Dave and I drove to the nearby rural airport early that morning for a wolf-monitoring flight. It was still thirty below when we took off and I was huddled in the backseat of the plane shrouded in down, my Steger mukluks peering out of my bulky bibbed pants. I scraped the plane's back windows like I used to scrape the Maverick's windshield, peering through the frosty portals in utter ecstasy. We saw ten packs that day—forty-six wolves total. We watched a reunion of a single animal returning to his pack, obviously after some sort of winter walkabout. We watched greetings and pinnings and straight-lined travel through deep snow. One alpha male chased our plane. Talk of courage! I saluted him, thinking he should get the canine medal of honor. One pack was out on a frozen lake and within seconds, as the plane did a low flyby, managed to vanish into unlikely hiding. There was only one small tree on the end of the small peninsula, but somehow the wolves managed to disappear as we circled back above. There was nowhere for them to hide, and yet hidden they were. The now-you-see-us, now-you-don't behavior of these mysterious creatures sent shivers down my spine.

On the way back to the airport we had a rather unusual sighting. A fisher, a large member of the weasel family, very rare in Minnesota, galloped down a narrow plowed road just below the plane. It was my first sighting of the mustelid. Dave hadn't seen one in years and was thrilled in the way only one who truly loves the discovery of wildlife can be. He was as enthusiastic as a small child, grinning and exclaiming and instructing the pilot to circle just one more time. Watching Dave that day reminded me of Sam Keen's lovely comment, "Forests are enchanted enough without elves or hobbits. Did you ever see a ruby-throated hummingbird?" I've never heard Dave, an ardent mink trapper and no-nonsense biologist, lapse into reveries of animal myth and mystery, but I greatly respect Mech's sincerity and clarity in approaching a relationship with animals. I trust his way because he brings such a passionate curiosity and vitality to that relationship, a sort of tireless hunger to learn more, to ask more, to enter into an exchange built on intricate knowledge and attention, rather than rhetoric and righteousness. Although his approach and ethics differ greatly from my own, I learned much more from him about what it means to "know" a species than I have ever absorbed from reading countless animal rights books.

That second night at the lab I fell asleep with that marvelous sense of flight still in my bones, the room turning softly. All my dreams moved as though I were floating through them. Wide-open white dreams with long-legged wolves drifting across snow-dusted ice. Shadows moving easily through the winter trees and along the ridges. The world was shining and light and the Douglas firs were the deepest, most miraculous green, as though light gathered and glowed and spilled from their boughs. I awakened the next morning thinking about the deep hypnotic green of those trees, and then remembered there weren't any Douglas firs in Minnesota—Doug firs were in Wyoming. I prayed my dream might be a far-off omen that indeed someday I would watch wolves weaving though the trees of Yellowstone.

On the last day of my stay I was to speak at a small community college in the Minneapolis suburbs. It was a howling, blizzarding winter night and yet Dave cheerfully volunteered to drive me to the lecture. We got completely lost and wandered back roads and streets for what seemed like hours. When we finally arrived we were led through a cavernous maze of buildings and halls to an auditorium in the heart of the campus. I was highly skeptical that any of the general public would go out in the storm, let alone ever find such a hidden auditorium. To my astonishment over a hundred people showed up.

On a last-minute impulse I added a slide of Natasha at the very end of the program. I had never talked about her or my thesis experience in front of an audience because it felt so private and sacred, but for some reason on that windblown, forsaken night on the Minnesota plains, now tamed by the Minneapolis suburbs, I felt I needed to invoke her memory. As was my habit, I ended the program with a passage from Henry Beston's *The Outermost House,* but that evening, for the first time, I dedicated it to the memory of Natasha, "a wolf I once loved."

> We need another and a wiser and perhaps a more mystical concept of animals. Remote from universal nature, and living by complicated artifice, man in civilization surveys the creature through the glass of his knowledge and sees thereby a feather magnified and the whole image in distortion. We patronize them for their incompleteness, for their tragic fate of having taken form so far below ourselves. And therein we err, and greatly err. For the animal shall not be measured by man. In a world older and more complete than ours they move finished and complete, gifted with extensions of the senses we have lost or never attained, living by voices we shall never hear. They are not brethren, they are not underlings; they are other nations, caught with ourselves in the net of life and time, fellow prisoners of the splendor and travail of the earth.

After the program a group of people gathered near the podium to ask questions and offer comments. A young woman stood there a long time, kind of hanging back, allowing the others to finish their queries. After they all had left she approached and introduced herself as Kathy Traylor. She asked if by chance Natasha had been born at the North American Wildlife Park Foundation in 1980. I nodded. She asked if I knew what had become of her. My eyes teared. I apologized, explaining that it was a difficult topic for me. Once I was a bit more composed I told the young woman that to my knowledge Natasha was taken to a research facility in North Dakota. The woman smiled gently. She said she just wanted to confirm that we were talking about the same wolf. She put out her hand in offering before her next statement. I took it with both my own, a mid-conversation gesture common in Africa. "I'm the woman who took her," she said. "You were too upset to speak with me then. It was nearly ten years ago, but I thought I remembered your face."

I could hardly believe that after all these years, there, in front of me, holding both my hands, stood the woman who had taken Natasha. The sheer impossibility of it all—the storm, the remote college, my impulse to mention Natasha that night—all of it seemed surreal. Neither had Kathy any idea in coming to the lecture that I was connected to a wolf she, too, had cared for so long ago. We sat down, or rather she sat and I crumpled into an auditorium seat, and she began to tell me about Natasha as an adult wolf.

She said in all her years as a caretaker of wolves at this facility she had never encountered an animal quite like her. She had a "presence" about her, and a focus that was very unusual. She described her as the "sweetest" of all her wards, and very much her favorite. She said Natasha had a steady calm about her, a softness that the other wolves didn't possess. About seven months after Natasha arrived at the facility in Fargo, she said, a skunk got into the enclosure and the wolves tore it up pretty well. In late January of 1981, Otter, another one of the pups that I had raised, began to behave oddly. That was on a Sunday. Otter started convulsing and, in spite of the efforts of several vets, died on Wednesday. They did an autopsy and on Friday the test results came back: a paralytic form of rabies. On Saturday the four other wolves from Wolf Park that had shared the pen with Otter were euthanized, including Natasha. Even though they had not yet shown symptoms, Natasha and another female tested positive for rabies.

Natasha dead? Dead all these years? On some level I guess I had known; on another, the idea of her physically gone from the world was inconceivable. I was overcome by relief and happiness that 'tasha had been loved like that after she left my care. On one hand I think I was grateful that she hadn't had to endure a long life of captivity, so contrary to her nature; on the other, the finality of her absence was crushing. The woman was very kind and gentle, and had obviously suffered from Natasha's loss as well. She said it had broken her heart and that she had left the facility not long after Natasha's death.

I felt such a collage of emotions: grief, devastation, joy, bewilderment—I staggered out of the lecture hall awash in confusion. Somehow Dave delivered me to my hotel and I got on a plane home the next day, but I have little recollection of the trip. What followed was a period of turmoil and anguish. I wondered if Natasha's death made my promise irrelevant. I had, in essence, lost my guiding star. Without the strong sense of Natasha's life my direction and determination faltered.

Sixteen

❖ ❖ ❖

Into my head rose
the nothings
my life day after day
but I am leaving the shore
in my skin boat.
It came to me that I was in danger
and now the small troubles
look big
and the ache
that comes from the things
big.
But only one thing
is great
only one
this.
In the hut by the path
to see the day
coming out of its mother
and the light filling the world.

ANONYMOUS ESKIMO

TRANSLATED BY W. S. MERWIN

FTER LEARNING OF Natasha's death I went through a period of despondency and aimlessness, as I had when she was taken from me the first time. My office had become a prison with an endlessly overflowing in box and a stack of unreturned phone calls that haunted me even in my dreams. I had created this insatiable creature called The Wolf Fund, I had fed it for years with will and passion and purpose and certainty, and then one morning I awakened with nothing left to give it.

To keep myself going and focused I developed a habit in my work. During this period of faltering, every decision, trip, meeting, phone call, and memo I did while working for The Wolf Fund was guided by one question: How will this action put wolves on the ground in Yellowstone? I needed this litmus test to dictate how I spent my time, knowing how easy it is to get sidetracked in conservation matters. Given the sheer multitude of needs, the danger is even greater when you've lost your focus. So it was against all odds that in the spring of 1991, when I was invited to attend a conference/retreat on humanizing the conservation movement hosted by the Natural Resources Defense Council and the Nathan Cummings Foundation, that I would accept. The retreat's purpose was to bring a more human and humane approach to environmental activism and was led by Thich Nhat Hanh, the great Vietnamese Zen teacher and Nobel Prize–nominated peace activist. I was desperately behind in my work and could imagine no relevant argument for attending the retreat, but in the end I betrayed all my self-imposed rules and just followed the truth of my heart which said, "You need to do this."

Thich Nhat Hanh opened the retreat with the statement *"To take care of the environment, we must first take care of the environmentalist."* I am still coming to fathom the amount of wisdom packed in that short phrase. Like myself, many of the attendees had not fully absorbed that this was a meditation retreat, almost entirely conducted in silence. Fortunately I felt somewhat "trained" for the experience by my year in Africa, although this time I didn't have the *poyo* to lubricate the transition from frenzy to stillness. For five days nearly a hundred participants sat, ate, walked, and lived in silence—a silence only broken by the ringing of bells marking mealtime, meditation time, walking time, and the times of teaching by Thich Nhat Hanh.

The retreat was held at a rustic camp built into the Malibu hills where hawks circled in the high afternoon light and the hillsides crackled in the baked California quiet. In spite of the serene surroundings, emotions ran wild among the many who had never gone a waking hour without speaking, let alone five days. Activists and lobbyists stripped of language are like birds plucked of their feathers. Some of us squawked and flapped and panicked, others resigned themselves to what was perceived as a flightless existence, submissive and listless. Still others found a contemplative peace rarely experienced in the context of our frenetic lives. Like so much of what is profound, the essence of what Thich Nhat Hanh was trying to convey was taught through example, not sermon. No one left the retreat unaffected.

Two important things happened at that conference that would have a fundamental effect on my work and life. The first arose from the simple act of buying a book from the small selection of merchandise being sold at the conference headquarters, a book by Thich Nhat Hanh called *The Miracle of Mindfulness.* It contained the following story written by James Forest about witnessing a lecture by the peace activist given during the time of the Vietnam War. The anecdote sparked a whole new direction for The Wolf Fund.

Thich Nhat Hanh had been speaking in the auditorium of a wealthy Christian church in a St. Louis suburb. As always, he emphasized the need for the U.S. to stop their bombing and killing in his country. There had been many questions and answers when a large man stood up and spoke with searing scorn of the "supposed compassion" of "this Mr. Hanh."

"If you care so much about your people, Mr. Hanh, why are you here? If you care so much for the people who are wounded, why don't you spend your time with them?" At this point my recollection of his words is replaced by the memory of the intense anger which overwhelmed me.

When the man finished I looked to Nhat Hanh in bewilderment. What could he—or anyone—say? The spirit of the Vietnam war itself had suddenly filled the room, and it seemed hard to breathe.

There was a silence. Then Nhat Hanh began to speak—quietly, with deep calm, indeed with a sense of personal caring for the man who had just damned him. The words seemed like rain falling on fire. "If you want the tree to grow," he said, "it won't help to water the leaves. *You have to water the roots* [emphasis added]. Many of the roots of the war are here in your country. To help the people who are to be bombed, to try to protect them from this suffering, I have to come here."

This, I thought when I read it with the clarity of five days of meditation under my belt, is the compassion that needs to be brought to conservation. I wasn't sure how, but I knew that the answer lay in understanding that we needed to water the roots of our problem, to nourish our perceived enemies in order for growth and healing to occur. This notion of entering the place of the so-called other and listening, offering, understanding, was a profound lesson.

The second thing that happened was meeting a woman who would have a pivotal effect on my future. On the final day of the retreat, I was hurriedly packing to race off to a fund-raising meeting when a lovely, dark-haired woman approached me in the parking lot. She had patient, calm hands and solemn brown eyes and a manner that was intent, eager, and insistent all at once. Someone had told her of my efforts on behalf of wolves in Yellowstone and she asked if I might have a few minutes to tell her about my work. I glanced at my watch, already a half hour late. I took a deep breath and suggested we go sit on a nearby park bench.

This woman asked the kinds of questions everyone wishes they would be asked about their work, the kinds of questions that allow one to tell one's story, to say one's truth, to utter one's vision. I called and rescheduled my fund-raising meeting for later in the day, and she and I talked for nearly an hour and a half. I gave her a handful of newsletters and articles and left, realizing only after I'd driven away that I hadn't even written down her last name. All I knew was her first name was Mollie. What I didn't know was in that hour and a half the powers of synchronicity and serendipity had touched my life once again. This woman was to become the single most important comrade I would have in the next three years of fighting for the return of wolves.

Seventeen

❖ ❖ ❖

there is always movement, toward or away
below the most innocent conversations
movement, silent and inevitable, as moss
growing on moist rock, as undulating
as sea ferns in a tidal pool.

beneath any language, there is the language,
which eddies past the granite words
like a tiny underground stream, you may
bathe in this flow, this warm or cool
rhythm, or you may ignore it and find

the ground you stand upon become mud,
unexpectedly, or wash away altogether.
beneath any language, there is the language;
cup your hands, lean toward the silence
and drink there.

CHARLES LEVENDOSKY, "there is always"

I RETURNED TO Wyoming after the Thich Nhat Hanh conference re-
freshed, reinspirited. Partly it had given me some breathing room—
figuratively and literally—some time out off the firing line to rest and
recuperate—and partly it had opened a new way of thinking for me.

I was now driven by the belief that the next most critical step was to disarm some of the direct rage that was focused on the idea of wolves. I began to
put together a regional outreach effort to try to communicate with the communities and constituencies most ardently opposed to wolf reintroduction. I
thought of it as my humble effort at what Thich Nhat Hanh had described as
"watering the roots." My staff, however, called it "the behind-the-enemy-
lines lecture tour."

Unquestionably, one of the greatest inherent challenges of the work for
me personally was confronting and managing the growing rage that the issue
incited. By nature I am a peacemaker. I don't enjoy conflict or confrontation
the way some of my male colleagues seemed to, nor am I tough-skinned in
facing it. Entering and embracing the rage that lapped and licked and boiled
around and within the wolf issue was at best extremely depleting, and at worst

virtually crippling. At times the anger was so thick and vitriolic it was palpable, a saplike ooze one had to scour and scrape to remove from one's psyche. It was during this time that I started getting hate mail and, even worse, hate messages. The following two capture the kind of rage I'm trying to describe.

The wolves are a sack of monkeyshit. Why should we give a FUCK about 'em. I think we should shoot all the FUCKING wolves. Each and every in Yellowstone. You FUCKIN' bag of shit. Go there, I'm gonna go up there, there, I'm gonna blow each every FUCKING one of 'em away. So FUCK YOU you FUCKING environmentalist, butt-FUCKING assholes. My contribution is this: FUCK YOU! FUCK YOU! [A Wolf Fund answering machine message transcribed verbatim]

Another caller, equally refined and eloquent, said,

Yeah, as far as I'm concerned you can just fuck all them wolves. Shoot every one of those motherfuckers right between the eyes. Skin their pelt. Sell it. Only thing you can do with 'em. Ain't worth shit. All they fucking do is eat sheep and chase cows. They fucking suck. Just like goddamn coyotes. Just shoot the motherfuckers. Kill every one of the last bitches. Fuck 'em all. And fuck your nonprofit organization. All you're doing is fucking over people and trying to make 'em feel sorry for the bastards they don't know what the fuck they can do. Them wolves are more fucking problems than a guy knows what the fuck to do with. The guy that gets this fucking message can shove it up his ass. If it's a bitch she can suck my dick, all fucking eight inches of it, down her fucking throat. [A Wolf Fund answering machine message transcribed verbatim]

Under those words is a terrible despair. A helplessness, a fury, a madness that is both terrifying and at the same time somehow compelling. I assure you there were a lot of deep breaths, bubble baths, quivering nights, and teary moments during those years, but the basic truth I had to confront is that we can't run from this stuff, because there's no place to run. No matter where you turn it exists—because it is the state of humans struggling with their shadow.

We can't conquer it or crush it or stomp it out or wipe it away. To disarm or transform this rage we have to know it, we have to understand it, it has to be palpable and real. The only way to disarm it is to go straight into it. To begin to live next to it, to enter into the place of its origins and its home.

There were many aspects to the rage: there was the anger that people felt at having their assumptions, their habits, even their "worldview" challenged. This was often expressed as a sort of righteous indignation: "It's been this way for sixty years. Who the hell are you to think it should be different?" Although sometimes these sentiments came from western natives, often they were parroted by individuals who had recently moved to the West and seemed to have a deep attachment to living, or at least preaching, the myth of western independence.

Removing wolves from the West nearly one hundred years earlier expressed what settlers *perceived* as their right—to control wildlife and the natural world. So putting wolves back was perceived as an effort to take away that control. No matter how substantial the scientific evidence that wolves kill few livestock and would have minimal effect on game populations, or that there would be very few restrictions associated with their presence (as there indeed had been with other endangered species efforts), it did not change the perception that wolves meant loss, limits, and outside interference.

"At the end of the open road we come to ourselves," wrote Louis Simpson. We have come to the end of that open road, and now it is ourselves that we must face in matters of environmental degradation. Water shortage, nuclear waste, spreading erosion, overgrazing, water pollution, and strip-mining are catching up with us. The changes that must happen ARE about giving up some control and acknowledging limits. We take less, we have more. Once there was a lot of wild country and a few of us. Now there are a lot of us and only a little wild country. The inevitability of change, however, doesn't make it any less painful for those caught in its midst.

Another kind of rage people felt was the fury that arose from believing their livelihoods were being threatened. Often the wolf was referred to as "the spotted owl of the Rockies." The notion that wolves would directly undermine livestock operations or outfitting businesses was very common. I felt tremendous compassion for these people. That their fears had no basis in fact did not make them less painful. Our approach with this group was to listen, to allow the fears to be aired and echoed, and then, when appropriate, to attempt to provide accurate information, oftentimes about the behavior or biology of wolves that addressed the specific concern.

And then there was the rage felt by a few select men who believed their dominion, their supremacy, their sense of manhood was being threatened not only by the idea of wolves returning, the symbol of the uncontrollable, the fellow predator, but that a *woman* dared represent or advocate such a thing. I wish I could say we developed a helpful response to these guys, but basically we didn't. Even though they were often the boisterous, outspoken hecklers at talks or meetings, I found they were rarely respected by the community, and when it came down to forging a cooperative plan, seldom were they nominated as representatives of any constituency or given any standing at the negotiating table.

I don't want to mislead you. On the whole I found the men of the West a kind and valiant lot. I attribute much of their polite treatment of me to a deep and embedded code of civility and chivalry that still pervades the rural West. In fact, once, at a lecture in Cody, Wyoming, a hotbed of wolf hatred, an elderly rancher—lean, weathered, hat in hand—came to my rescue. He stood up in the packed conference room of the Holiday Inn and gently but firmly silenced a vitriolic attack by a woman wolf hater (newly arrived from Greenwich, Connecticut) during the question-and-answer portion of a lecture. Even though the room was filled with locals who were clearly opposed to the presence of wolves there, nonetheless a sense of fair play and presentation prevailed among the native westerners.

I considered myself fortunate to have received only occasional death threats and perverted phone calls. (The letters that were merely nasty or the comments that were only snide seem pleasantly mild by contrast.) Only once was I threatened directly with bodily harm, and that occurred in Alaska, not Wyoming. I had spoken at a conference in Fairbanks, to a hockey rink packed mostly with hunters and trappers, many adorned with their wolf-fur hats, mittens, and coats for the occasion. I had expressed some dissenting opinions about machine-gunning wolves from helicopters. Later that night, having a beer with some of the conference's other speakers, I was set upon by a drunken hunter who had been dragging a dead wolf around behind his pickup. I was whisked out of harm's way by Ted Williams, one of my advisory board members, who scolded me for having even responded to the guy's incendiary taunting. I think Ted quoted Schiller's "Against stupidity, the very gods themselves contend in vain." I hung that quote on my office door.

In October 1992, a year and a half after I had attended the Thich Nhat Hanh retreat, a lone wolf arrived in Yellowstone, having traveled several hundred miles from southern Canada or Montana. It should not have shocked me that the first wolf to make it to Yellowstone in seventy years was met with a bullet rather than a cheer, but it did. It brought me to my knees—on a cement loading dock in Mammoth, at Yellowstone's park headquarters, on an overcast day in early fall.

I had received a call from Yellowstone headquarters and had immediately driven up to see this animal with my own eyes and hear the story firsthand. Leaning over the wolf, running my fingers through his thick black fur, I somehow wanted to convey to it, in whatever realm it had come to occupy after its death, that all of human impulse wasn't directed at killing animals. A coolness had infiltrated the warm autumn days, a quiet chill permeated the day, suggestive of both the coming dark days of winter and the cold indifference of the killer's act. There I thought of Thich Nhat Hanh's enormous courage, his extraordinary example of reaching out to those who had destroyed his homeland and murdered the people he loved. For at that moment all I felt was a deep and residing anger—anger that took my breath away and left me reeling in the acidity of its fury.

The wolf was a large black male with a splash of silver under his chin and across his chest, possibly a disperser from a wild pack in Canada. He had been shot by a hunter who supposedly mistook the ninety-two-pound black animal for a thirty-five-pound tawny brown coyote. The carcass was being prepared for shipment to the Fish and Wildlife Service lab in Ashland, Oregon, for an autopsy. The shooting had occurred near Fox Creek, approximately two and a half miles south of the Yellowstone border, an area believed by many to be the wildest country in the lower forty-eight. Over twenty miles from any road, great grizzly habitat, lots of game, it is particularly dear to me because many years ago I saw my first mountain lion there. It is a place where one would have thought a wild animal would be safe, but because it is designated as wilderness, not national park, coyote hunting is permissible—at any time of year. There was no question as to cause of death. The blood had dried to a maroon crust around the bullet wound. The only question for the authorities was about the wolf's origins. The only question for me was about our own.

I called the wolf Odysseus. As I sat there stroking that animal, all I could think of was the thing that had led to its death. Rage—like the rage I felt at that moment toward the hunter who had killed the animal. Helpless, pulsing, defensive rage. For the first time I could actually recognize the rage, feel it coursing through my body, understand its power. For the first time, I really saw that *I* was capable of the emotion that I had been so patiently working to extinguish in others.

It was an odd experience to be sitting in Yellowstone stroking a dead wolf, smelling the sweet scent of sage and meadow grass carried by his body, touching the flesh of an animal that had traveled hundreds of miles to reach this wild place. For the four years preceding Odysseus's death I had spent my time ricocheting back and forth between the Rockies and the East Coast talking endlessly about the *idea* of wolves, the possibility of a multitude of scenarios all built on the mythic, imagined wolf. Here he was, dead.

The Wolf Fund had by now developed into a full-fledged organization, able to hire full-time staff and set up permanent offices in Moose and then later in Jackson. We started out in a weathered one-room schoolhouse located at the Dornan compound in Moose; then, as staff was added, we moved a couple miles east to Mormon Row, where Clark and Vita Moulton, then in their eighties, rented us several cabins on the ranch that Clark's daddy had homesteaded. It seemed right that we were sheltered and launched from the bosom of one of the first ranches in Jackson Hole, as our physical location always reminded us that the way to a solution must be derived from the people who had lived in the West their whole lifetimes rather than imposed by those who had not.

Year after year on the East Coast had been spent in a frustrating dance of lobbying and appropriations efforts to get an Environmental Impact Statement under way, the last formidable obstacle to implementing a reintroduction program. But rather than chronicling the endless political battles, conservation infighting, strategic lobbying efforts, and countless meetings during that time, I want to turn to the sounds under the surface. It is the pulse of the subterranean activity that bubbles up into my memory of that time.

One of the problems of national conservation organization is that the true dilemmas of local conservation action stay remote and alien, an abstraction not only to the staffers at national conservation group headquarters but to the vast majority of the national public. It is easier to hate the enemy, or who we imagine the enemy to be, if they are abstract. We can easily diminish the debate into the simple theater of US against THEM, acted on a stage where the colors and complexities of human life and struggle dwindle to insignificance. Things can be black and white only if you don't have to stare the "villains" in the face and note the color of their eyes. I learned that the villain whose blue eye is settled behind the rifle scope might be a hundred-pound woman whose beloved pet heifer was just left half eaten and hardly breathing by a grizzly, or a red-haired twelve-year-old boy whose daddy just lost his family's third-generation ranch to a bank for reasons that a young mind cannot comprehend. Real people, real lives, real dilemmas. These days ranchers, in particular, are having a hard time of it—the burdens are numerous: drought, falling stock prices, rising taxes, and, yes, predators. Predators may be the least of their problems, but be assured it is much easier to hate and kill a coyote, or a wolf, than it is to change weather patterns, market trends, or the government.

For many people in the West a value system is at stake, the way they view themselves and their relationship to wildlife and the land is being challenged because national attitudes toward wilderness and wild animals have been shifting. When I began working on wolf recovery I believed it was wolves we were arguing about; I thought conservationists could win the debates if we just assimilated enough solid biological information, filed enough successful lawsuits, or marshaled enough political support. I no longer believed that. These confrontations did not center on biological facts or abstract laws. These were moral questions, and moral questions are resolved on a cultural level, within the context of personal emotion: love, passion, and anger. Our value systems are called into question by issues like wolf reintroduction, and we're asked to examine what we believe and feel on a profound and intimate level.

On a profound and intimate level, I admit I felt angry. When I held that dead wolf I felt very angry. When a rancher has a cow or a herding dog killed by wolves they feel angry. There has to be room for those emotions. Denying emotion *on either side* is simply another way of trying to disarm effective protest and sterilize the debate. As Jack Turner wrote in an early essay, titled like his later book, "The Abstract Wild,"

Effective protest is grounded in anger . . . anger nourishes hope and fuels rebellion, it presumes a judgment, presumes how things ought to be and aren't, presumes a care. Emotion is still the best evidence of belief and value.

But to feel and honor your anger does not mean that you cannot also feel compassion. In fact, experiencing your own anger can give you more empathy for how others might experience theirs. That is, after all, the root meaning of compassion, "to feel or experience another's passion."

As I had discovered working on whooping cranes and mule deer, fundamentally the conservation issues being debated today are all moral issues, whether it's reintroducing wolves to Yellowstone, a rancher's right to protect his livestock, or the implementation of the Endangered Species Act. At their heart, these are not debates about wolves killing livestock, or ranchers killing wolves. These issues, at their deepest level, are battles over man's control of the natural world, over defining our relationship with animals, and the dignity and honor with which we approach those relationships. Again, this is why it is so important that we recognize the disease, not just the symptoms.

One of the counterproductive aspects of these sorts of debates is our attempt to sterilize the language when we talk about highly charged issues. It is very difficult for us to face cultural changes directly, so we try to blur the language, to disarm the emotion, to render the words impotent and meaningless by using euphemism, shibboleth, or jargon. But when the language has become sanitized of emotional honesty people leave exchanges frustrated because they can't say their truth, nor can they hear it echoed back to them.

The government and the agencies that represent it are particularly at fault in this regard. Attendance at any of the so-called hearings where government officials were dispatched to "listen" to the public's concerns revealed an antithetical strategy. Bureaucrats essentially developed their own locution on the wolf issue to disarm the debate. They did so by emasculating the language with phrases like "renewable resource," "reduction strategy," "management tool," "control action," "game units," "predator control," "remove," "cull." Sterile words. Words devoid of emotion and meaning. Most conservation debates, whether about acid rain, global warming, mining, or water rights, are filled with jargon that dissolves under scrutiny—"strategic plan," "interest groups," "consumptive use," "control program"—words that suggest anything but what they truly mean. I suppose we all use language this way. We see it all the time—a missile is called "the Peacekeeper," a wolf hate group is called "the Abundant Wildlife Society," and a campaign to undermine critical environmental protection of wildlife and public lands is called "the Wise Use Movement." To at least be conscious of the language is a step forward—to believe oneself accountable to words, as if what we said and how we said it might be used as a gauge of our honesty.

Language is power. Control the way people talk about an issue and you control the parameters of the debate. Reduce talk about people's lives and their sense of loss, or the act of killing wild, innocent animals, to talk of benefits, resources, game units, and control actions and you've succeeded in sterilizing and abstracting the debate. The vocabulary shapes the discussion to fit a certain worldview, and that worldview seems too often to forget that people and their fears and their rage are a part of the equation. Sterilized language deepens the rage because it essentially ignores it—as if by ignoring it we will cause it to disappear. Many of us want to discount the rage. We want to expose how irrational and unreasonable the other side's assumptions are. The point, however, is not whether their pain is logical or rational, but that it exists. We will not abate this rage by trying to discount it or challenge it. People who fear loss feel pain, and in the West one of the ways they will express that pain is through the raging act of killing animals.

We conservationists need to take a long hard look at our current tactics and strategies—our lawsuits, our attack ads, our letters to the editor. We need to really evaluate whether maneuvers formulated to protect animals may not be inadvertently killing them, whether our approach might function more to vent our own rage (or sell memberships by polarizing sides) than to achieve our stated objectives.

I never understood how we could profess love for animals but not humans. Walt Kelly's wisdom, "We have met the enemy and he is us," echoes in my mind. We need to go straight into this rage with compassion and with care, and that means we need to fundamentally transform the process by which we attempt conservation projects and remove a basic foundation for abusive attitudes—both ours and theirs. We need to be more physically present in the local communities where we are trying to enact change. The most effective change I've witnessed has been facilitated by conservationists living in and working from within communities. It makes all the difference to share the passions and pains of the people whose lives our actions affect.

We also need to listen—listen to the stories, come to understand the rhythm and reason of these lives we think of as antithetical to our own. We might find we are an awful lot alike. We need to come to understand their arguments and their fears, and be able to articulate these fears and threats as well as or better than they can. Help them hear their own voices. It is a very powerful thing for people who view you as an outsider to hear you name their concerns.

It is interesting to ask, What does it sound like to hear a culture talking with itself? There is always the shrill background noise, the sense of riots and rage from one direction, and from the other you can hear the religious din of righteous rhetoric. You can hear the grandstanding and sideshows; but if one is drawn toward the heart of the conversation, as one nears the center a quietness descends. There is the soothing murmur of people talking, of calm, of people listening to each other, of sentences finished and thoughts matured, of reason, compassion, wisdom, and humor arising from experience and patience. The din is democracy, the still pool at its center is where a culture hears and heals itself.

What we're talking about is social change. Attitudes toward predators and our treatment of them cut to the very marrow of how people view their relationship to animals, and our relationship with animals reflects our capacities and openness to other cultures, other countries, and, most important, to the earth itself.

The wolf debate is an example of how a single wildlife issue can change attitudes toward all animals. Changes don't happen easily. Almost every major movement that has involved value shifts in this country has begun with an underground trickle, a small dribble that slowly eroded and shifted the bedrock of a value system. The trickle becomes a stream and over time—a long time—it spreads and rises and becomes a river, and then changes are made. This was true of the civil rights movement, the suffrage movement, and the peace movement. It will happen, too, with the values related to wildlife and wild lands in the United States.

Eighteen

❖ ❖ ❖

Yes, and when the love of life disappears,
no meaning can console us.

ALBERT CAMUS

.

T HE REAL WAY I came to understand the rage and sense of inconsolable loss the people opposed to wolves felt was to learn it through the prism of my own experience. That lesson would, like so many, be taught by my dog.

From the time she was quite young Bristol seemed to have an enchanted relationship with coyotes. When she was just a couple of years old a friend and I took her on a backpacking/fly-fishing trip on the Greybull River. It was a hot, cloud-speckled afternoon when we took a break from lashing the waters—or rather my friend took a break from lashing, I from extracting my fly from the riverside botany—when I noticed Bristol's absence. I stood up to scan the surroundings and saw her on a slope about two hundred yards away racing full speed across the sage-pocked incline. Suddenly she stopped, splashed her front legs down, and arched her rump up in what behaviorists call a "play bow." Out of the sage in front of her exploded a coyote, dashing by her in a dead run. Bristol whirled and rocketed after him in full chase.

At first I was anxious that she might be lured toward a pack that could overwhelm her, but my fears were allayed seconds later when the coyote pivoted around in a 180-degree leap and dropped into another play bow. Bristol raced by him and he followed in full chase. I stopped, whispering in awe, "They're playing." I turned around to my friend and said, "Bris is playing with a coyote." He nodded and grinned. We watched the two frolic on the hillside for about half an hour. When they started getting closer to the ridgetop I called Bristol in.

Over the years, usually on backpacking trips or on long backcountry runs, Bristol had several play encounters with coyotes. Never did I witness an aggressive encounter, rather bewildering because most wild-domestic encounters do involve some element of aggression. I've also never understood why coyotes were so attracted to her. Usually coyotes are extremely wary and suspicious of strange canids in their territories—their typical response is to flee or to threaten; to frolic is quite unusual. Obviously some communication or quality beyond the reach of my senses was at play in the fields of the coyotes.

I had graduated from Yale in 1988, but continued to split my time between Wyoming and the East Coast until 1990, when I moved back to Moose permanently. By then I had been seeing Tom Rush for several years, and we had fallen in love. Soon TR joined me and we moved into the log house at the foot of Shadow Mountain, on the border of Grand Teton National Park and the Bridger-Teton National Forest. The house was actually within the boundaries of the park and, as described earlier, was a haven to local wildlife. This move would turn out to be profoundly important to my work because the location, with its abundance of wildlife—bison, elk, deer, moose, antelope, coyotes, cranes, owls, hawks, and many others—would become the place of my healing, the place to which I could return from The Wolf Fund night after night, depleted and exhausted, only to be lifted up and rejuvenated by the calm and beauty of this refuge and its constellation of creatures.

To our delight we discovered that a coyote pack denned very close to our new home, so close that we could watch the adults regurgitating for the pups, and a myriad of wild canid activities—rallies, howls, and the daily comings and goings of the pack. Bristol and I would often encounter these coyotes on our walks. She was trained not to chase wildlife of any sort, but one afternoon I was hunkered down in some high sage lost in a reverie, examining the spring's first yellow fritillaries through the wide end of my binoculars, and looked up to find Bristol racing around with one of the neighborhood coyotes. It was one of the subordinate males, distinctive because he had a faintly cocoa-colored ruff and snowy white chest. The two seemed to take to one another, for after that he would often appear when we were out walking or we would see him around the yard or hanging out in the sage plain, like a lovesick teenager near the house.

The next fall Bristol and I were out walking on the west side of the valley in a maze of trails crisscrossing the lower slopes of the Tetons when she disappeared ahead of me, beyond a willow-thick bend in the trail. The sound of dogs snapping and growling and then a series of yelps sent me sprinting up the trail to find Bristol slinking away and a mountain biker and his yellow Lab coming toward me. As I ran toward the biker I yelled, "What happened?" He shrugged his shoulders in silent dismissal. I was puzzled by Bristol's strange retreat and kept running past him and his dog to reach her. She greeted me with a feeble tail wag. I examined her and found no visible marks. The biker and dog had disappeared down the trail behind us so we continued onward. As we approached a stream crossing Bristol balked, which I found odd because we had crossed the same stream many times before. With a great deal of coaxing she gingerly picked her way through the current and rocks, but her hesitant behavior began to seriously alarm me. Eventually I got her across and made it back to our car. She refused to jump in the car. Finally I had to pick her up and put her in. At home, again, she refused to jump out and had to be lifted from the car.

I checked her over again. Still finding nothing, I was bewildered. The phone rang not long after. It was the mountain biker. Back on the trail he had recognized me from photos that had been run in the local papers. He was calling to see how my dog was. I told him she was not doing well, but I couldn't figure out what was wrong. To my shock, he told me, "The two dogs started fighting, and admittedly, I might have overreacted, but I was concerned for my dog's safety, and I kicked your dog in the stomach several times, pretty hard, to drive her away from mine." He had been wearing pointed, steel-toed biking boots. I told him I thought his response was extreme, but thanked him for calling and telling me what had happened. I returned to Bristol. I took her outside and found she was urinating pure blood.

From that day forth I had Bristol in and out of vets' offices weekly. Superficially she appeared to heal from the incident, but she was never the same. I suspect her immune system was severely knocked down and she simply couldn't recover. I hold forgiveness as one of the great virtues in human life, but I have not been able to forgive this man—this is part of the shadow that I carry, and it has become part of my life's work. He hurt an animal that I loved with all my heart and soul, and no matter how I argue with myself about his intent and good manners for calling me afterward, the anger I feel toward him is so visceral and primal it resides far beyond reason or will.

Eight months after Bristol's trauma we discovered a tumor in her chest cavity the size of a small pumpkin. We took her to the nearest canine oncology unit in Fort Collins. Because of the location and positioning of the tumor they were unable to biopsy it, so we had no way of knowing whether it was malignant, but if we left it, it was likely she would die quickly in any case. One lung had already collapsed due to the tumor's pressure. I was given an all-or-nothing choice. I chose all.

About an hour into the operation the surgeon came out to say it was going badly and that he doubted she would make it through. He offered a less than 5 percent chance that she would survive the surgery. I remember my refusal of the notion of her death in that way. I looked him straight in the eye and said, "She is a wild thing and she will not die on a stainless steel table under artificial lights with a bunch of tubes in her. Finish. She will not die."

She didn't. We brought her home to Moose. She healed quickly, but we now knew the tumor was malignant, a highly aggressive and very rare cancer. We went for long walks, and on several occasions her cocoa-colored coyote friend showed up as an escort. In late June she began to decline again. Her breathing became more labored and she stopped eating. I had begun to sleep on a mattress on the floor with her, although it was difficult for her to find a position to lie down in that wasn't painful. By early July she was in such discomfort that I had begun to consider the option of euthanasia.

To be truthful, I could not fathom the idea of taking her life. I admit with some shame I simply did not have the courage to let her go. It was an act that was incomprehensible, as merited or right as it might have seemed. One night Bristol could barely lie down, and mostly stood or paced, panting, laboring for the precious oxygen she needed. I was crazed with her pain and her struggle. Finally, at 2 A.M., I did what I had only done on a very few occasions, and only for the sake of my work. I called on, for want of a better description, the spiritual realm of wolves. Where the wild edge of our ancestor and animal guardians reside, where our spirituality wanders and prayer travels, I invoked the memory of Natasha. I appealed to my sense of the beyond, to my trust in a meaning-filled universe where our actions and dreams matter. "For eleven years I have worked on your behalf, Natasha, and for the wild rights of your kind. I ask only this—that you take Bristol now. She is of your nature, take her now and stop her suffering because I cannot." In less than two minutes Bristol died. Tom held her as she collapsed. I remember most the peace that replaced her anguished gasps for breath and the quiet offering of silence that held our relieved sobs. The wild's mercy.

In the gift of Bristol's immediate death that night and the cessation of her suffering lies the reciprocity that I fiercely believe exists between animals and humans, between the spiritual and the earthly. Bristol's soul came from the wild and to it we were determined to return her. We made a makeshift sling out of a blanket and two poles, and on it we carried her out in the predawn dark toward the soft slope a half mile away where the coyotes denned. At the top of the slope we found a place near the den where four aspen saplings bowed together, creating a shaded awning. There we laid her on a bier of long grasses and boughs and covered her with a brilliant blue blanket of lupine flowers. I felt strongly that Bristol did not belong under the earth. She was a free-flying spirit; no rocks or mud should cover her lightness. There the coyotes would consume her and through them she would still roam in both worlds, ours and theirs.

We sat near her on the edge of the slope overlooking the expanse of the Tetons to the west and our home and the ridges of Shadow Mountain to the east, and drank a bottle of champagne while the sun lifted from the dark, lighting the shadowed granite of the mountains. As we rose to leave I howled. Just once. A howl that screamed the agony of letting her go. Seconds later it was as if the earth came alive. Coyote howls surrounded us like a sonata breaking from the sage and buttes and islands of trees. Howls from every direction, rising up and filling the dawn as it spread to light the peaks and ridges of Shadow Mountain.

Nineteen

❖ ❖ ❖

I believe there is some kind of consciousness in all creatures, but it is probably different from ours. One of the facets of our consciousness is the ability to think our way into the Other in a way that perhaps other creatures don't do, and, this is all speculation mind you, we can therefore bring them into our consciousness—not as mirrors of us, but as their own selves. When that happens it is a kind of miracle. It is a miracle to experience that between species there can be an electric connection, a shining.

GALWAY KINNELL, INTERVIEW, *Wild Duck Review*, AUGUST 1977

L OSING BRISTOL AFFECTED my life as forgetting how to breathe or walk might have done. In the months following her death I had to reconstruct my world from fragments of remembering how to function. I was ambushed by the devastation wrought by her death. I didn't see it coming—the leveling and destruction of this grief-wave wiped out the sensibility of my psyche. Although I had been numbed and deeply saddened by Natasha's loss, because she hadn't died at our separation the blow hadn't been as acute. It didn't feel as final as the wall of death. While there were some friends who could feel the enormity of my loss and offered tremendous compassion, the world in general has little patience or empathy for loss of an animal companion. Many people were unable to fathom the level of my grief because they could not fathom that level of connection with an animal. To me this is yet another reflection of the alienation from the animal world that our culture feels.

All the things I thought I would do when I no longer had a dog became irrelevant. The long walks in national parks (where dogs are not allowed), the leisurely trips to Europe (during which I would not fret about the animal left behind), the two-seater sports car instead of the chunky station wagons—none of it held the least enchantment in the reality of Bristol's absence.

My coping mechanism for assimilating Bristol's loss was the haunting of dog pounds—not just a few but dozens and dozens. Almost everywhere I went—big cities, small towns, anywhere in the great outback of America—I somehow found the "animal shelters," as they are now called. The fall after Bristol's death I visited twenty-six dog pounds on one trip. I now find it amusing that the places I considered a horror and prisons of death as a youth became my havens and places of healing as an adult.

I still don't understand it, but something about being in the presence of those dogs who were, in the most profound way, lost in the world and without a home was soothing and healing. After Bristol died I felt turned out at sea. I went through all the motions of life and work, but underneath I felt like a land bird who could never find a place to light, no place to rest. When I walked into those acrid-smelling shelters I could breathe again. I felt calm and happy, even hopeful. They were almost like a hit to an addict. Maybe I thought I might find some essence of Bristol there; maybe they just seemed familiar when everything felt alien. Maybe it was as simple as sharing the company of animals who, too, were clawing at the barriers of their world, sure that a better life, or just life, lay on the other side.

Many shelters have exercise areas where you can take the dogs out to play or go for a short walk. At the very least most pounds will allow you to go into a dog's run area to have a little chat and petting session. So I would just go and spend time with the strays, as they were called, and over the months slowly I began to heal. My friends used to be in awe of my ability to visit these "prisons" and not get depressed or at least come home with a dog every time. But after Bristol died I had no home. Regardless of the fact that I lived in a physical structure, there was no place *in me* to offer shelter to an animal, and I think the dogs understood that. They accepted what I could give, even though I knew that the little romps or walks or scratchings I could provide them in their confinement was a meager acknowledgment of the gift of empathy they gave to me.

Since The Wolf Fund offices were by then located in the town of Jackson, I had got in the habit of going down to our local shelter on my lunch breaks and hanging out with the dogs. Karen, the warden, was usually gone from noon to one, so I would just sit outside the runs and share my sandwich and a pocketful of dog cookies with whoever might be in residence.

On one occasion, after I had been on the road for nearly a month, I returned and began my usual lunch shelter-visit routine. There was a young and gangly black shepherd mix with vanilla highlights around her eyes and chest in one of the runs. She immediately drew my attention, in part because her yowling and yelping were so utterly jangling. She acted like a lap swimmer gone berserk, racing from one end of the run to the other, leaping and throwing herself against the cage wall, and then pushing off from the chain-link and twisting in midair for a one-bound heat to the other end of the run. If nothing else, her athletic finesse and stamina were astonishing. All at once she stopped in mid-lap and sat perfectly still and silent on the cement, ears pricked and eyes completely focused on something on the far horizon. I sat munching on my tuna fish, squinting at the sky trying to see what she saw. Slowly, out of a pearl white overcast materialized a raven, flying so high I could barely make it out. She sat in rapt attention, her nose and eyes following the perfect arch of the black speck of feathers directly overhead and slowly into the opposite distance. It disappeared back into white oblivion, and the second it was gone she was back to her frenetic laps.

Just then Karen drove up in her white sedan. I wandered around the runs and up to the front office. "What's up with the shepherd mix?" I asked. "Crazy," she replied. "Loco, insane. She's been here for over three weeks, someone dumped her." Karen started shuffling through some papers. "We would have put her down a long time ago, but I've been gone on my vacation for three weeks and I just got back today. We made a deal with my replacement that she wouldn't have to euthanize any of the dogs while I was away. We're putting her down tomorrow." My silence made Karen look up. She saw the glint in my eye. "Renée, you do not want that dog. She's nuts. She has been screaming and pacing and yowling from the minute we got her. She's totally unmanageable, no training, freaky as all get out. She's been badly abused and she'd be an utter nightmare. She's completely wild." I said nothing.

I persuaded TR to make the eighteen-mile trip into town that afternoon because "there was something very important" I had to show him. As we pulled up to the shelter, he knew he'd been suckered. As we stood in front of the run of this screaming, leaping, lunging, lunatic dog, he clapped his palm to his forehead, wagging his head back and forth, muttering, "Oh no." Exactly my father's response to the pony. He laughed feebly at my notion of consulting him. "I know you're going to bring her home whether I agree or not, so let's just get it over with." "I'm just going to train her and find her a home," I promised for the third time. "Yeahyeahyeah," he said as she dragged the two of us clutching the leash out the door of the shelter. "Why THIS dog of all the hundreds, no thousands, of calm, quiet, sweet-natured dogs we've seen over the past year?" I had no answer. But the dog had no hesitation. She beelined straight to the open back door of our car and jumped in without pause or consideration.

Once in the backseat, she lay down, head on her paws, completely silent, not a whimper or a sigh the whole way home. We couldn't believe this was the same animal we had watched minutes ago in the pound. As we sped north toward Moose, I stared out at the somber green blanket of sage that stretched along the highway, wondering how I would behave on death row the day before my execution. Would I have noticed the raven? We christened her Zany, for obvious reasons.

We knew little about Zany's history. The vet guessed she was about nine months old and had had a rough start in life, which is perhaps why she appeared to live every second as though it were her last. It was obvious that she had been badly abused. For the first three months she hid under an old rocking chair, quaking like an aspen leaf every time someone new approached her. With training and time she gained confidence and matured (sort of) into a wonderfully extroverted dog with great charm and panache.

We were able, by chance, to learn a bit about Zany's sordid past. I had coerced Tom into participating in what is called in dog-training lingo a "setup" to "proof" Zany's heeling concentration. The idea is quite simple. Because you want the dog to be able to focus and obey under *all* circumstances, *especially* when faced with surprises or when things get chaotic, you "set up" situations the handler can anticipate and control to work the dog under potentially frightening or threatening conditions. This particular "setup" consisted of going to downtown Jackson, where there was traffic and other distractions. Tom dressed up like a madman, with a stocking cap, goggles, and a big flapping coat, and would come running out from behind a wall roaring and screaming just as Zany and I heeled past. Zany, way ahead of the game, cocked her head at Tom's bizarre behavior, wagged her tail amusedly, and kept on going.

Meanwhile, a blond-haired guy in his early twenties who looked like he'd just jumped off his snowboard noticed Zany from across the street and approached us, exclaiming, "I know that dog, I know that dog! I knew this dog when she was young. I can't believe she's still alive." He didn't know much, but enough to confirm my worst fears.

The snowboarder loved dogs and had noticed how unusual Zany was even as a pup. He had wanted to rescue her, although he couldn't keep her himself because his landlady didn't allow pets. Apparently Zany had been born into a litter of thirteen. The jerk owner of Zany's mother had killed all the other puppies right after birth by breaking their necks, but for some reason decided to spare one. Having a puppy around was great "to meet girls," but the realities of an active, unhousebroken dervish ultimately led to the puppy becoming the guy's punching bag. He used to hit her and kick her around. Eventually he got fed up and Zany got passed from home to home, ultimately ending up at the shelter.

Playing on death's edge seemed to be part of Zany's karma, having brushed up against it twice before she was even a year old, first as a pup and then at the pound. Zany nosed death yet again a few months later. It was an incident that left me with an even deeper and more profound sense of her will to live and of the laser-beam ability of animals to communicate with us in realms for which we have no words.

It was a late spring morning and I had an appointment with an important funder early that afternoon. I knew I had to ask him for money; The Wolf Fund was broke and desperate. For some reason being broke and desperate makes it even harder to ask: you feel backed into a corner and the consequences of failing seem all the more dire. After going to the dentist and having my picture taken, asking for money is my third most hated activity. One would think I would have gotten used to it after so many years but I never did, and I approached every fund-raising meeting with dread and foreboding. To bolster my willpower and quell my anxiety (it was not uncommon for me to have these meetings and never get around to actually asking for the money), I decided to take Zany for a run before going to the meeting.

We ran up an old two-track that winds up Cache Creek Canyon just east of the town of Jackson. The trail runs a couple hundred yards above the creek, which at that time of year is more of an icy river boiling down the mountains, sweeping everything in its way into deep narrows. Often the branches and debris clog up in these chutes and create logjams against which the water pounds and pours in a frothing torrent. When we ran Zany usually ranged a few hundred feet in front of me like the canine Secret Service, sweeping back and forth with her impeccable radar to locate any places, people, or situations of interest ahead. She would occasionally disappear for two or three minutes and then reappear, galloping past me to resume her endless sweep for land mines and ground squirrels. On that particular morning we were coming back down the canyon and I was running fast because I was already late and didn't notice Zany's absence for some time. When I did, I stopped and called. I tried to whistle, but my lips were numb and sluggish from the cold spring air and no sound would come. I called again. Nothing.

I walked over to the shoulder of the embankment and called again. The roar of the creek drowned out my call. I looked down at the creek and from my perch high above I could see three logjams. Something clicked. Although Zany is not afraid of water, she's not particularly drawn to it, especially ice-cold crashing torrents, and to this day I have no explanation for what prompted or guided my action in the next few minutes. There was no sound, no sign, I just went barreling down the embankment toward the middle jam, breaking through willow stands, over logs, and through briers as though an iron cable was attached to my belly, dragging me ahead. I reached the bank just upstream from the jam and plunged into the muddy water, fighting not to be dragged under by the pounding pressure. Still I saw nothing.

I think the shock of the frigid water penetrated to my rational mind, because I remember repeating out loud to myself like a chant, "Don't fall, or you're dead." I edged my way toward the middle of the creek and down toward the jam. The water was above my waist and slammed me into the branches protruding from the blockage. I inched along the jam, the branches digging into my legs. Still nothing. Then I felt something with my calf. I still couldn't see her. The froth of the current combined with the muddy runoff made the water opaque. I groped around, fighting to keep my balance. I found her shoulder, her head, her neck, and then her collar. It was hooked on a branch about three feet under the surface. Her body was totally limp and being smashed by the current against the wall of branches. I finally got her collar unhooked and managed to haul her to the surface. She weighs about seventy pounds, probably more soaking wet, and was completely limp. I got my arms wrapped under her front legs and hooked around her torso. Pulling her back to my chest, I carried her like a burlap bag dangling in front of me and started back across the current, praying that I wouldn't slip. I have no recollection of getting back to the bank. I tripped just as we were climbing out. Heaving forward, I landed with my full weight on top of her back.

I lay there stunned for a second, then rolled off her limp body, sure that I had broken her ribs. I had no idea what to do. Before I could entertain something like mouth-to-mouth resuscitation (my vet later confirmed mouth-to-nose is possible), she coughed, a sort of sputtery, raspy hack. Then she vomited, and vomited again. She stood up, shook, coughed again, then looked down at me as though noticing me for the first time, muddy and soaked, lying on the ground next to her. She gave me a definite "Whatareyoustaringat?" look. She shook again, shimmying every last part of her body down to her toenails, and then set off trotting up the steep embankment toward the two-track as though nothing had happened.

I started laughing. Laughing and sobbing and rolling in the muddy, soaking grass realizing how much I had come to love this dog when I was sure I couldn't ever love again. Zany reappeared. She bent over and licked and lapped at my face, her characteristic response to me when I'm down on the floor acting like a madwoman, and then she turned and bounded back up toward the road. I dragged myself up and clambered up to the ridge on all fours, and I stumbled back down to the car with my running shoes squishing and sloshing.

Forever prepared, I always carry a pair of jeans and a sweatshirt in my car. Modesty not being one of my virtues, and with no one but the trees and a picnic table as witness, I peeled off my wet clothes in the parking lot, wiggled into my jeans and sweatshirt, stuck my damp bare feet in a pair of clogs, and jumped in the car. I was now thirty-five minutes late for my meeting. I raced across town and down among the cottonwoods to the funder's home. Forty-five minutes late. In the second happy ending of the day, I didn't have to grovel—the check, a generous one, had already been written. Zany had brought not only life back into my paralyzing grief but apparently luck as well, because that check marked the shift in momentum, like cresting a hill—everything started to fall into place.

Twenty

❖ ❖ ❖

*It makes the most material difference whether a thinker stands personally related
to his problems, having his fate, his need, and even his highest happiness therein;
or merely impersonally, that is to say, if he can only feel and grasp them
with the tentacles of cold, prying thought.*

FRIEDRICH NIETZSCHE

For nearly seven years The Wolf Fund had worked toward the goal of getting an Environmental Impact Statement (EIS) under way, and twice in that span of time, when we were on the brink of success, powerful western senators and congressmen had subverted our efforts, calling for more research studies rather than initiating the legal process necessary to actually reintroduce wolves. It was frustrating to be so close then have the power plays of well-positioned politicians whose campaign coffers had been lined by the livestock lobby (a lobby whose political influence was totally disproportionate to their contribution to the western economy), behind closed doors, sabotage the clear will of the nation's majority. It was also difficult to keep all the conservation groups and their lobbyists pointed in the same direction, delivering the same message to the politicians and staffers who championed the wolf project.

I recall a late night encounter after a local environmental conference where one conservationist counseled me after a disappointing, contentious day of trying to bring factions together, "Renée, you shouldn't take it so personally." I remember thinking at that moment, "It *is* personal, though!"

Conservation still needs people personally invested in the outcome of their work. I felt that the raw emotion and imagination and ingenuity that come with true passion are still the most compelling tools in effective conservation.

And there were a number of such people who *did* take it personally. For instance, much could be said of the dogged efforts of numerous staffers, especially those working for appropriations committee members, who round after round willingly carried the wolf banner. Neil Sigmund, an aide to Congressmen Sidney Yates (Democrat from Illinois), who was chairman of the House Interior Appropriations Committee, and Sue Masica, the minority clerk who worked for Yates's counterpart in the Senate, Robert Byrd (Democrat from West Virginia), were tireless in their efforts.

Not having had the usual indoctrination period in a D.C. internship or "Hill" position, I found myself continually astonished at how arbitrary the process seemed. That conservationists would pour months, even years, into influencing the wording of a bill or the position of a congressman on an issue, only to find on the day of the critical vote that he or she was absent, or had switched sides due to a last-minute donation, or that in the backslapping and swapping of conferencing (the process of reconciling the House and Senate versions of a bill) the critical wording, or the money, or some other essential detail was irrevocably obliterated. I'm sure after a while people just come to accept this reality, become inured to the possibility of so much work for so little return, but I never could make peace with it and remained dismayed by the capricious nature of this thing we call the political process.

My response to the indifferent face of democracy was to make the issue personal, because in the realm of the personal I could at least trust the substance of human intention. In the chaos of a political system subject to such whim and manipulation the only thing my instincts really trusted was the fact that behind this arbitrary machinery clanking along were the hearts and minds of real people with real values and morals. And since I believed we had stumbled our way into this wrongful state of a wolfless West by losing our true and emotional connection to the natural world (the absence of wolves in Yellowstone obviously being only a simple example), I likewise believed we could only find our way back by engaging personally. Once again, the invocation of Wordsworth's words carried me through those days: "What you have loved, others will love, and you will teach them how."

I suspect most of the people I met with who found themselves persuaded by my arguments said things like, "Her personal passion for the issue was infectious," or "Her arguments were very compelling because she seemed so personally invested," or something of the sort. My effort wasn't really to tell my story, but rather to allow the personal nature of my story to open theirs, which I believe it did. *People respond to people,* and our own honest stories invoke and mirror the experience and intuition of others' stories. I have no way of measuring how effective our work was, but I do think that The Wolf Fund's approach augmented and complemented seasoned lobbying efforts of groups like Defenders and the National Wildlife Federation precisely because we did make it personal.

In the late eighties and early nineties several important shifts were taking place on the political front of wolf recovery. Years of grassroots efforts were reconfiguring the political ranks in ways that none of us could really measure, but that all of us could feel and ardently welcomed. One important development was the involvement of Idaho senator Jim McClure (Republican from Idaho), a powerful member of the Senate Interior Appropriations Committee. McClure was judged by most conservationists to be a sort of environmental anti-Christ, but when he seemed open to discussing the wolf issue a number of conservationists, both individually and collectively, started exploring options with him. That we would even sit down at a table with him appalled some of our colleagues, but as it ultimately turned out his contribution was significant.

Since wolves were already beginning to show up in his state on their own—single sightings, but a hopeful omen of potential natural recolonization—McClure could read the writing on the wall. He wanted to leave the Senate having carved a solution that both accommodated the presence of wolves and protected his primary constituency, ranchers and the energy extraction industry. After several years of effort, McClure ultimately couldn't get his own constituents to buy into a proposal that would allow reintroduction even with extraordinary concessions that protected them. It never really got to the point where we had to rally support for McClure's proposal among conservationists. His position and efforts did, however, cause the majority of other western senators and congressmen to face the reality that wolves were returning and that it would be in their best interests to make a deal before the opportunity was lost.

Meanwhile, the director of the Fish and Wildlife Service, John Turner (an important but largely unrecognized player in the ultimate success of wolf recovery), was busy trying to engineer a compromise solution that had biological integrity but could survive the political gauntlet. Turner happened to be, by some strange turn of luck and fate, a wildlife biologist and former state senator from Moose, Wyoming. I had (and have) tremendous respect for John, and believe strongly that his leadership and fairness on the wolf issue, under nearly impossible political circumstances, contributed enormously to the ultimate success of the project. Finally, in 1991, McClure's and Turner's efforts resulted in establishing a sort of blue-ribbon committee, funded yet again by money diverted from what Congress had intended to be an EIS. It was called the Wolf Management Committee, and its mission was the equivalent of throwing all the constituencies in the closet together for a preset amount of time and seeing what they came up with.

The ten-person committee contained representatives of all the major interests. On the supposed prowolf side: the Fish and Wildlife Service, the Forest Service, and the National Park Service, and two conservation representatives. On the antiwolf side: the state directors of the Game and Fish departments of Idaho, Montana, and Wyoming, a representative of the hunting industry, and one for the livestock industry. The committee was instructed to begin on January 23, 1991, and to reach a consensus of at least six of the ten representatives by May 15.

Predictably, after four months of intensive efforts, the rhetoric won out and no consensus was reached, but the process had provided a very valuable map for the EIS. We all knew by the end where the minefields were and who had planted them and who played and guarded critical positions.

It was in the next round at appropriations that we were at long last successful. In November, Congress passed an appropriation to fund an EIS on the reintroduction of wolves to Yellowstone and central Idaho, to begin in 1992.

The process was broken down into three phases: one, the scoping, alternative scoping, and review of the draft EIS; two, the final EIS; and, three, the subsequent federal rule-making. This process took from April 1992 until June 15, 1994. The amount of effort the government put into creating opportunities for citizen feedback was extraordinary. During the exhaustive two-year period of grassroots organizing around the EIS and rule-making comment periods, open houses, hearings, and press rallies, The Wolf Fund's most important role was that of herding dog. The Liz Claiborne and Arthur Ortenberg

Foundation gave The Wolf Fund a generous grant to bring the conservation groups together and keep them headed in the same direction so that they wouldn't be replicating efforts, stepping on each other's toes, or undermining each other during that critical period.

Undoubtedly, launching the grass-roots contribution to the EIS process was one of the most comprehensive, far-reaching endangered species efforts western conservation groups had ever undertaken. It was a difficult challenge because it promised to be a long-drawn-out process, and keeping the public engaged and responsive to every phase of it was like asking them to watch old reruns over and over and stand up and cheer after each viewing. Still, I was impressed because all the groups, local and national, *did* work together. They put their differences and competitions aside and rolled up their sleeves to get people to turn out for the hearing and to send in comments. After witnessing so many years of backbiting and turf wars among the groups, I was very struck by how, during that one period, everyone rallied to cooperate. Mailing lists and phone trees were shared, press conferences were jointly hosted by competing groups. The power and pulse of grassroots efforts really shone and the results were extraordinary.

After two recovery plans, an extensive, federally mandated wolf management committee process, thousands of pages of research on the potential effects of wolves in Yellowstone, the public involvement really began. Beginning in April 1992, there were thirty-four open houses held in the three regional states, and seven in other parts of the country, to identify what issues people wanted to be considered in the EIS. More than 1,730 people attended these meetings and nearly 4,000 comments were received. In the next phase, the alternative scoping which examined all the different methods that might be used for wolf recovery, twenty-seven open houses and seven formal hearings were held in the three regional states and three national locations. Nearly 2,000 people attended the meetings and about 5,000 comments were received. In the final phase of the process, stretching from July 1, 1993, to November 26, 1993, twelve formal hearings were held in Idaho, Montana, and Wyoming; and four more hearings were held throughout the country. Never had there been such an extensive effort to poll public opinion on a wildlife issue. The results overwhelmingly favored wolf restoration.

This was one of the most difficult phases for me personally, both physically and emotionally, so exhausted had I become from the endless grassroots efforts. During this time I lost a critical staff member, funding had dried up, I was suffering major health problems, and burnout was careening toward blackout. I had started running—maybe trotting is a more accurate description—again in the hopes of finding a means to keep going. One dim cold spring day I went out for a run along Antelope Flats Road, set a modest goal, and somewhere midway collapsed. I came to, my body curled in a fetal position amid the wet sage. I lay there for a long time rocking and sobbing and for the first time in my life completely resigned to quitting. I walked home to Shadow Mountain. I called my brother, Craig, in Ann Arbor, Michigan, and said, "I've trained for twelve years for the big race, it's next week, and right now I don't even have the strength to tie my shoes." He listened, comforted, and quieted me. I was nonetheless sure that I could not go another step.

My brother arrived in Jackson Hole the next day. After I got over the initial shock of seeing him, hugging, crying, speechless, he threw his arm around me. He pointed to a large cottonwood tree towering above the rest along the river bottom. Grinning, in a low-voiced chant he began, "See the tree, aim for the tree, little hill after that, nothin' big, you've done it before, use your arms, push with your arms, come on, one foot in front of the other." Once again, my dear brother granted me the physical gift of accompaniment. He stayed to work alongside me for long days and late nights, laboring for nearly a month at The Wolf Fund on the EIS until we crossed the finish line.

I'll never forget the kindness of so many people and the hard work of my staff during this time. One of my oldest friends in the Tetons, Lyn Dalebout, a poet and activist, helped to organize the ranks of friends and volunteers to deliver one of The Wolf Fund's greatest goals. In one of the truest expressions of friendship I will ever experience, Lyn helped my brother and the staff do everything from sticking, stamping, and stuffing to cooking meals and walking the dogs, so the legions of Wolf Fund workers could work late into the night, sending letters, organizing phone trees, planning press events, and the myriad other things associated with the grit of grassroots organizing.

The results of all the conservation grassroots efforts bore fruit. Thousands of people showed up at the hearings, wrote supportive letters and postcards, and made phone calls. A record-breaking 160,000 comments were received on the EIS alone, the most on any EIS in history, and in the final count they favored the return of wolves by a two-to-one margin. Clearly Americans were ready to see wolves back in their oldest national park.

Lyn told me poets have a phrase for the work that must be done that ultimately adds up to a poem, the countless hours of contemplation, of scribbled drafts, of squeezing out the meaning in chaos. They call it "shadow work." In my mind the true heroes of this last leg were not the conservationists or even the citizenry, but the silent government workhorses who labored hour after hour, month after month, and even year after year assimilating and delivering the various studies, reports, and then, finally, the EIS documents that formed the scaffolding of wolf recovery. I admire them not for their outward achievement, but rather for their courage and endurance. Their stamina and commitment were largely unseen by the world because they played out their parts in the late, silent, echoing rooms of government buildings, passing unnoticed in the hubbub of controversy and media hype.

Three principals come to mind immediately: Ed Bangs, hired in 1988 to oversee Montana wolf recovery for the U.S. Fish and Wildlife Service, who ultimately became the intrepid government leader of wolf reintroduction; Wayne Brewster, a Fish and Wildlife employee in the early years of recovery efforts who ultimately moved over to the National Park Service to oversee reintroduction for Yellowstone (I first met Wayne in 1982, when he was a principal engineer of the wolf recovery plan and a key individual in the fifteen years of cutting through the bureaucratic underbrush to reach reintroduction); and Steve Fritts, a wildlife biologist, who spent hours compiling, sorting, and organizing the material for the studies that led up to the EIS, a key compiler of the EIS documents, and then the team leader for gathering wolves in Canada and overseeing the technical reintroduction process.

Life mysteriously offers us, at the perfect time, signposts and teachers for the challenges we face. During the EIS process, when The Wolf Fund was called upon to play one of its most important roles—that of herder—life would offer the perfect guide: a herding dog. It came about that a friend had a purebred German shepherd bitch who gave birth to a litter of ten pups. The runt was almost one third the size of the rest of the litter and the vet predicted she would die because she seemed unable to nurse. I was called in because of my experience in getting wolf pups to take bottles, and with some luck I was able to get the tiny mouse-sized canid to nurse from the pet-size bottles filled with Esbilac. My friend's home was near The Wolf Fund offices, so feeding the tiny puppy, christened Mocha, became the calm in my otherwise harried life. Her little squeaks and mews and coos were the sounds I most hungered for after hours on the phone with ranchers, activists, reporters, and politicians debating EIS complications. It came as no surprise to Tom when a couple of months later Mocha joined our household.

From a very early age Mocha illustrated the fine art of herding on our long walks together in her constant dance of driving, steering, navigating, spurring, wrangling, and nudging. Her habit and movement were driven by genes honed for the job through hundreds of years of breeding. Watching the antics of this herding dog never ceased to absorb and teach me. She never stopped, never gave up, never gave in. Mocha taught me the physical meaning of what the phrase "endless pressure applied endlessly" really meant. It became The Wolf Fund's mantra.

Late in the fall after Mocha came into our lives I set off on my annual sojourn to Washington, D.C., to play herding dog to the usual suspects involved in wolf recovery. A key character, if not *the* key character, in that lineup was John Turner, the aforementioned director of the U.S. Fish and Wildlife Service, technically the agency responsible for implementing a wolf reintroduction. I was deeply disappointed when I heard the Clinton administration had decided to replace him. When I called John to let him know of my visit he kindly offered to facilitate an introduction to his successor. I gratefully accepted his offer, knowing how difficult it is to get access to high-level bureaucrats. The meeting was set.

As I was escorted, high-heeled and linen-clad, into the new director's office, I stretched out my hand in formal introduction, "Hello, Ms. Beattie, my name is Renée—" She interrupted me mid-sentence, ignoring my hand and enveloping me in a big hug. "I know who you are." Stepping back but still holding my shoulders, she said, "You don't remember me? Mollie Beattie, Thich Nhat Hanh? California?" My mouth dropped open in astonishment. For once in my life I was speechless. Mollie started laughing, as she had assumed I had made the connection. I finally burst into incredulous giggles. Having walked into her office straight-backed and tense with the burden of having to "pitch" yet again the importance of the controversial Yellowstone wolf project to a watch-glancing, probably ignorant political appointee in the position of making or breaking the project, I collapsed on her office couch in relief and disbelief.

We chattered for nearly two hours that afternoon. She canceled her appointments and refused phone calls and thus began a friendship that would enable, shelter, and empower each of us over the next three years. Although in my eyes Mollie's responsibilities running an agency of seven thousand employees with a budget of over $500 million made my little microcosm of The Wolf Fund mere dabbling, she would always point out how we both fundamentally faced the same difficulties in trying to enact a personal ethic in our professional lives. We both navigated the same male-dominated profession of natural resources, faced the same ignorant, sexist, and haughty Republican politicians who dominated the committees overseeing resource issues, and struggled with the same painful challenges of living and embodying an example of whole, loving, compassionate humanness in a frenetic and cruelly competitive profession.

Mollie became a champion of the Yellowstone wolf project not just because of our friendship or my passion but for the same reasons I had devoted my life to it. The project provided an ethic and action true to her beliefs in the world on many levels. She invested a lot of time and personal effort on the project, not only to make it happen but to make it happen the right way. She shepherded, facilitated, opened the closed doors, and slammed through the locked ones.

Ours was a friendship born of intuition fueled by commiseration. We saw each other infrequently but shared a lot of time on the phone and did a number of long road trips from which emerged a relationship which was somewhere between Butch Cassidy and the Sundance Kid and Thelma and Louise. We had been guided and influenced by many of the same mentors. Among them were Michael Bean of the Environmental Defense Fund (we both agreed, the finest endangered species advocate in the history of the Endangered Species Act); Don Barry, who had counseled me on strategy and lobbying many years before when he was a staffer for Representative Walter Jones (Republican from North Carolina) on the Merchant Marine and Fisheries Committee and who had by then become the assistant secretary of the interior, Mollie's boss and best friend; and Tom Collier, Secretary of the Interior Bruce Babbitt's chief of staff, one of the critical figures in the final stages of wolf recovery. Mollie and I had many things in common: graduate degrees from eastern Ivy League universities, training in forestry, residency in Vermont (I lived there briefly, she for nearly two decades), husbands who were musicians, athletics as a formative part of our adolescence, an interest in Zen and meditation, a bewilderment as to how conservation had gotten so far off-track, a deep connection to the West, a hatred of panty hose, and, perhaps our most profound bond, our love of dogs.

It was through Mollie's sister, Janie, that I would find myself nudged inadvertently into the world of exotic dog fancy. For nearly a year I had looked for a dog for my mother-in-law. Mary Rush (everyone called her Mollie, but that would get confusing here) was a lovely tiny woman, then in her early eighties, and I thought a smallish dog would be most suitable, but I knew she wouldn't suffer a yappy half-witted midget very well. So I set out to find an intelligent, gentle, well-mannered diminutive mutt. It's a habit of mine to match things, to introduce lives that seem to fit. Perhaps it's the neurotic, messianic part of me that likes to bring things together, or maybe it's just the harmony one feels in finding things that fit when the whole world seems to be falling apart. I don't know, but I like bringing people together with other people (eight couples I have introduced are married), and animals together with other animals, and people and animals together. After many visits to many animal shelters I had still, after nearly a year, not turned up the perfect dog for Tom's mother.

In early October 1994 I went to Ketchum, Idaho, to participate in a panel on the Endangered Species Act which Mollie was also on. It so happened that Mollie's sister Janie was arriving the same evening to move in with their mother, Pat Beattie. However, unknown to Pat, Janie had two dogs with her. Just before leaving the East Coast, Janie had rescued from a dark future two puppies of a breed I had neither heard of nor seen called Chinese Crested. I loved them the minute I saw them. They were inquisitive and quick, alert but not yappy, and full of merriment and lilt. Mollie's mother was a bit overwhelmed by the prospect of two new puppies and a daughter come home to roost, and had it in her mind to refuse both dogs; but the three of us somehow persuaded her that one dog would be manageable, and the other, christened Chico, soon came to Wyoming, on his way to Tom's mother.

I decided to keep Chico for a couple of months to housebreak and obedience-train him. Big mistake. I fell totally in love with the little critter. He turned out to be such a merry elfin soul that when Christmas rolled around and it was time to give him to Tom's mom I was an inconsolable mess. By then Mollie Beattie's mother had taken possession of Chico's brother and was totally in love with him. To cheer me up and help me let go of Chico, Mollie Beattie used to joke that when I did give him to Tom's mother we would truly be related, having our two mothers (her mother, my mother-in-law) owning blood-related Chinese Crested brothers.

In the tangle of the EIS's slow march toward completion there remained many potential land mines waiting to sabotage a final decision. During this phase Tom Collier stepped in to usher the document through. Without his personal intervention I believe the EIS would still be languishing, unsigned, in the backwash of Interior's legal department business. I had met Collier on his first trip to Yellowstone the year before when I was asked by Bob Barbee and John Varley, my two Yellowstone guardian angels, to join the secretary of the interior's entourage through the park. Collier was reputed to be a hard-bitten, no-nonsense corporate lawyer. He had been hired to streamline many of Interior's antiquated policies, and some of his "makeover" strategies had spurred the wrath of environmentalists. Once again I found myself conversing with an environmentalist-listed pariah, and once again I found the person behind the myth a fair-minded, exceedingly bright, and potentially committed conservationist who simply needed to be more personally engaged in the issues.

Collier fell in love with Yellowstone. Watching him being seduced by the sheer beauty and measure of the park—the creatures, the geysers and canyons and vistas—reminded me of my first trip into the park, nearly twenty years before. Tom Collier and his wife, Anne, would become good friends to TR and me in the years to come, and he would, like Mollie, find his own reasons to believe in and become fiercely committed to the rightness of wolves in Yellowstone. In a wonderful gesture, Collier invited TR and me to come to D.C. to witness the secretary sign the record of decision on the Yellowstone wolf EIS. When we arrived in Washington on the appointed date, rumor rushed through the Department of the Interior like a rising flood that the signing would be delayed, that the lawyers were still nitpicking. The talk in the halls was that it could be weeks, even months, before each of the principals would agree to approve the record of decision on such a controversial issue. TR and I waited in the secretary's office lobby, wondering if, after all these years, the delay would yet again give opponents the opportunity to squash this final move.

One hour passed, then another, and the secretary's assistant suggested we leave and return a few hours later. TR and I were losing hope in the face of what seemed to be an ominous omen of another delay in the dark string of delays that had obstructed the EIS for nearly ten years. Much to my astonishment, when we returned a beaming Collier escorted us into the secretary's office. With Mollie on one side and me on the other, Bruce Babbitt—with the courage of a lion, given the political pressure he faced—signed into law the decision to reintroduce wolves into Yellowstone National Park and central Idaho.

Twenty-one

❖ ❖ ❖

The spirit wanders, comes now here, now there,
and occupies whatever frame it pleases. From beasts
it passes into human bodies, and from our bodies into
beasts, but never perishes.

JOSEPH CAMPBELL

JUST AS THE actual reintroduction was to get under way in the fall of 1994, the livestock industry, in a predictable last-ditch effort to halt reintroduction, filed suit. We saw this coming, but completely out of left field came a suit filed by the Sierra Club Legal Defense Fund (later renamed the Earthjustice Legal Defense Fund). Their suit challenged the legality of reintroduction in Idaho based on the notion that the few wolves that might be already present in Idaho might lose a level of their protection should reintroduction take place under the experimental population provision which granted wolf managers more flexibility in responding to wolves that threaten livestock. Their rationale was bewildering both to me and to Mollie, who had moved mountains to achieve the completion of the EIS and put reintroduction on a timetable. Conservationists had worked for nearly twenty years for this, and numerous wolf biologists in the country deemed it a solid plan providing adequate protection. In my view, there are few cases that so clearly illustrate the high-minded conservationist's penchant for missing the forest for the trees.

In spite of the fact that the legal battles ground on, the reintroduction wheels were also turning. The logistics were a complicated tangle of biology, bureaucracy, and politics. International agreements had to make their way through the maze of both Canadian and U.S. customs; each department whose jurisdiction was involved in either country had to give its stamp of approval. Then there was the biology, the logistics of identifying likely packs and individuals, the mechanics of trapping and holding and shipping, the challenge of handling the media and working cooperatively with all agencies. This was the phase of the project that I dreaded most. On one hand, it represented the reality of reintroduction—real wolves brought to real sites. On the other, it was the most highly manipulative, invasive, potentially animal-harming phase of the project. The notion of invading these packs—the thud-thud-thud and whoosh of the helicopters, the dark, hard pain of a dart, the processing and, perhaps worse, the waiting, the indefinite time in holding pens and kennels—added up to an expression of arrogance and presumption that made me, at best, extremely uneasy and, at worst, horrified.

The problems started with the snaring equipment. The U.S. Fish and Wildlife Service, the coordinating agency on the reintroduction, agreed to supply the Canadian trappers participating in the reintroduction effort, via Alberta Fish and Wildlife, with snaring equipment and to pay each trapper $2,000 for every live, uninjured wolf. The equipment turned out to be faulty. The cable that was supplied was ³⁄₃₂ inch cable, suitable for coyote snaring but too light for wolves, and the construction of the snares was inappropriate for the style of snaring used by Canadian trappers.

Many of the trappers were frustrated by the inadequate equipment and the follow-up of the U.S. program (which had been delayed because of the lawsuits). Some trappers were probably just frustrated by the locking-neck snares that the United States required that they use because it was possible for wolves to struggle out of the neck loop. The locking system used aircraft cable, bated at a wolf's head height, with an antislip stop to prevent the loop from closing too tight. By nature these trappers were a pretty independent lot, and even though the right equipment was ultimately provided, not all of them felt compelled to follow the guidelines or use it and opted to chuck the guidelines and take their chances with regular snares. The result of all these variables was a number of dead or injured wolves. The Fish and Wildlife Service then decided that one of their agents would accompany the designated trappers to check the lines, a not so subtle means of imposing the lock-ing system, but still at least ten wolves were killed.

I found myself with deeply conflicting feelings. The joy of winning was tempered with an urgent concern for these animals. Walking the line of com-promise was the balancing act of reintroduction. A thousand times I was haunted by the ways this project manifested our arrogance—our assumption that by intervening we were doing the right thing, that we were "righting a wrong" that had been done seventy years before out of ignorance and greed. However, once again, none of us asked the wolves. Would they choose, each of them choose, to subject themselves to the myriad manipulations that were inherent in the pioneering phase of this project?

Intellectually, I could justify the compromises. The wolves that were taken the first year from Alberta lived in a virtual free-fire zone. Trappers could snare anywhere on "Crown" or public land from October 1 to the end of February; resident hunters could shoot any wolf they encountered from September 1 to June 15, no license needed and no limits imposed. The mor-tality rate was estimated to be as high as 70 percent of the population in any given year. I liked to imagine that the wolves that were relocated from the Alberta collection area to Yellowstone were wolves that were saved. To cap-ture and move these animals to a place where they would have an abundance of prey and near-total protection seemed to be justified, at least on a biologi-cal level.

I prayed—prayed to whatever spiritual entity, energy, element that might be out there—that the wolves captured would be those that in some way of-fered themselves; that we would be able to, in the process of compromising their autonomy for a period, honor their dignity, as a hospital staff might in taking away the autonomy of a patient for the purpose of surgery. I prayed that the wolves would understand, or at least forgive. I prayed that the biolo-gists would understand. I know we all tried, I know we did the best we could. I don't know if that was enough.

Between November 16 and December 11, 1994, seventeen wolves were snared or darted, fitted with radio collars, and released back into their home territories so that when the actual collection phase began their packs could be located easily. These were called the "Judas" wolves because their function was to betray the location of their pack when, a month later, biologists would be-

gin collecting animals for the actual reintroduction. On January 3, 1995, Judge
William F. Downes of the U.S. District Court for the District of Wyoming
issued an order denying the Farm Bureau's request for a preliminary injunc-
tion. Finally, all systems were go! A couple of days later I was on a plane to
Canada to join the ranks of biologists, veterinarians, bureaucrats, and media
gathered to execute and document the actual collection of wolves for reintroduction.

I arrived in Hinton, Alberta, on a dim, cold afternoon. It turned out to be
a rather cheerless town, lined with strip malls, cardboard-looking motels, and
fast food restaurants, located approximately three hundred miles west of
Edmonton on the east shoulder of Jasper National Park. The headquarters for
the Canadian wolf collection operation was the maintenance compound
for the William A. Switzer Provincial Park, located about fifteen miles from
Hinton.

The location, like the project, seemed to balance on the edge of beauty. To
the west broke the snow-glistened peaks of Jasper National Park; to the north,
east, and south lay the broken lodgepole and spruce that were home to one of
Canada's hardiest populations of wolves. Day after day the legion of biologists,
bureaucrats, and media would gather in and around the corrugated-metal
maintenance buildings at Switzer. Although it was numbingly cold, lingering
the whole week well below zero, the region had received relatively little snow,
very uncharacteristic for that time of year. The lack of fresh snow made tracking wolves quite difficult, and locating them from the helicopter was equally
challenging without the contrasting white backdrop. Only one wolf had been
captured early in the week, and it huddled alone in a chain-link enclosure,
buried deep in several feet of straw bedding that served as insulation and as a
floor to the holding runs.

I had no official role in Hinton, except perhaps that of witness, which
forced me to fully absorb the uncomfortable reality of intervention necessary
to carry this nearly fifteen-year-old mission to its completion. Dave Mech arrived midweek, and after a quick analysis of the operation made some gentle
suggestions to the coordinators that improved the conditions for incoming
wolves. One was that the enclosures where wolves would have to wait for
days, perhaps weeks, for transport to the States be enclosed and darkened. To
that end Dave and I spent an afternoon stretching and securing tarpaulins

over the individual runs. I was relieved to be able to take some small action to assuage my anxiety over the discomfort of wild wolves suffering captivity.

Dave was also concerned about the wolves mouthing the chain link, and in the end his fears were realized. Several animals cut their gums and mouths and broke teeth on the wires both in the runs in Canada and then in the holding pens in Yellowstone. For all the criticism Mech has received from animal rights groups over the years because of his manipulation of Minnesota wolf populations, I found it moving that he would be the one among all of us who instinctively sensed most strongly what would give comfort and protection to the animals. After nearly thirty years in the field with wolves he has come to think and move in their skins.

As a few more wolves trickled in, the processing system was perfected. The animals were carried from the helicopter to the maintenance building on stretchers, often swathed in old quilts to protect their anesthetized bodies against the bitter cold. Each wolf was fitted with a nylon eye mask to protect their pupils from overexposure to the light due to hyperdilation from the tranquilizing drugs. The vets did their best to create a subdued, quiet atmosphere in the echoing metal, cement-floored building pummeled by wind and occasionally by pelting snow.

The wolves were put on a stainless steel table; their temperature, respiration, oxygen, and pulse levels were constantly monitored. During the processing their bodies were thoroughly examined for wounds, skin and coat condition, lice, parasites, breeding status, and any possible abnormalities. They were measured and weighed and blood was drawn. Next, a hole was punched in each ear, the flesh sample bottled in a vial to be used for DNA fingerprinting, and ear tags were inserted in the holes. The vets worked quietly and quickly, murmuring to each other in hushed tones.

Having watched and participated in a number of wolf captures in the field, I was comforted by the extra effort the biologists made to minimize trauma. Rarely do you see field biologists quite so attentive, but of course rarely do you see television cameras so close and focused. Underneath I did feel the intention was true, even though I was aware that some of the biologists and vets who had worked on hundreds of wolves viewed the extra measures as a sort of charade. I was, nonetheless, grateful.

The onlookers watched in a sort of mesmerized mix of awe and discomfort. A sense of greatness subdued permeated the room. No one could quite name the emotion evoked by seeing consciousness manipulated, but there was an uneasiness, a feeling of ambivalence, and, yes, a sense of hope mixed in like the streaks of sunlight that seeped through the dirty windows and warmed the fluorescent lights in the brewing gray of that cold corrugated building.

On the eighth of January, misfortune struck. As the helicopter swooped in on a young female wolf, fate scowled and a dart pierced her chest cavity. By the time the crew reached her on the ground she was dead. Somberness hung in the air. I returned to the hotel that night chilled, pierced by the long inactive day in the cold so thoroughly that all I could do was huddle under the hotel's cheap polyester comforters, curled with my knees against my chest, my head buried under the covers, shivering, rocking in a fetal position, and praying that we were doing the right thing.

Per the reintroduction plan, biologists were trying to capture packs that would be habituated in the holding pens in Yellowstone, whereas individual wolves caught in Canada would be "hard released" in Idaho without any habituation in enclosures. On January 10 the helicopter happened upon a group of wolves in the open. Four wolves were darted from the Petite Lake pack area, two of them were male pups, brothers to two wolves already caught earlier in the week. The alpha male and female were also caught. At last a family group suitable for Yellowstone.

Later in the day, two additional females were darted. They were presumed to be mother and daughter, from a group designated as the McLeod River pack. Even before they arrived I was painfully aware of the history of this pack. Carter Niemeyer, one of the heroes of the wolf collection phase, was one of the first people to lay eyes on this pack. Carter is a statuesque man who had spent his whole life in the field as what he describes as a "wildlife cop" working for Animal Damage Control, whose name was later changed to the more benign sounding Wildlife Services. His career has been "to keep the peace between the wild and the domestic," a job which he performed for nearly twenty-five years throughout the western United States. Once wolves recolonized Montana, Carter had become the key responder to wolf depredations, a job he undertook with uncharacteristic fairness and compassion, given the history and habits of his agency. He had been asked by the U.S. Fish and Wildlife Service to help coordinate the Canadian trappers because he was one of the few who could skin, cuss, drink, and trap with the best of them. His presence undoubtedly resulted in a lot fewer dead wolves.

The story of the McLeod River pack began on December 3, 1994. Carter got a call from Wade Berry, one of the trappers who had signed up for the project. Apparently Wade had a trapping buddy over near Edson who had snared five wolves. Three of them were dead, but two were still alive and might be suitable for the Judas phase of the project. It was late and near twenty below zero, but Carter agreed to drive the seventy miles to check out the animals. He, two vets, and the project photographer drove to the Robb turnoff fifty miles east of Hinton. There they met Wade's trapping buddy, Rick Stelter, and his brother Dave, and followed them another twenty miles over a maze of seismograph roads and two-tracks to an old burn area grown up in thick poplars. The brush was exceedingly dense, ideal for setting snares.

Among the poplars were five snared wolves. It was cold, dark, and late. Carter and his crew didn't really look over the three dead wolves; their attention was quickly absorbed by the two that were alive, who were quite subdued. Carter used a jab stick, a pole with a drug-filled syringe, to immobilize the two wolves with Ketamine. They turned out to be two young juvenile females, one gray, one black. He threw the wolves over his shoulders and beat a path back to the car. They agreed it was too cold to try to process them there, so they put them in one of the station wagons and drove back to Hinton.

The next day the two radio-collared females were taken back to the McLeod River region by helicopter and released. A few days later Rick Stelter would be out checking his traplines on his snowmobile and would encounter a group of three wolves near the snaring site. One, a very large gray-colored wolf, most likely an alpha male, had its jaws clamped on the nose of a moose calf, blood covered the snow; one, he would notice before they fled, was a small, dark collared animal. He figured she had been one of the five he had snared a few nights before. He was right—little did he know how important two of those wolves would become in the Yellowstone story. A few days later he would find the remains of the moose calf.

When they carried the alpha female from the McLeod River pack into the maintenance building, where I had been helping with the four wolves brought in from Petite Lake, something happened. My body felt her presence before I even saw her, much as I used to feel the deer on the slope before I could find them. My skin prickled, my breath quickened, my belly felt that old feeling like I was being drawn in by some invisible cable. I had a very eerie and distinct feeling that I knew this wolf.

I can't explain the powerful sense of familiarity I felt with this female. I hovered near her the whole time she was being processed, experiencing an uncanny sense of recognition. She was a dark charcoal color, not exactly black but a sort of sooty warm darkness, grizzled and highlighted in a beautiful interpretation of dusk. The guard hairs on the ridge of her withers and back were flecked with a thousand shades of smoky gray and her chest revealed an undercoat cloud of cinder and pearl and opal that prickled through the carbon shine of her overcoat. Her muzzle, underneath, had the peppered sheen of lilac gray just starting to hint at full maturity. I loved this wolf from the moment I saw her, or, more accurately, felt her.

After they finished processing her, Dave, noticing my intense interest in this particular wolf, asked if I would sit with her while the anesthesia wore off. All the runs were full, so she was put back on a stretcher in a corner of the building. I have no explanation for the emotion, but I could feel Natasha's presence. I sat with the wolf as the drugs slowly loosed their grip and began to babble as if the same were happening to me. The words gushed out of my mouth unintended and unattended. I whispered stories about this magical place called Yellowstone with its bounty of elk, bison, deer, and moose. I told her the truth about the chain-link pens she would have to endure for a few months and the pissed-off ranchers—but, I pointed out, they were no worse than the Canadian free-fire and poison zone she had survived the last five years. Even though it was against the rules, I stroked her gently, running my fingers through the deep frosted-ivory black of her coat. Whispering low, I told her her daughter was there, how sorry I was about her other missing offspring, the three unidentified dead wolves caught in Stelter's snares. At that point no one knew the fate of her mate. I told her we needed her to survive because we might not have another chance. The politicians were already trying to cut the funds for any future reintroductions.

As my babbling diminished to a dribble I did a rather odd thing, odd even for me, who has a penchant for oddness. I leaned close to her ear, buried my nose in the snowy scent of her neck, and told her we needed a mother of Yellowstone wolves. I guess I should tell you that she didn't respond. The biologists teased me all week about my attachment to this wolf. They called her

"Number 9," bound for the Rose Creek pen in Yellowstone. I called her Natasha in memory of a wolf I had once loved.

On January 11, 1995, I said good-bye to Natasha in her gleaming metal shipping kennel on the tarmac of the Hinton airport. We had spent the morning readying the eight wolves bound for Yellowstone and the four for Idaho for the long trip south. I raced from Hinton back to Edmonton. Only by the grace of some kind airport cop who offered to return my rental car did I catch the flight down to Montana. TR picked me up in Bozeman and we proceeded down to Yellowstone late that night. Very early the next morning we convened with Mollie, who was torn between exuberance and concern, for once again, even after the wolves were already in transit, the Farm Bureau had attempted a last-minute legal maneuver to stop the process. The horrifying aspect of their action, a request for an emergency stay filed with the U.S. Court of Appeals in the Tenth Circuit Court in Denver, was that they demanded that the wolves not be released even into the acclimation pens. This meant the animals had to be kept in the steel kennels, which were only designed for short-term shipping use and allowed little room for the animals to move or be fed or watered. Even though the action could have been taken much earlier, the Farm Bureau filed their request only after the wolves were airborne.

The wolves had been flown from Hinton to Edmonton to Great Falls, Montana. From there the shipping kennels were moved into large horse trailers and complete with ranger car escorts set out for their respective destinations—Yellowstone and central Idaho. At dawn's break a crowd of people had gathered near the Roosevelt Arch, the soaring basalt entrance monument at Yellowstone's north gate in Gardiner, Montana, constructed in 1903 to commemorate the park's creation nearly three decades before. Some of the classes at the Gardiner schools had let out so the students could witness the historic event; in other classes, where teachers were less than enthused about the arrival of wolves, students had simply walked out, expressing their own eager sentiments. The road leading up to the arch was decorated with the rainbow-colored jackets, hats, and mittens of the elementary school children, their excited voices calling out like a colorful flock of snow buntings along the roadside. Spectators and media had gathered on the hillsides near the arch and a general air of festivity and expectation permeated the crowd.

At last the procession of ranger cars and the horse trailer appeared on the horizon. I couldn't help but squeal from my hillside perch, "Here they come!

Here they come!"—words I had only dreamed for fifteen years. Within minutes the entourage carrying the eight wolves, Natasha included, passed under the arch to the cheers and tears and jubilation of the crowd. Wolves had been listed as endangered in 1975; this moment had been twenty years in the making.

The trailer made its way to the Crystal Creek trailhead where Mollie and Bruce Babbitt and several Yellowstone personnel helped carry the kennels holding the first wolves into the Crystal Creek acclimation pen. Then the shadow fell over the sparkling event. The Tenth Circuit Court judges had issued a statement that they needed forty-eight hours to consider the Farm Bureau's request. Until they ruled, no wolves were to be released, not even from their shipping kennels. The dignitaries returned to park headquarters, where a press conference was scheduled, while the wolves were forced to remain in the kennels sitting silently in the expanse of their new chain-link home.

At the press conference Bruce Babbitt had to amend his celebration speech with angry comments about how these kennels could become coffins. The wolves trapped in the kennels became the lead media story and the public's outrage was lit. Mollie and I decided to start a phone-warrior campaign. We began making calls, first on the media phones in the large hall which had held the press conference, and then, as the afternoon wore on, we moved to the private phones in our hotel rooms at the Mammoth Inn, adjacent to the media hall. All I could think of was Natasha confined in that kennel, her daughter somewhere nearby, both of them fed little more than ice chips squeezed through the ventilation holes for the last thirty-six hours. Their anesthesia would have worn off long before, and no one really knew how any of the wolves were faring in their cramped quarters.

It seemed like an eternity, but the phone calls finally paid off and just before six Mollie rushed into my room with the news that the stay had been lifted and the park biologists were on their way to release the wolves out of the kennels. We hugged and hooted and whooped and finally opened the bottle of champagne that had been sitting in an ice bucket since five-thirty that morning.

At last the wolves were turned over to the able hands of Mike Phillips, the newly appointed project leader for the Yellowstone wolf project. Mike had spent the preceding eight years working on the reintroduction of red wolves in the southeastern United States and stepped in to guide the Yellowstone project through the early years of political hurricanes, lawsuits, and biological challenges. I felt tremendous relief, once the wolves were released from the kennels, knowing that Mike would be charting the course of recovery for the next several years.

The wolves had all survived their long incarceration without significant injury. A few, out of frustration, had chewed on the inner parts of their kennels, cutting their lips and gums, but the wounds appeared superficial. The wolves were released into the acclimation pens to await their final freedom in Yellowstone National Park.

Twenty-two

❖ ❖ ❖

If we can't live among them in their natural order,
we bring them to live among us in our unnatural order.

JIM MASON

NATASHA AND HER daughter were released into the Rose Creek pen on January 12, late in the evening. With the next shipment of wolves to Yellowstone, which arrived on January 20, a beautiful large caramel-colored 122-pound alpha male was released into the pen to join her. Officially he was called "10," but behind the scenes he'd been nicknamed "Arnold" or "the Big Guy" because of his physique and macho, fearless swagger. It was most definitely a risk. No one knew how the two adults, both formerly alphas in their respective packs, would respond to each other. According to his captors, the male unquestionably "had an attitude." He immediately tried to dominate Natasha, but she took no guff and soon, with Arnold appropriately starstruck, the two became deeply bonded.

The months between the wolves' arrival at their acclimation pens in Yellowstone and their release into the park were some of the most harrowing times we were to face. A myriad of legal and political moves were afoot to block their release from the holding pens and send them back to Canada. Canada, of course, didn't *want* them back, so a court order to that effect would have amounted to a death warrant. It was perhaps the most nerve-wracking period of my fifteen years—so close, but so much hung in the balance. There was also the ever-present fear that someone might try to vandalize the pens or harm the wolves, and the Park Service had to maintain constant security around the pens.

The stress was considerable and I felt quite helpless in that I was unable to physically or politically guard the wolves from all the forces bent on sabotaging their release to freedom. My despondency was heightened by the fact that I missed Chico, the little dog I had gotten for Tom's mother, with all my heart. A few weeks before leaving for Canada I had given him to her, and he became her most cherished companion. Nonetheless, the loss of that little dog on top of the ominous threats to the wolves sent me into a deep, inconsolable sadness from which Zany and Mocha and Tom couldn't seem to lift me.

In early February I was invited by Yellowstone Park officials to attend a meeting to discuss the logistics of releasing the wolves from their pens. I drove up to Yellowstone a day before the meeting to fit in a visit to Natasha. I knew seeing her would be enough to carry my faith a little further through the tangle of lawsuits and political maneuvering. It would be on this trip that I would have the great pleasure of meeting the future guardian of Yellowstone wolves, Doug Smith. Doug served as the principal biologist, alongside Mike Phillips, the project leader, overseeing all the logistical and biological decision making on wolves once they arrived in Yellowstone.

In another twist of fate, I would learn that day that Doug's interest in wolves had also originated when he spent a semester at Wolf Park as an undergraduate, a passion that would lead him to commit several years of study to the wolves on Michigan's Isle Royale for his master's and ultimately on to Yellowstone. It would have been difficult to imagine a scientist more deserving of or better suited to the privilege of protecting Yellowstone's wolves than Doug Smith. In the years to come Doug had to navigate the gauntlet of warring values, interests, and philosophies that would define wolf management in Yellowstone, and he did it successfully, with grace and style.

After a day of helping Doug haul the bloody quarters of a bison carcass up to the Crystal and then the Rose Creek pen, I got to watch Natasha, now unanesthetized and full of flight and power, race around the chain-link perimeter. Arnold held himself like a proud dancer. Snowy golden, alert and undaunted by the visitors to his enclosure, he circled us in a show of curiosity and belligerence as we dragged the carcass into the pen. After a few laps around, Natasha watched from the far corner of the pen, inquisitive but cautious. I was overjoyed to see her seem so quiet and untraumatized. I whispered my greetings and slipped out.

Back at park headquarters, in a fit of last-minute political paranoia, one of the bureaucrats decided I shouldn't be allowed at the meeting because I was not a government employee. It was typical of the government boys during their war games to want to exclude the women from the final huddle, but this time I was so angered and frustrated by the small-mindedness and stupidity of the agency jockeying and game playing that I didn't bother to argue. I had spent far too long fighting my way into and through the spectrum of male paranoia, and I didn't have the heart for another round.

When I learned I would be barred from the meeting, in spite of having driven half a day to attend it, my response was predictable. I did what I always do in times of frustration and distress—I went AWOL to search for another dog. Only this time I didn't head for the animal shelters. In the blink of an eye, I cashed in some frequent flyer miles, jumped on a plane, and flew to New York to go to the Westminster Dog Show, where I hoped I would find a thousand little Chicos.

I didn't anticipate what a leap it would be from wolves to Westminster. Although Tom denies it to this day, when I sank into such sadness over Chico's absence he muttered, "Honey, why don't we look for another one?" So there I was in New York City at Madison Square Garden marching straight into the bizarre and inbred world of exotic dog fanciers.

I carried a picture of Chico about, asking complete strangers where can I find a dog like this? I learned that he was a particularly small Crested (in the trade called "teacup"), caramel-colored (called "apricot"), and hairy ("powder puff"). So in my quest to find a dog like Chico, I had come from Yellowstone, feeding wolves bloody bison quarters, to New York City, looking for an apricot, teacup, powder puff Chinese Crested.

I couldn't have chosen a better breed than Chinese Crested as an entryway to the strange, inbred weirdness of dog fancy. As an outsider who has never attended a dog show, let alone considered dogs as a commercial enterprise or trading commodity, I was flabbergasted. I was to learn that Chinese Cresteds are primarily valued as a hairless breed and have great appeal to the exotic pet crowd. Centuries ago the hairless versions, the result of a mutant gene, were originally favored by boatmen because they were good ratters and, due to their hairless condition, didn't carry fleas and so weren't vectors for the plague. The hairless dogs continue to be crossed with the hairy versions, or "powder puffs," because the hairy dogs are physically more sound and have much better dentition.

Entering the Westminster Dog Show was like stepping through the looking glass. The fantasy of my worldview underwent a drastic reconfiguring. My notion that a "human-dog" relationship might return us to or reconnect us with the wild was shaken to its very core with the discovery of this weird world of dog fancy. I began to realize that even though the human-animal relationship might offer an avenue toward a healthier relationship with the natural world, it could also serve as an example of just how far removed we had become.

There in the white picketed rings, on the shiny green indoor/outdoor AstroTurf, circled like circus ponies, were the man-molded derivatives of wild wolves. Bred for thousands of years to please human need, utility to humans had driven selection. Health, herding capacity, hunting instincts, strength, loyalty, protection, fleetness, stamina had all influenced our manipulations of the original wolf stock. But in the last hundred years, largely as a result of American Kennel Club (AKC) pageantry, function had become sublimated to form—to extremely standardized form.

As I watched the Chesapeake Bay retrievers circle their corral, I thought they looked like a group of gingerbread-cookie-cutter dogs, so perfectly were they molded to meet the standard of beauty imposed by the AKC rule books. It was virtually impossible to distinguish one dog from the next. Their demeanor varied slightly, probably influenced by how famished the dog was, withholding food being a dual pre-ring strategy for avoiding showtime "accidents" and making the dog respond to the dried liver treats used to tease them into an artificially chirpy state in order to impress the heavily bejeweled judges.

Backstage the prep crews were busy in the hubbub of pageantry, plucking and poofing, clipping and blow-drying. Patient dogs stood on steel pedestals, stretched by their neck and suspended by their girth for the perfect grooming in anticipation of their brief trot around the white-picketed ring. There were aisles and aisles filled with gold-linked leashes and diamond-studded collars, porcelain figurines of every breed imaginable, books and toys and T-shirts—

the canine merchandise that spurs Americans into spending nearly $8 billion a year pampering their beloved canine beauties.

Unfortunately, an extremely arbitrary notion of beauty somehow became the driving force in selective breeding, and the results have been tragic. Because of our impulse to control and manipulate, one out of every four purebred dog today suffers from a serious genetic problem. Sadly, the problems are not limited to physical maladies. Rough estimates indicate that some 20 percent of the 52 million to 57 million dogs in American households are afflicted with genetically driven behavior problems. What we reached out for, seeking reconnection with some wild heritage, has turned on us and, quite literally, attacked us for our tinkering. There are an estimated 4 million dog bites a year. Of course our response to this betrayal by "man's best friend" has been to abandon them. Approximately 4 million dogs a year are dumped at shelters and, in a terrible twist of irony, over half of them, about 2.4 million, are euthanized because their natural instincts can't be made to fit into the unnatural order that we created.

In the end, I did find several breeders of Chinese Cresteds who I felt were honorable, compassionate people, fiercely fond of the breed but determined to serve the animals' best interests and health, rather than have the animals serve their interests, financial or otherwise. In the months to come two unrelated Chinese Crested puppies, a female named Roo and a male named Rye, would arrive in our household, and Chico would become firmly ensconced in his new Connecticut home as Tom's mother's best friend, brightening and blessing the anguish of her aging with his clowning antics and loving spirit. With my own pack of four distant wolf descendants I would be left to contemplate the potential of potential wild wolves in Yellowstone.

Twenty-three

❖ ❖ ❖

Everything with substance casts a shadow. The ego stands to the shadow as light to shade. This is the quality that makes us human. Much as we would like to deny it, we are imperfect. And perhaps it is in what we don't accept about ourselves—our aggression and shame, our guilt and pain—that we discover our humanity.

CONNIE ZWEIG AND JEREMIAH ABRAMS, *Meeting the Shadow*

ALTHOUGH MUCH MEDIA attention had been focused on the actual arrival of wolves in Yellowstone, the most significant event in my mind was the release of wolves from their acclimation pens into the park after ten weeks of captivity. This was the point at which I felt the project really started, in part because it was the point at which the success or failure of the whole effort became dependent upon the wolves themselves. Would they adapt to the new terrain? Would they flee north, driven by an abiding homing instinct? Would the infrastructures of the packs, like the new pairing of Natasha and Arnold, or those that had been seriously disrupted in the relocation, as the Crystal Creek pack was, hold together? None of this had ever been tested before, and what happened once those gates were opened would determine whether the compromises these fourteen wolves had endured in the last several months and the twenty years of effort by so many people had been worthwhile.

On March 21, at about four-fifteen in the afternoon, the gate to the Crystal Creek acclimation pen was opened. At that moment The Wolf Fund staff hung a sign on the door that read SHUT DOWN, and our answering machine message was changed to explain to all callers that the organization no longer existed. I was up in Yellowstone in the superintendent's conference room with a smattering of reporters, park personnel, and wolf colleagues awaiting word from the field. No one really knew what to expect. Would the wolves charge out behind Mike Phillips and Steve Fritts, who performed the release honors, or would they wait until nightfall? Would they go one by one or dart out in a group in a dead run toward Canada? Instead, nothing happened.

On the twenty-second, the gate to the Rose Creek pen was opened. Still nothing happened. Hour after hour, nothing triggered the remote monitors at either pen that would transmit a signal if anything entered or left the pens. Utter silence. It made me laugh. It was so perfectly WOLF. Expect nothing or expect anything, but fully honor that wolves do not function according to the predictable notions of man. Since the park had adamantly discouraged people from gathering anywhere near the pens, I stayed hour after hour, day after day, in that overheated, sterile conference room, holding vigil, awaiting word. The longer we waited the more confident I became that the wolves message was: "This will be on our terms." By the twenty-third, the press was having a field day with the wolves' reluctance to leave the pens—Paul Harvey declared them "welfare wolves," preferring free food to freedom.

Eventually, the biologists collectively surmised (an insight proposed by Dave Mech) that the wolves were nervous about the gates, where for ten weeks humans had been entering and exiting the pens. They speculated that the wolves would be far more confident if an exit option existed in the back of the pens, an area that was termed the pen's "comfort zone." So, late in the day on the twenty-third, a four-by-ten-foot hole was opened in the chain link at the edge of the comfort zone of the Crystal Creek pen. A deer carcass was tied to a tree outside the pen (so that the wolves wouldn't simply drag the carcass back into the pen) to lure the wolves out. At 9:14 the next morning the remote sensor was triggered. By 2 P.M. it had fired nine more times. The wolves appeared to be going in and out, and according to the telemetry readings from their radio collars, they were either returning to the pen or staying very close to it.

On the twenty-fourth, biologists hiked up to Rose Creek pen to cut a hole in the comfort zone there and leave a deer carcass. Just before cresting the last hill in their approach to the pen, nearly blinded by a swirling snowstorm,

Mike Phillips and Doug Smith heard a loud howl. They had assumed all three wolves were still in the pen, but much to their surprise the howl was coming from behind them, from less than fifty yards away. With a shift in the horizontal blowing snow, Arnold appeared, almost an apparition, as though in a dream, the snow and wind blowing through his fur, his insistent howls hanging on the storm. He was out! And obviously waiting for Natasha and his stepdaughter to join him. Mike and Doug were ecstatic and alarmed all at once. They desperately didn't want to spook him or drive him away from the other two wolves. They dropped the carcass they had been hauling up the mountain and hightailed it down the trail. Being spooked didn't seem to occur to Arnold, however, for he followed Doug and Mike down the mountainside, keeping a distance, howling and every now and then appearing in silhouette just above them in the trees or on a ridge amid the haze of blowing snow, gently but firmly escorting them out of his territory. The men both described it as one of the most exciting and surprising wolf encounters of their careers.

So it was the bold and beautiful Arnold who would be the first to really depart a Yellowstone acclimation pen. He would wait for several more days before Natasha and her daughter followed, but by March 30 the three were located in the first wolf-monitoring telemetry flight, fifteen miles north of their pen in some very wild country near the headwaters of the Buffalo Fork. By the thirtieth, all but one of the Crystal pack had also vacated their acclimation pen and were making reconnaissance forays nearby. The pattern of the Soda Butte wolves, the animals in the third acclimation pen, was similar to those of the other two. By the end of March the Yellowstone wolves were free, and none of them showed any signs of fleeing northward.

A few weeks later, on the eve of Easter Sunday, in the tall, wind-washed grass that stretched across a Yellowstone slope a single ear twitched, appearing and then disappearing in the swaying stems like the flickering of a single life in the reach of history. That was the first evidence I personally witnessed of the presence of wolves roaming free, wild in Yellowstone at last. For a long time I studied that ear through my binoculars, thinking I saw it, then losing it, then with the flutter of movement it reappeared. At last the wolf to which the ear was attached lifted her head. It was the alpha female from the Crystal Creek pack. Blood from a recent kill had stained her grizzled muzzle a warm pink, reaching down her chin and neck in a crimson bib that faded into the dense black hair of her throat. In spite of her pink muzzle she was nearly invisible in the sage and flaxen-colored clumps of grasses sheltered by an overhanging fir. It was only when she stood up to survey the four wolves that emerged from behind a rock outcropping below that she became fully visible.

The pack was lolling about in the shade of a scattering of aspen and fir, all of them looking a bit comical, with their pink muzzles and distended bellies. The hint of comedy, however, was punctured by the broken rib tips of the elk they had killed only hours before. The faint ivory arch of carcass bones silhouetted against the ribbon blue sky illustrated that their intentions had been anything but comic. Aside from the rib cage little of the elk was left, its presence mainly evidenced by the collection of ravens and magpies that hovered and dipped above it. Now and then one of the wolves would manage to rise and make a halfhearted charge at the marauding ravens, which would erupt like a feathered fountain in a cloud of protesting caws and iridescent flashing. The wolf would then return to the slumbering shade, the birds to their furtive feeding, and the afternoon drifted on with the sleeping wolves oblivious to their significance in an unfolding human history, their sleep only nature's reminder that so much of the essence of the wild lies in the heart of the mundane.

Coming upon that pack along the Lamar Narrows was one of those freeze-flashes in life I will always remember. I was overjoyed by our good luck, which came by way of Bob Crabtree, a coyote biologist who flagged us down along the road to point out the wolves. With me were several members of The Wolf Fund board and staff, my family, and several close friends and colleagues who had worked with us. We had come to Yellowstone for the day with little expectation of seeing any of the released wolves—although I won't deny a glimmer of hope—but just to honor the place and the animals that gave us reason to come together. We were gathered for a party at Chico Hot Springs in Montana to celebrate the closure of The Wolf Fund.

I'd had the heady sense that once the wolves were free, so then would I be free from the driving mission and focus of the last fifteen years of my life. My impulse to announce the change to the world seeped into all aspects of the day. For the party that evening I had chosen an uncharacteristically short slithery dress, silk stockings replete with lace and glitter, and three-inch come-hither spike heels. No one in fifteen years of working on wolves had seen me in anything but conservative, mostly western garb. I was determined to make a point. I even had my fluffy little dogs attend the party to ensure that no one had any lingering ideas of continuing to define me as the "wolf woman." I was as hungry to break out of the confines of the role that had defined my existence as those wolves must have been to escape human domination.

Little could have darkened my jubilant mood that day, but one small detail penetrated my consciousness, planting itself in the future of my thoughts where memories of that wolf sighting would lie strewn like my pearls after the party. *Each wolf wore a collar.* This, in itself, was not a surprise. I had even seen each of these wolves wearing a telemetry collar in their acclimation pen at Crystal Creek. But seeing these wolves outside of their chain-link prisons, silhouetted against the wild landscape of Yellowstone, each with a collar and ear tags, left me troubled, plagued by a feeling deeply incongruent with the joy I felt over their freedom.

Ostensibly the purpose of the telemetry collars was to monitor and protect the wolves in the vulnerable early months after their release. But that day the reality of those collars, the black bands visible even on the necks of black wolves, left me feeling uneasy. Perhaps it was the sterile straight line on a wild, organic creature. Perhaps it was the limber, sinewy movement that contrasted with the square black box attached to each collar, the battery-driven transmitter which allowed biologists to locate the wolves at any time, day or night, and determine their activity level. I'm not sure what it was that troubled me, but images of Huxley's Brave New World haunted my dreams that night. I feared the presence of the collars revealed something darker than the altruism we all professed. Under the surface of our intention was a far more dangerous impulse—the need to control what we had pretended to set free.

Twenty-four

❖ ❖ ❖

If only it were all so simple! If only there were evil people somewhere insidiously committing evil deeds, and it were necessary only to separate them from the rest of us and destroy them. But the line dividing good and evil cuts through the heart of every human being. And who is willing to destroy a piece of his own heart?

ALEKSANDR SOLZHENITSYN

IN EARLY APRIL Arnold, Natasha, and Number 7 abruptly moved south-east back into Yellowstone where Number 7, Natasha's daughter, set out on her own. Number 7 would wander alone in the north-central part of Yellowstone for many months before at last, in late January of 1996, pairing with Number 2, one of the males from Crystal Creek, thereby forming the Leopold pack, Yellowstone's first naturally occurring wolf pack.

Meanwhile, tragedy swirled and boiled like a darkened storm front in the life of Natasha. Back in Canada a huge gray male with a stiff hind leg, proba-bly injured by a rancher's bullet or a trapper's snare, would visit again and again the lonely stand of poplars where his five pups had been snared one dark night in December. Three had died. His mate, Natasha, had avoided the snares, and his two daughters had survived that night, reappearing the next day with collars and ear tags. A month later his mate and one daughter would disappear after the whoosh and thud of a chopper had descended above them. Rick Stelter, the trapper who had snared most of Natasha's family in early December, would tell me later that after Natasha and her daughter, Number 7, were darted and brought to the States he would frequently see the male near the original site. Stelter had set snares for the male, and when they didn't work he tried traps, but the wolf was exceedingly smart and very trap-wary. It took six weeks of effort, Stelter often seeing the male's tracks, easily identified because of the heavier imprint the hind leg left along his own Ski-Doo trails. Finally one day he caught the male. Stelter confessed to me he was disappointed, almost sad, when he caught that wolf, so great was his respect for the animal's cunning. Stelter told me in a gentle voice, "He was kinda special, he was so doggone smart." The trapper, a taxidermist, skinned and tanned the pelt, but in spite of its considerable value he kept it for himself, a reminder of the secret communication, the depth of the solemn relationship between hunter and hunted.

On April 12 Natasha's other daughter who had been snared and collared that fateful December night in 1994, sister to Number 7, was shot by a farmer near Carrot Creek, just east of Edson, Alberta. She was seen standing near some calving cattle. No cattle kills or other wolves were reported in the area.

One wonders whether, in the mystical ways animals seem to know what has happened to their loved ones, Natasha, so far away from her former mate and daughter, perceived their deaths. She and Arnold were located on April 13, the day after her Canadian daughter was shot, after which the two disappeared for nearly eleven days. I can't help but wonder whether that time was some sort of canid walkabout, whether Natasha was driven into constant movement by some deep grief that we humans could never have fathomed, even if we had known about the death of her remaining family far to the north.

In spite of numerous monitoring flights, Natasha and Arnold went undetected until early in the morning of April 24, when they were seen by Mike Phillips just outside Red Lodge, Montana, well outside Yellowstone in the far northeast corner of the ecosystem. Not long after they were sighted by Mike, the plane possibly having flushed the wolves down the mountain, Arnold was spotted by two local men who were drinking beer and digging a truck out of a ditch after an aborted bear-hunting expedition. Upon spotting the wolf, Chad McKittrick, a forty-one-year-old unemployed carpenter who seemed to limp on the edge of Red Lodge's hard-drinking populace, pulled out his scope-mounted Ruger M-77 7-millimeter magnum rifle and settled the gray gun barrel against his unshaven jaw. He said to his companion, Dusty Steinmasel, "That's a wolf, I'm going to shoot it."

Steinmasel argued that it might be somebody's dog, McKittrick dismissed the theory and focused the scope on Arnold, silhouetted on a ridgeline some hundred and forty yards away. This proud, fearless, indifferent beauty didn't even turn toward his assassin, though he probably knew the men were there. Natasha, probably not far from Arnold but hidden from the two men, must have heard the shot. She likely witnessed his midair spin, his anguished attempt to bite at the wound high on his back as he fell to the ground, the quick spasm of his legs kicking, and then the stillness. The stillness that each of her three pups had come to, hung in neck snares outside Edson, the stillness that had descended on her Canadian mate and daughter, and now this stillness. She knew it well and wearily. Heavy with pups, she fled from her companion, away from the half-dug den up the slope, alone again.

By the time the sound of the shot reached Arnold the bullet had ripped through his upper chest cavity, most of it exiting the other side, leaving massive bleeding and organ destruction. He died before the men reached him. I am glad that they didn't watch him die, that his last few rasping breaths were sighed without the shadows of men darkening his view of the open sky, that he died wild, the mark of their hands only born by the fingerprints on the bullet that entered and left him, murdered but not broken by some pathetic hunger to conquer.

The cockiness began to drain out of McKittrick as soon as the gun was fired. The victory was empty and thin. They reached Arnold. His radio collar with Yellowstone National Park printed on it confirmed that indeed he was a wolf, one of the reintroduced animals from Yellowstone. Steinmasel, according to a later account, was feeling anxious, confused, disgusted, and mostly terrified. He pleaded with McKittrick to report the incident. Again, he was ignored. They jointly decided what was needed was more beer. Leaving the carcass bleeding and cooling, they headed down the mountain to a small corner store for a twelve-pack.

On further consideration, after a few Miller Genuine Deluxes, they realized the collar was probably still transmitting. Better lubricated but hardly clearer-minded, they decided to return to the carcass. The beer facilitated a rejuvenation of some of their earlier bravado and McKittrick decided he wanted the pelt. Steinmasel dragged the carcass, too heavy to carry, down the slope and tossed Arnold's remains into the back of McKittrick's pickup truck. McKittrick yanked out the ear tags; Steinmasel removed the bolts of the radio collar with a wrench and tugged it off Arnold's neck but kept it. The area was treeless and exposed, and fearing the plane might return or someone might show up, they drove down the mountain to an area with more cover, near some cottonwoods, and found a spot to hang the carcass. Together they strung Arnold up by his hind legs with orange baling twine. When I think of Arnold suspended, the horrid binding of the Day-Glo orange against the cool caramel-and-snow color of his coat, I think of Miracles, the whooping crane hung by barbed wire, I think of the suspended deer my daddy shot, whose hide I wore as mittens, I think of the chickens from the chicken plucker. I think this is our story—man and creature. But I wonder: must this always be our story?

McKittrick cut Arnold's head off. He wanted the skull and skinning out the head could be done later. Next, between slugs of Miller Genuine, he started hacking away at the hide. Impatient and inept, blood sullying the task, Dusty realized it could take the whole day for McKittrick to finish. A far more skilled hunter and skinner, Steinmasel took over and removed the caramel-colored fur from the thick musculature of Arnold's shoulders and back and legs, leaving only the paws, fur-covered and blood-drenched. The two men slung the pale blue bloody carcass down the slope. It settled in the dry brush in the bottom of a gully, soon shiny with blood.

The brittle edge of the morning's beer wore thin as the day weighed into the afternoon. Steinmasel's anxiousness seeped back. He implored his buddy to report the incident again. McKittrick ignored him and instead commented on bear hunting. They headed down to Dusty's cabin, where McKittrick hosed down the cape and piled the pieces of his trophy, the head and pelt, in a thick plastic bag that once covered a mattress. He heaved the bag into the back of his truck. Steinmasel kept the collar, promising to destroy and dump it. They ferried the trucks down to McKittrick's and Chad returned Dusty to his cabin. The beer's glow had been gone for a while. Dusty sat in his cabin turning the collar over in his hands. He was incredulous. He couldn't believe he had got himself into this mess. He thought of shattering the black box with a hammer, but instead wiped it clean of prints and wandered down the road toward the highway, where he tossed the collar into the rush of spring runoff coursing through a culvert, wishing he too might be carried elsewhere by the gush of clear scouring water.

On April 26 Doug Smith was in the air over Red Lodge. He picked up the mortality signal—a fast series of beeps indicating the death of an animal—from Arnold's telemetry collar. Although I suspect Doug would be hesitant to admit it, Arnold, whom he had called "the Big Guy" since his arrival in the Rose Creek pen, had been his favorite ward. Doug had fed him in the pen countless times, and admired his courage, his indifference to human presence, his Zorba-like willingness to push the envelope. The day Arnold left the pen and followed Doug and Mike down the mountain was one of the most memorable—perhaps spiritual—days of this young biologist's life. Doug's response to the mortality signal was first shock, then disbelief; he wanted to believe it was just the signal bouncing in an odd way from the gully below, he desperately wanted the signal to be wrong. Maybe Arnold shed the collar, maybe it's malfunctioning, maybe the receiver is messed up—maybe anything, but please not this wolf. Still, he didn't find Arnold that day.

On the twenty-seventh of April, at the first hint of light, Doug was back up in the air over Red Lodge. He picked up Natasha's signal in a place virtually identical to yesterday's reading. She hadn't moved. He feared she had denned in none too good an area. Exposed, near Red Lodge, close to a road, very vulnerable. He switched to Arnold's frequency. That day it was clearer, although still muffled and still in mortality mode. Finally they were able to isolate the signal's origin in the vicinity of Bear Creek. Once on the ground Doug drew a map for the local sheriff, Al McGill, and a U.S. Fish and Wildlife special agent, Tim Eicher. The hunt for the collar and clues had begun.

On the ground the two men, equipped with a receiver, homed in on the collar's signal. Late spring runoff had swollen Bear Creek and the back roads were muddy and rutted, but slowly the team of searchers, led by the steady beeps of the receiver, focused in on a track off the Bear Creek highway that led to a feeder creek. Water crashed through a culvert that ducked under a section of road where dead grass and debris covered the new shoots of green that peeked through the old dried stems and sticks that covered the road's shoulders like mulch. Eicher yanked on hip boots and waded into the creek. The ache of the icy current made his legs sluggish and numbed his arms and hands as he felt his way up the stream, the signal from the receiver on the bank beeping strong and steady. Eventually his hands bumped into the collar in the ashy-colored water, like a lost treasure. He clambered back to the bank, pleased, grinning. They had the scent.

The collar that Eicher had found had been unbolted. He knew that no wolf could shed a collar like that on its own, he was definitely looking at the work of a wrench and human hands. Was it fate, or was it synchronicity expressing its power, the shadow side of destiny's unfolding? Whatever the case, just after Eicher found the collar Steinmasel arrived on the scene, a very ill-timed appearance for him. Of all the moments Steinmasel could have chosen to return home and drive up that road, this was the worst.

Steinmasel's yellow Jeep turned in from the main road. He saw the group of lawmen. Shit. Bad timing. He stopped, thinking a wave-on-by might appear too nervous on these western back roads. He innocently inquired, "What's going on?" Eicher immediately sniffed something. Steinmasel, whom he knew years ago from working down in New Mexico, was furtive and nervous. They asked him if he'd seen anyone in the last few days. Nope, just him and his neighbor Dave Oxford, claimed Steinmasel.

Later the team questioned Dave Oxford. He said he hadn't seen anyone, well, that is, except Steinmasel and McKittrick unburying the latter's truck up the mountain on the twenty-fifth. Eicher decided to let Steinmasel stew for a bit. Less than two weeks later, on May 7, Evert Armstrong, a ranch hand from the Sunlight Ranch, came across Arnold's carcass. It was headless, the pelt hacked off, but the four furry huge paws suggested it had to be the missing wolf. The ranch personnel talked it over. It sure would have been easier to shovel and shut up, but they decided the law was the law and ultimately contacted Al McGill, who in turn called Eicher. On May 10 Eicher and another interrogator from Denver visited Steinmasel again. This time Steinmasel cracked. No, no, no, well—yes. He didn't admit ever touching or handling the carcass, but the story started to unfold. Eicher persuaded Steinmasel to "write it up in his own words and sign it." He did. They then had enough for a search warrant.

The next day Steinmasel told McKittrick what he had done. McKittrick, who had been drunk for two weeks, just shrugged. He had kind of felt it coming and was just waiting for the heat to arrive. They did, in force, on May 15. Eicher, calm, easy, got McKittrick to go for a walk with him. McKittrick talked openly about the shooting. He claimed he thought the wolf was a feral dog. The fact that Arnold's head and pelt were found in McKittrick's half-finished cabin did little to bolster his story. Even in Montana, they rarely mount dogs as game trophies.

The heartbreak we all felt over Arnold's loss was softened by some uplifting news from the field. Natasha gave birth to eight pups (four females, three black and one gray, and four black males) in early May. The loss of her mate had obviously disrupted her denning because she gave birth on open ground near a road just outside the park boundary. She would be extremely vulnerable for the first few weeks, as would her pups, so after very difficult deliberations the decision was made to provide supplemental food. Because of Arnold's death, Natasha would have to leave the pups unattended to hunt, so by providing food biologists could lessen the time she had to spend away from her young. Ultimately, because of Natasha's vulnerability, biologists made the difficult decision to move her and the pups back to the Rose Creek acclimation pen, where they could better protect them during the early stages of the pups' development.

Even though Natasha's reincarceration troubled me, I understood, and in the end agreed with, Mike and Doug's decision. At the time of her return to the Rose Creek pen, Natasha and her eight pups represented 43 percent of the entire Yellowstone wolf population. Still, I was heartened that the wild had its own unexpected and irreverent response to our well-intended control. On July 29 a freak windstorm hit northern Yellowstone and two huge spruce trees fell on the Rose Creek chain-link fence—news I received with some glee. Natasha remained in the pen, but five of the pups escaped. Biologists caught two of the wily little critters, but three remained outside the pen, frolicking, unfenced, and free. In the next month one of the three found his way back in. The remaining escapees were left carcasses every few days and fared pretty well that summer.

In late September I visited Natasha in captivity, I hoped for the last time. Her pups were actually teenagers in wolf years; they paced the perimeter of the pen, gangly and wild-eyed, as we hauled the bison carcasses in. She and the pups looked great, filled-out and sleek. Then, in the final days of their captivity, something rather miraculous happened.

All summer the biologists had been leaving meat outside the pen for the two pups whenever they fed the gang inside, and all was going smoothly until a young grizzly showed up in mid-September and decided *he* wanted the semiweekly free lunch—no doubt the two young pups looked like a fitting dessert as well. This was a bit of a problem until the improbable, perhaps unprecedented, happened. A dispersing wolf from down the valley, a young male from the Crystal Bench pack, Number 8, abandoned his clan and showed up at Rose Creek and began regurgitating food for the two pups. For an unrelated male to tolerate, let alone feed, another pack's pups is uncommon if not unheard of. Number 8 hung around with the two wayward teenagers for several weeks, putting up with their relentless ambushes and antics, waiting for their fetching mother to come out and thank him.

On October 11, 1995, Natasha was released for the second time from the Rose Creek acclimation pen. Upon emerging from the Rose Creek pen, she surprisingly did not drive Number 8 off, but instead rewarded his ardor with the introduction of six more adoring and hungry teenage wolves. Apparently the two adults took a liking to each other, because all ten of them, Natasha in the lead, Number 8 bringing up the rear, and the pups between them, began exploring northern Yellowstone together. Number 8's presence and contribution increased the pups' chances of survival tenfold, and he and Natasha proved to be good predators and providers. In fact they showed such promise I started calling them "my little serial killers."

Not long after Natasha's release Mike Phillips and a film crew witnessed and filmed a sensational scene in the ongoing drama of our Natasha, whose legend was growing. While out for a Yellowstone stroll, Natasha, her new mate, and the eight pups chanced to encounter the Crystal Bench group, Number 8's natal pack. The prodigal's parents and three brothers were, I'm sure, more than a little astonished to find their lost pack member hitched up—and with offspring.

The two Crystal Bench alphas took off running in the opposite direction to show just how uninterested they were in getting to know their son's entourage. Looking at the footage, I guess I have to admit Natasha didn't act all that enthusiastic about her in-laws either and took off for a couple hundred yards in the other direction, woofing and making her general disapproval known. Number 8, on the other hand, was delighted to see his brothers, and the pups were more than exuberant about the idea of uncles and the expanded prospects for food-begging that three new wolf bellies offered. The brothers were indeed curious about, perhaps even smitten with, their brother's choice of a mate—that is until Number 8, the proprietary new husband, in an act of destiny, attacked a brother who got a bit too friendly, putting to rest any future confusion over where his allegiances lay. Natasha jumped in to join Number 8 in roughing up his sibling, lest the brothers have any doubt about *her* allegiances. Together they chased the bewildered wolf away and returned to their pups. The two established a territory that summer in Yellowstone's northern range which stretches from the Lamar Valley along the Yellowstone River, reaching almost to Gardiner, Montana.

On December 20, 1995, loss licked at Natasha's life once again. One of her pups, Number 22, a strapping black male, was killed by a delivery truck in the park. The pup was not actually hit by the truck, but rather ran into the side of the truck and was killed by the rear wheels. Somehow it made me feel better that he was not run down but chose to leap into his death.

In the spring of 1996, I watched Natasha at the opening of her den site. She had excavated a deep hole under a large boulder high on a ridge with views of the Yellowstone River, shaded by arching Doug firs. Her coat had already started to glint with the onset of gray, her muzzle had shifted to a soft pewter. Her pups frolicked around the den opening in the cool early summer breeze. The legacy of her Yellowstone life and the enormous contribution she would make was just beginning.

Twenty-five

❖ ❖ ❖

This is what youth must figure out:
Girls, love, and living.
The having, the not having,
The spending and giving,
And the melancholy time of not knowing.

This is what age must learn about:
The ABC of dying.
The going, yet not going,
The loving and leaving,
And the unbearable knowing and knowing.

E. B. WHITE, "Youth and Age"

O N MAY 31, 1995, after all the files and office equipment and numerous boxes of grant materials had been moved, I closed The Wolf Fund, literally locked the door and returned the key. I drove home feeling like my life was just beginning. I had thought of this act of locking that door for so long, now that it was here I wasn't sure how I should toast it. Tom was away, I was too exhausted to meet anyone, and I had a desperate need to be alone, to savor this notion of freedom. On contemplating it the night before, I had decided that a cold beer was the proper thing, not a smooth, swift scotch or the sweet-and-sour complication of a margarita, not the spring juniper aroma of gin or the icy trout-belly gold of Chardonnay, but the basic simplicity and foam of a very cold beer. A simple libation for the simple pleasure of finishing a job and fulfilling a promise. I walked into the house, greeted enthusiastically by the dogs, and fished the Snake River lager stowed there the night before for just this moment, out of the back corner of the fridge. I opened it and sat down on the couch thinking, "IT'S OVER! I am FREE." The phone rang. It was my sister, Robin, who is only two years older than I. She said, "Renée, you better sit down." I replied in a gay voice. "I AM!

Not only am I sitting down, but I have a very delicious, very cold beer in my hand." She said, "Good." There was a long pause, then she said, "Renée, I have cancer."

I packed the dogs in their flight kennels and flew to Atlanta the next day. Robin's first surgery was the following week, and thus started my journey into the realm of a different kind of wild, a wild that grows within us, a wild that is as hungry, cunning, indifferent, and voracious a life force as wild animals such as bears, wolves, whales, and sharks, those creatures capable of killing us, of humbling us, of teaching us proportion and scale, which I cherish so much in the outer landscapes of my world. This wild we call cancer is not unlike them, only it stalks us from the inner landscapes.

My sister fared well on her first surgery; the news was dark, but not devastating. The cancer had spread to her lymph nodes, but as far as the doctors were able to determine was not present elsewhere. She started on a regime of chemotherapy and radiation that we hoped would subdue, even exterminate, this horrific wild cell growth that raged in her body.

On Monday, June 26, my brother came down to Atlanta to stay with Robin and care for my dogs while I drove from Atlanta to Chattanooga, Tennessee, where both Mollie Beattie and I were speakers for the Outdoor Writers Association annual meeting. Mollie and I had connecting rooms and sat up nearly all night in our pajamas talking about everything from my sister's cancer to panty hose—both of us despised them. We talked about our sisters and the pain of witnessing and enduring illness, we talked about dogs, and long-ago lovers, husbands, and mothers.

When the phone rang in my room at two in the morning we were both wide awake, sitting cross-legged on the bed; each looked at the other quizzically, wondering what ominous harbinger this might be. It was my brother calling from the emergency room of a vet clinic in Atlanta to let me know Zany had been very ill and was vomiting blood. She had become sick at 9:15 but was now quiet and resting. They hadn't figured out what was wrong, but she was at that moment stable. In retrospect, it is no surprise that Zany would, that night, physically manifest the grief my sister was going through and what lay ahead for Mollie, for it would be exactly one year later, at the exact moment Zany had become ill, 9:15 P.M., on that day, June 27, that Mollie would die.

Six days after our pajama party in Chattanooga, July 3, 1995, Mollie had her first seizure. She called me two days later to tell me what had happened. The assumption was epilepsy. I began researching the disease immediately. When I called a few days later to report that "I've got a ton of research and guess what I found out about these seizure dogs—" she interrupted me mid-sentence. "Renée, we just got the MRI results an hour ago, it's not epilepsy, it's cancer, I've got a brain tumor." For the second time in the course of our relationship I was speechless.

One month later I sent her a letter.

August 5, 1995

My dearest Mollie,

I've been feeling a bit like the doe in the headlights, frozen, still, word-less. Standing by without utterance or ability. But slowly the shadows are returning, the outline of a forest, the meadow's edge, the sounds of night. With the redawning of the dark I'm seeing my way again, the outline of the world emerges and our place in it becomes clearer. I love you. I bow to you and all you must feel—your pain, your fear, your sadness. I've been wondering if you feel alone, if this place to which you have journeyed seems far away from home.

I sit here facing my beloved grove of aspens, their twinkling leaves, merry, in spite of my mood. Each tree stands alone, each single trunk and its slender limbs drinking in the morning light, but I know last night they were bent by 65 mile per hour howling winds, some fell, some withstood. Year after year each tree has faced the storms alone, the droughts, the unrelenting winter snows, the violent fight for sur-vival as fate licked at its trunk. Each slender white column stands apart in this little grove of deep calm summer grass, and yet they are con-nected underground, nurtured by the same sweet soils, watered by the same falling rain. Outwardly their long limber trunks stand alone, sin-gular, but underneath, secretly, silently, they all hold each other, roots shared and entwined. Mollie, you stand that way, like a young willowy birch, erect, lean, strong, and we all hold you underneath, en-twined, connected together. We all face the storms fundamentally alone, but we endure them together.

I sent her a red bandanna with shimmering glitter to wear on the "warpath," and a black Venetian point lace garter belt with beautiful lace-topped silk stockings and a note that read "FUCK PANTY HOSE."

Accompanying these two women through the span of their battles with this mysterious disease was a gift of unspeakable proportions. To embrace life's precariousness we must first embrace its fleetingness. Each had a different story and a different path. My sister's cancer seemed to respond to the on-slaught of drugs and radiation, and by the end of a year the wild cell growth and even the cancer itself appeared to be eliminated. Mollie's cancer went into remission for a short while, but returned with a vengeance in the dark of winter, taking over her body in shaking, quivering seizures that left her spent and silent.

I felt very entwined in Mollie's cancer. Some months after her first surgery Tom and I were in D.C. and were scheduled to have dinner with Mollie and her husband, Rick, the following evening. That night I dreamt that Mollie's cancer had returned. I saw it very clearly, two strands in very precise places on the upper left portion of her brain. My dream shifted to Mollie and me in a fighter jet, reminiscent of a scene in the Tom Cruise action/drama *Top Gun.* I dreamt Mollie was for some reason unable or unwilling to respond to some threatening enemy presence, and I awakened myself screaming at the top of my lungs, "ENGAGE! ENGAGE! MOLLIE, ENGAGE! ENGAGE!" It was a hor-rifying dream.

The next night Tom and I were already seated at a table when Rick and Mollie arrived at the restaurant. As they approached the table Mollie's face was hard, resolute, unreadable. Rick was pale. Mollie apologized for being late and sort of slumped into a chair. She opened the conversation, "I had another MRI this week, we just got the results an hour ago. My cancer is back." We talked for a long time that evening about choices, about life, about death. Standing outside the restaurant after dinner, I put my forehead against Mollie's and said, "I dreamt it last night. I knew." She said, "I knew too. I've known all along." I said, "Mol, what do you know?" She said, "I *know.*" We both knew. The unbearable knowing and knowing.

We had lunch with Rick the next day and I told him about my dream and screaming "ENGAGE." He told me Mollie had always believed she would die young. Her father had, and she had always had a strong premonition that she would. It was then that I begin to sense that Mollie was moving toward a destiny, something preordained or already known. It wasn't that Mollie was resigned, or didn't fight, or didn't desperately want to live. She loved life with a fervor and depth known to few. I think she literally had another job to do, another calling. On some level she knew.

Our friendship was deeply intuitive, perhaps because we spent five days in silence together, meditating at the Tich Nhat Hanh retreat, before we ever met. I felt very entwined in Mollie's cancer and still struggle with the WHY? Although I know it is natural for people close to people diagnosed with cancer to feel guilty, to feel it should be they who are ill, that the cancer is somehow their fault, I feel not guilty but grateful, as though Mollie endured that cancer for all of us, taking it out of the world via her body, like a soldier using his body as a shield to protect others.

When I saw Mollie in Grace Cottage Hospital in Townsend, Vermont, two weeks before she died, she wanted to know every detail of the wolves' movements and progress. She was so elated that Natasha had succeeded in producing a litter of pups that spring. She gave much to the wolves. They would not be in Yellowstone had it not been for her efforts. In the end, they too gave to her. The project became the legacy of which she was most proud.

When Mollie and I talked about the experience of grief and grieving around her coming death, our context was the loss of our dogs. For her it had been the loss of a dog named Rosco, whose favorite thing in the world was Oreo cookies; for me, as she well knew, it had been Bristol. Mollie was one of the few people I took to the site where I gave Bristol to the coyotes. In an act of sweet generosity Mollie asked for a picture of Bristol before she died. She wanted to be sure to find her in this other world she would soon occupy. I gave Mollie a Polaroid shot taken the day before Bristol died. The picture shows a strange span of light originating from Bristol's eyes and fanning in front of her, a sort of brilliant ray invisible to the eye but somehow captured by the camera. I reassured Mollie that Bris would find her, probably greeting her next to Rosco's side as she entered that golden world.

And so it was on June 26, 1996, that my dear friend and comrade, dying as she had lived, would ask to be taken off the life-sustaining drugs that held the cancer-driven swelling in her brain at bay. Mollie Beattie would choose to enter death on her own terms, on her time, wondering at the last moment if she would need her shoes, for hiking, in that other world. The gift of her death was as precious as the force of her life. Before we left we gave her a package of Oreo cookies for Rosco. Rick, Mollie's husband, later told me that at her request, Mollie had been cremated with two things—the Oreo cookies and a stuffed wolf she kept beside her in her hospital bed, a totem of Natasha.

Twenty-six

Without words, it comes. And suddenly, sharply one is aware of being separated from every person on one's earth and every object, and from the beginning of the things and from the future and even a little, from one's self. A moment before one was happily playing; the world was round and friendly. Now at one's feet there are chasms that have been invisible until this moment. And one knows, and never remembers how it was learned, that there will always be chasms, and across the chasms will always be those one loves.

LILLIAN SMITH, *The Journey*

I AM REACHING into the darkness, pawing and straining and screaming to reach my dogs. Mocha, now sixty-five pounds, has seven-pound Roo in her jaws and is shaking her like a limp ground squirrel. Everything is black. We are in the car, which I've just driven off the road in response to Roo's panicked screeches. They are behind my seat. I am fighting and twisting to reach them, bound by the seat belt that has locked down in response to our jarring stop amid the sagebrush. Over and over I am screaming Mocha's name. Screaming for her to come back. I can't reach her.

This is the mouse-size canid I fed with baby bottles, this is the dog I know through and through, this can't be her. She has left me. She has forgotten me. She is gone. She is possessed by something I don't recognize. She has retreated too far, too far into the darkness, into wildness, into predator. I am clawing at her face, at her gums, at the cold pulp of her nose. My hands are in her mouth, prying with all my strength to open her jaws, which are clamped on Roo. Roo is shrieking in a staccato, ear-piercing frenzy. Roo's teeth are digging into the flesh of my hands in a panicked effort to defend herself. I can feel the pulse of this thing in Mocha, I can feel it coursing through her as I pry at her mouth; it is pumping "predator" through every muscle, sinew, nerve, and cell in her body. Her back teeth rake over my hands, and I dig my fingernails into the roof of her mouth, pulling at her locked jaws.

The other two dogs are adding their voices to the madness. Zany is yowling from the far back, where she is trying to escape Mocha's frenzy, and little Rye is howling in a high-pitched plaintive call of fear and panic in the front next to me. Everything seems to be in slow motion. I am sure Mocha's jaws are crushing feather-boned Roo, and I am not strong enough. I am straining with all my might to open the casket of Mocha's jaws. I feel like a mother trying to lift a car that is crushing her trapped child. I am not strong enough. A line I've used a thousand times in my lectures on wolves flits through my head. *Wolves can exert up to 1,200 pounds per square inch with their jaws. . . . Imagine the concentration of pressure being applied . . . something equivalent to the weight of balancing a Volkswagen Bug on a broomstick. . . .* What did I know. I knew nothing.

Suddenly Mocha drops Roo. I scoop up my little dog's limp soft body, sure she is dead, or soon will be. She feebly licks my face with her petal-size tongue. She is still alive! I cradle her, sobbing, begging her, "Please don't die, please don't die." Her vanilla-colored coat is covered with blood and shit. In her terror her bowels released. She is trembling. I wrap her in my coat and hold her in one arm, digging in my backpack for the car phone with the other. I only notice how badly my hands are shaking as I fumble to push the phone plug into the lighter receptacle. I start the stalled car. Somehow my fingers know the vet's number. I reach the answering service. I announce my name, my voice quavering, and say, "I have an emergency, please get a vet to the clinic." The woman asks the name of my dog. I reply, "Roo." She says, "Spell that please." I scream, "R-O-O, as in Kanga. What the fuck does it matter what her name is, get a vet there NOW!" I hang up.

I put the car in gear. The tires spin on the embankment. I retreat to my early years of Catholicism and pray, "Please God, don't let us be stuck." The tires grab, we pull ahead, the sage and snow scraping and crunching underneath the carriage, and the car heaves back on the road. I race toward the clinic, praying once again that no cops stop me for speeding. The vet clinic is dark. I rock Roo and dial the number again. The woman on whom I've just hung up recognizes my voice and replies coldly that the vet is on her way. We sit there in the dark, all four dogs silent. I rock Roo, who is limp. I'm too afraid to look to see if she's dead. I moan over and over in a mantra, "Please don't die, please don't die."

The vet arrives, a warm-voiced southern woman named Laura Hulsey whose calm, reassuring demeanor immediately eases my hysteria. Remarkably, aside from her psychological trauma, Roo's wounds are relatively minor. She has a light puncture wound in her shoulder and neck, and will be bruised, but has suffered no damage to vital organs or structural or muscle damage. She is not even showing signs of shock. As if to penetrate my disbelief Laura shakes my shoulders and says, "She can go home with you tonight." I am incredulous. I am joyous. This imp of a dog has faithful angels. I thank them. I sink to my knees on the clinic's linoleum floor and thank every single angel in the world.

As I kneel there on the cold linoleum babbling incoherently about angels, the throbbing in my hands rises up through the layers of my consciousness like bubbles coming to a boil. I look down at my hands as though they were someone else's. They are covered with blood. I find only three or four puncture wounds, all from Roo's sharp little teeth. My penance. This whole thing is my fault. I didn't see it coming. I am responsible. I thought I knew my dogs. How could I have missed the onset of Mocha's aggression? I didn't protect Roo. These wounds are my reminder. Laura's sharp order to "hold this little snapping turtle!" jolts me out of my guilt-and-blame wallowing session. Roo is obviously returning to her incorrigible self.

My relief over Roo's miraculous escape from death is momentary. On the way home I begin to confront the dark specter of choice. One dog or the other must go—an impossible choice. I cannot fathom giving up either of them. I try to force myself to the edge of the precipice of decision. The thought is simply unthinkable. I think of a running jump. My brain is unwilling to encompass the idea of life without either of them, I can't get my legs to move toward the edge of decision. I am so deeply bound to both. I turn back to find another path. The odd question arises in my mind, Why didn't Mocha kill Roo? She could have effortlessly crushed her, she was capable of inflicting massive wounding with little effort. But she didn't. Why? What is Mocha teaching us? What is the lesson? What was Mocha telling me? It was clear what she was telling Roo.

Thus begins my journey into the nature of domestic dog aggression.

Unfortunately, Roo, who barely weighed two pounds when she arrived, entered the house with the attitude of an arrogant ruffian. She seemed to lack the most basic of canine social graces, like knowing when to submit, when to look away, when not to challenge and charge. Mocha in the first year showed admirable maternalistic tolerance toward this incorrigible, ill-mannered waif of a dog, but something must have shifted in the car that evening. Perhaps Roo challenged her and Mocha, already feeling crowded in those close quarters, snapped. I will never know just what precipitated the attack, but the shift seemed permanent. Once Roo elicited that predatory response, no amount of behavior modification, drugs, obedience work, or distraction would change Mocha's behavior sufficiently for me to trust that Roo was safe. Thus began my divided household. Mocha and Roo had to live separately.

The complexity increased several months later when Mocha and Zany had their first altercation. Zany had been the uncontested dominant dog, and Mocha, reaching her own maturity, began to test the relationship. They declared war on an occasion after they had been apart for several days and then, with little thought, had been thrown back together, both stressed and excited, and I quite ill with walking pneumonia. Apparently the structure of the dominance hierarchy was too unstable, and in the space of seconds an explosion of canine fur and teeth led to the permanent separation of Mocha from all the other dogs.

The search for answers or solutions or remedies that I undertook in the aftermath of the dissolution of my peaceful pack is too detailed and lengthy to offer in the space of these pages. All four dogs remain in our household, Mocha isolated from the other three. Friends find the degree of complexity around the "dog dance" in our home amusing if not ridiculous (TR likes to joke that going to bed at night is like locking down Leavenworth), but anyone who has confronted near-impossible circumstances with a beloved set of dogs knows the ends to which we will go to accommodate creatures we love.

What has been most interesting to me is how much I have learned about my own presumption and attitudes toward animals and wildness in attempting to navigate this domestic canine minefield.

Wolves and humans occupy two different cultures, and dogs act as the go-between, the translators for both our worlds. Dogs are not wolves, nor are dogs human. Dogs occupy some middle ground in a spectrum that reaches between the absolute wild of wolf and the absolute tamed of human. My relationship with my own dogs has been a means for me to continually confront and learn from the wildness that inhabits the domestic, a stepping stone that makes the wild more accessible.

It is easy for us to forget or underestimate the wild nature in our tame dogs. Of all my dogs, I thought of Mocha as the most domesticated, the most attuned to me, and the most tamed. She has the characteristics of a working breed, and is always aware of where I am, what I am doing, and whether she is a part of the activity. In other words she is always checking in, keeping track, a habit which after centuries of breeding is part of her genetic code. Unlike the other dogs, she is constantly "registering" my activity and intentions. We have come to know each other, anticipating one another a bit like synchronized dancers or skaters.

However, Mocha is teaching me not about the domestic, but rather about the wild. Our dogs are still wild, they still have wild natures and a social protocol we need to learn and respect. This is the nature of their otherness, this is how their differences can reflect and define our human identity. The ends to which we go to make them similar to us, to treat them as our children, to breed them like slaves, to show them in competitions according to some arbitrary, contrived aesthetic, directly diminishes the ways in which they are different, other, and autonomous, and therefore valuable to us as teachers.

Convenience has become one of the driving factors in how we breed and acquire pets. We need to embrace that it is the inconvenience, the ways in which animals are wily or self-willed, the ways in which they don't fit neatly into a predesignated notch, that alerts us to their uniqueness, to their contrasts. For it is that separateness that beckons our curiosity and learning. A dog which is a robot, granted little right or identity of its own, is indeed only a means of perpetrating our alienation from the spiritual sense of the animal world.

We also need to recognize how we use dogs. I will be forever aware of how heavily I leaned on Mocha in her early months. How her tiny little existence gave my exhausted, broken human one meaning and direction. I am sorry that I put so much emotional weight on her. Sorry that, so young, she picked up on the need that I had at that time, to be rescued, to be protected. It was too much for her. She grew up too fast. Her genes, selected for hundreds of years, told her she had to serve, but she was given an impossible task for one so young.

Mocha's attack on Roo, the incident that shattered my presumption of control, was both a sobering and a humbling reminder of my wrongful assumption that our pets can be tame and completely knowable. I forgot to honor the mystery, the essential autonomy of these animals and the separate world they occupy. It was in fact this incident and my search to understand it, to understand the animals I thought I knew so thoroughly, that took me back into the work of Paul Shepard.

Shepard's denouncement of pets has rocked the ranks of pet lovers the world round. His assertion that pets are essentially biological slaves that cringe and fawn and perform, engineered to conform to human wishes, creatures "created" by humans over the last ten thousand years, mere vestiges and fragments from a time of deep human respect for animals, needles the ire of even goldfish owners. What is most disturbing to Shepard is the notion that pets have become substitutes for the authentic relationship we once had with wild animals, that using domestic animals as surrogate companions, siblings, lovers, victims, workers, parents, and competitors has enabled people to avoid the dimensions and edges of relating to true wildness, that it has not only tamed the creatures but tamed our psyches, and that has led to a culture overrun by neurosis.

Although I find myself agreeing with parts of Shepard's arguments, I find them a bit too black and white. I believe that our relationship with pets reflects the reality of man's experience in a world in which wildness has been pushed to the corners of our psyches. It is my opinion, however, that our animal companions, rather than replacing our need for contact with wild animals, remind us of that need; they awaken it. I think they are our conduits, our stepping-stones back to the experience of the wild. They are able to knit us back into the fabric of the natural world through their own action and instinct, no matter how dramatically we have manipulated them to fit our sterilized world. As the chasm widens between the us and them, between civilization and wildness, we dearly need pets as interpreters and translators.

Shepard is not alone in his leaning toward a black-and-white judgment. We are a nation that longs for things to be black and white. We do not like ambiguity. We do not like the uncertain, the unpredictable, the uncontrollable. We like secure borders. We don't like the gray areas. Over the years my dogs have come in many shades of gray. Their colors have ranged from charcoal to ash, the same colors we see as our world turns from dark to dawn—the crepuscular colors. Mocha is all those colors, walnut to fawn, maple to coffee, pearl to pepper. The colors of her coat, like the dimensions of her personality, travel in those shadows between night and day, between the cultivated and the wild, between man and beast.

IT IS EARLY EVENING. The sun hovers above the cragged line of the Tetons, producing a lilac-tinged light which streams across the valley, bathing everything in a pastel glow. All the colors of the landscape appear more saturated and I feel that stirring hope and melancholy that is invoked with the sweet warmth of the setting sun. I scramble about the mud room, grabbing the accoutrements of dog-walking. This outing will be with three of them, three leashes, treats, sunglasses even though the sun's almost disappeared, brimmed hat, sweatshirt tied snugly around my waist. The dogs are agitated and eager as I lace up my hiking boots. They live for this moment. Zany, who continues her endeavor to live up to the full potential of each moment of her life, sits near the door talking in a variety of squeaks, yelps, howls, and yodels—most of which have no roots in her canid ancestry. Rye and Roo rocket around like ferrets on espresso, crashing into each other and Zany in their anticipatory exuberance.

I step outside the door and check for bison in the yard. I spot only two over a half mile out to the southwest. I open the door for the dogs and they explode onto the deck and into the sage as though fired by a cannon. I silently admonish myself for not making them sit before exiting, but rules are made to be broken now and then. Zany flies into the sage, stretching out in a belly-to-the-ground sprint as if in hot pursuit of something, which turns out only to be her freedom, arching in a huge half circle out and back to me like a furry boomerang. The little dogs, an eighth her size, follow in her wake like creamy-colored sage dolphins, somehow keeping up with her in this initial sprint of exuberance. Finally she slows and pauses to scent the air, and they, in turn, begin their comic "stotting," jumping up in the air on all fours like miniature deer. Each "yump" allows their little heads to pop up above the sage to assess their position and mine, before they are off again in a mad dash of glee.

I set off to the northwest, veering away from the bison. The walking is rough, the charred stubble of sage stalks create a minefield of broken sharp points which pierce up through the bitter brush and meadow grass unexpectedly. The burned sage is a remnant of a lightning-strike fire a few years ago that swelled out of control, nearly consuming our house and the outlying buildings of our little compound. I discover a thin game trail and follow its meandering path north. I crest a slight rise and there spread before us are twenty-three grazing elk. I count out of habit. Zany alerts, but ignores them. They too alert, forty-six cervid ears pinned forward in a serious evaluation of our appearance. They seem to recognize me and the dogs, having wandered around the house a good part of the summer, and sensing we pose no threat, one, then another, drops its head back to the cool evening grazing.

The dogs and I shift slightly east, away from the elk and back toward a tongue of aspen and conifers. On an impulse, just as the last sliver of sun sinks behind the granite lip of Avalanche Canyon, I pause, and do a coyote howl. I must sound different when I howl for a response, rather than howl for the hell of it, because the dogs, always willing to join my reverie, instead all sit down and cock their heads, listening. No response. We move on. Two courting ravens overhead catch my eye, and preoccupied with their dips and swoops, I manage to walk straight into a tangle of barbed wire, looped and twisted on the ground, no signs of old fence posts or how the heap arrived there. I am relieved one of the dogs hadn't run into it in their wild dashes. I gather it up and wade southward back toward our house, where the old corrugated-roof barn glints a green sheen in the afterlight of Shadow Mountain. I have come to love this place that holds the spirit of the wild, that has given me both refuge and sustenance all these years.

Later that evening storm clouds move in. Rays of rain like long gray veils interrupt the view toward Buck Mountain. A huge bull bison grazes under the bird feeder six feet from the plate-glass window in front of me. Mocha, lying next to me, is growling in a deep rumble, hardly able to obey the order of silence. The plate glass is an insufficient barrier. The bison is so close I am able to see the spots of rain, like freckles dappling the leathery hide over his hind hips where the heavy winter coat has sloughed off. Over his shoulders hair hangs in tatters and clumps, across his back there are still patches like great continents. I imagine Africa and India in two clumps, much like organizing cloud shapes. Small droplets of urine still cling to the hair that drapes his penile shaft and I note that the left dark coal-colored testicle hangs lower than the right. In spite of the huge head and baseball-bat-thick horns, caked with mud, his eyes still shine with a gentleness, brown and sweet. I remain still in the chair behind the glass, just happy that he is calm and greedily slurping up the long blades fertilized by bird droppings under the feeder. My dogs have taught me that the wild is where you find it, not in some distant world relegated to a nostalgic past or an idealized future; its presence is not black or white, bad or good, corrupted or innocent. Dogs can lead us to the bridges over the chasms of either-or. They can teach us the virtue of our vices and the vice in our virtues. They remind us that the imperfect is our paradise. A fallen tree, a barbed-wire tangle, a stream stone traverse, a daring leap—we need only follow them, for it is we, not they, who have forgotten how to navigate the nature of the "gray areas." We are of that nature, not apart from it. We survive because of it, not instead of it.

Twenty-seven

❖ ❖ ❖

Once we start managing wildness, the wildness is gone. . . . What we manage and control cannot nourish us with newness; it is like a "gift" we have arranged for someone to give to us.

SHIERRY WEBER NICHOLSEN, *The Love of Nature and the End of the World*

THE YELLOWSTONE WOLF recovery effort has been, by any measure, a grand success. The wolves are thriving beyond our most extravagant dreams and have, for the most part, stayed out of trouble. The project is seen as a shining light among conservation efforts. However, to really decide whether we deem this project a success, we have to determine what criteria to use to measure success, and how to assess the costs of that success.

And there have been costs. As Goethe said, "There is strong shadow where there is much light." Sadly, many wolves have been destroyed by our effort to restore them—some by accident, true, but more were lost to poachers and even more were killed in response to livestock depredations. There have been 97 known wolf mortalities as of November 2001, involving a combination of native and Canadian-born animals. Fifty-one (53 percent) were human caused. Twenty-seven were killed in "control actions," mostly in response to livestock depredations; 16 have been hit by cars or killed in other human/wolf accidents; 8 wolves have been illegally killed. Twenty-five of the deaths are attributed to natural causes, and 21 are "unknown."

I can comfort myself with the thought that this mortality rate is far lower than what these animals would probably have suffered had they been left in the free-fire zone in Alberta. But there are other, less quantifiable but equally important costs as well. It has taken many years for me to acknowledge what my heart knew the first day I saw wolves outside their acclimation pens, roaming the wild landscape of Yellowstone, adorned with ear tags and radio collars—we had *not* really set them free. To grant Yellowstone's wolves the true freedom they deserve seems the most basic obligation we might fulfill, given our treatment of the species in the past and the lives of the Canadian wolves we disrupted for the purpose of righting a wrong man perpetrated so many years ago.

The irony of the insight that struck me that day, when I finally recognized what the collars really represented, is that The Wolf Fund had paid for them. The Wolf Fund's final gift to Yellowstone before our closing had been funds for the purchase of the very telemetry collars those wolves had been wearing.

Since wolves were released in Yellowstone the biologists "managing" them have walked a razor's edge, trying to live the ideal of coexistence with a wild species in a culture which harbors tremendous ambivalence toward the wild.

With the appointment of Doug Smith as Yellowstone Wolf Recovery Leader, Yellowstone's wolves have been assigned the country's finest guardian. His team has been forced to travel that shadowland through no fault of their own, but rather because their freedom to *grant* freedom is restricted by our fear. The result of their mixed "marching orders" is that they too often have been forced, in my opinion, to err on the side of control and coercion.

Since the first release of wolves we have continued to intervene—collaring, ear-tagging, moving litters of pups that were vulnerable due to den site location, relocating wolves that posed a *potential* threat to livestock, attempting to rehabilitate wolves that had run afoul of civilization through the use of "adversive conditioning" and by rehabituating them to new locations—on and on. In almost all of the situations the actions undertaken, considered individually, have been completely justified from a biological standpoint. However, over time the habit of intervention—of darts, telemetry collars, ear tags, chain-link pens, and shock collars—has revealed a more troubling and insidious mind-set. It falls under the shibboleth of "management," but what it means in its application is *control*.

As of 2001, about 30 percent of the wolves in the Yellowstone population are collared and ear-tagged. In addition to trying to ensure that the alphas of every pack are radio-trackable, the objective each year is to collar at least 50 percent of the new pups. For many years leading up to reintroduction, biologists and advocates discussed the use of radio collars as a tool to monitor and protect the wolves in the early stages of the recovery program. I believe the collars have been very effective in accomplishing just that goal. There is evidence that the presence of collars can deter the illegal shooting of animals, and it can certainly help in prosecuting those who do kill wolves illegally, as Chad McKittrick learned to his sorrow.

Just how much sorrow? McKittrick, Arnold's assassin, was convicted on October 10, 1996, by a jury of eight men and four women (several of them ranchers) on all three misdemeanor counts: killing an endangered species, possessing it, and transporting it. He was sentenced to three months in jail, three months in a halfway house, and $10,000 in restitution. His appeal to the Ninth Circuit Court of Appeals was denied. In January of 1999 the Supreme Court refused to hear his case. According to the U.S. Attorney's office in Montana, McKittrick has served his sentence. The court recognizes McKittrick as indigent but has stated that as soon as he starts earning an income he will be expected to pay the United States of America $10,000 in restitution.

As illustrated by the McKittrick case, collars have always been very valuable in monitoring wolves, knowing where they are at what times, and working with ranchers and hunters to prevent conflicts before they arise. The collars have enabled biologists to better understand the distribution of wolves, their survival and mortality rates, and how they utilize habitat and prey. Telemetry has also contributed to numerous areas of research such as demography, predator-prey relationships, disease monitoring, livestock depredation, human-wolf interplay, and interactions with other predator species.

Each year as the population grows and stabilizes, the need for collaring and ear-tagging becomes more a question of science, ethics, and aesthetics, and less a question of necessity in terms of protecting wolves so they might recover. The truth is, we collar because we can. It's far more efficient for research (there is a limitless amount of knowledge to be gleaned), for management, and for control. But do we collar for the sake of the species? Some of the wolves have actively, physically rejected the collars. At least three of Yellowstone's packs have chewed each other's collars off. Clearly these animals are asserting their will. What might they be telling us? The Leopold pack chewed *all* their collars off, except for the alphas'. The response to this act of willfulness was to use the equivalent of spiked collars, adding brass brackets to the straps so the wolves couldn't chew through the leather. Rather than surrender to the wolves' volition we escalate the imposition of our own.

There are questions we can ask ourselves as a culture that might help us evaluate the appropriateness of such extensive collaring of wild animals within our most famous national park: How much autonomy and dignity are we willing to grant to a wild animal? We might also pose the question in the context of our national parks: What sort of expectation might we have for the treatment of wild animals inside a place like Yellowstone?

Remarkably, the policies governing the manipulation and research of wild animals varies greatly from park to park and superintendent to superintendent. In the case of Yellowstone, this flexibility is a blessing because the research department, with John Varley at its helm, is extremely protective of the park's wildlife and resources. Varley is one of the few scientists who does ask the sort of questions raised in this chapter. Nonetheless, Yellowstone is also subject to extreme political pressure, particularly from western livestock lobbies and the ranks of conservative western politicians—entities that have a different times advocated absurd policies such as fencing the park in order to contain its controversial migrating wildlife. Powerful conservative factions with considerable political clout, opposed to the return of wolves in the first place, would be delighted to see every wolf collared, ear-tagged, and aggressively controlled if they should venture outside park boundaries. Regardless of how much we would like to believe that science is objective, unfortunately its process is sometimes shaped by political pressures.

Unless the public conveys its sentiments, each park individually determines how much, how many, and how often animals are marked. Some park visitors feel that conspicuous markings, such as collars or ear tags, take the "wild" out of wild animals and contradict the original goal of preserving wildlife and scenic integrity in our national parks; they argue that the degree of manipulation necessary to use this technology is unacceptable within parks. Not only are these techniques rarely evaluated in terms of the risk they pose to individual animals, they are almost never judged on the basis of the aesthetic costs to wildlife observers, or in terms of the deeper ethical questions concerning the manipulation of wildlife in our national parks.

For me the issue of how much research is appropriate can be distilled into one question: Is the information we gain worth the invasion of a wild creature's life? If the answer is yes, then we must search further: How much information? How many animals? Does the information ultimately benefit the animals? Obviously there are circumstances in which compromising the safety or the autonomy of a few individuals is worthwhile because it benefits the population. I felt the Florida Panther Recovery Project in the Everglades provided an example of the ends justifying the means. Telemetry data obtained from collared panthers isolated the primary highway-crossing areas where many of the cats had been killed, and promoted the design of "wildlife underpasses" to reduce high mortality from automobile collisions. The panthers that have been collared have provided valuable information critical to the population's survival.

Unfortunately, researchers both in and outside national parks have become increasingly dependent on techniques that require the use of identification markers or telemetry equipment to carry out the most rudimentary fact-finding. Chris Servheen, a seasoned grizzly bear biologist in charge of grizzly recovery for the U.S. Fish and Wildlife Service, supervises numerous graduate students at the University of Montana. He claims that students, in particular, find a certain sexy mystique to be associated with radio technology. "It's gotten to the point that unless they're using telemetry they don't believe they're doing legitimate wildlife work. Using telemetry somehow ensures that research is 'modern.' I see graduate students who believe the only way to do any research is to slap a radio on an animal. There is an assumption that you have to trap and collar in order for research to be legitimate." Servheen believes very few research proposals seriously consider achieving their objectives by means other than telemetry.

Mardy Murie, in a discussion we had several years ago, expressed concern that the availability of technology may cultivate a "quick fix" mentality at the cost of real effort invested in observing wildlife. "Scientists nowadays have built up such a great reverence for all the technology," she said. "I guess people who question the technology are just considered to be old fogies, but I still have that feeling. I don't know how far we should allow ourselves to go with the technology. I think the concept of a national park should still be on the side of natural systems and natural activities. It seems to me there is a great deal of legitimate study that can be done in national parks without marking animals." Jack Morehead, the former superintendent of both the Everglades and Yosemite National Parks, agrees with Mardy. "Most researchers are not willing to go through the extra work. Frankly," he admitted, "I think researchers have gotten very complacent and lazy and they want a huge tag they can read from the road."

The collaring and tagging of Yellowstone's wolves has offered an unprecedented opportunity to watch the evolution of a canid culture. Much of the information contained in this book, ranging from Natasha's epic stories to the extraordinarily rich understanding of pack formation and individual mortality, has come from the research that collaring and tagging enabled. The genetic studies and the ability to monitor the interplay of packs, individual wolves, and other species has led to a new level of understanding in the fields of wolf biology and behavior. The research information has also given us insight into how ecological systems operate and into the extraordinary impact the presence or absence of one species can have on an entire ecosystem. We are fortunate to have such talented scientists as Doug Smith, and Mike Phillips before him, and recently Mike Jimenez, the Fish and Wildlife Service wolf recovery project leader assigned to Wyoming to collect, assimilate, and interpret the mind-boggling amounts of data into useful insights that inform and guide the management and protection of wolves.

On the other hand the technology sometimes make it easier to kill wolves; the tags and collars can be an asset in locating wolves that must be "removed" for "control purposes" because they have preyed on or pose a threat to livestock. If these tools were in the hands of individuals with less integrity than Doug Smith, Mike Phillips, or Mike Jimenez, Yellowstone could have troubling ethical issues to contend with. We still must weight the obvious benefits of doing the research against the costs it imposes on the wolves individually, their population collectively, and the public whose passionate voice and effort are responsible for the return of wolves in the first place.

Even though the act of restoring wolves to our oldest national park was biologically insignificant in the broader efforts of endangered species protection, it was a profoundly symbolic gesture by the American people, initiating a reexamination and recharting of our relationship with the wild. Wolves are symbolic and ours is a culture of symbols. We use symbols to tell our stories and to express our struggles. We have a way of distilling ideologies into incidents, processes into people. We understand the world through translation.

We create symbols—or attach symbolic importance to people and events—as a means of interpreting and translating our lives and our cultures. Rosa Parks's refusing to walk to the back of the bus was a minor event in the flood of life, but it had a major impact on the civil rights movement. Raising the flag at Iwo Jima was a seemingly insignificant accomplishment in World War II, but it had an electrifying effect on the morale of a war-weary nation. Restoring wolves to the West was more than just implementation of a law or the fine-tuning of an ecosystem, it was our nation grappling with its complicated relationship with the wild.

Bringing wolves back to Yellowstone was an act of raw faith, of abandon, of hope. It was an act that was intended to set free more than wolves. Perhaps we wanted to set free some part of ourselves by relinquishing a modicum of our precious predictability and control, to interrupt, if only symbolically, our dark march toward a world stripped of its wildness. It was an act of giving back something that we had taken, not just from the land or our first national park but from our souls. It was an act that conveyed the cultural desire and instinct to change, but it collided with the habit of our habit. As with the addict who promises to change, even desires to change, unless the underlying conditions and wounds that led to addiction in the first place are addressed, rarely is change possible. Thus the treatment of Yellowstone's wolves today offers a troubling reminder that history will repeat itself, the same madness will be enacted over and over, unless we succeed in healing the illness that led to our original action.

The bottom line is: the reintroduction of the gray wolf to Yellowstone has been a resounding success. (One is tempted to say "wildly successful.") They are reproducing at a great rate, have—for the most part—stayed out of trouble with the ranchers, and are expanding their territories into the surrounding ecosystem even faster than predicted.

On December 11, 1997, Judge Downes issued an opinion favoring the Farm Bureau and The Sierra Club Legal Defense Fund, ordering all reintroduced wolves and their offspring in Idaho, Montana, and Wyoming to be removed. He "stayed" his removal order, however, until the Tenth U.S. Circuit Court of Appeals could rule on the appeals that would inevitably be filed. In December of 1999 that court struck down all of Downes's arguments and completely upheld the Federal government and its actions. The other legal skirmishing has died down. These days the questions mostly revolve around when to downgrade the wolf, remove its statutory protections and make it just another member of the wildlife population.

But though this story has a happy ending, perhaps—like most real stories—it is the beginning of *another* story, another struggle we must have with ourselves, another opportunity to raise the bar. We enjoy the notion that we have been endowed by our Creator with "unalienable Rights," including "Life, Liberty and the pursuit of Happiness," but clearly those rights are of a somewhat philosophical, theoretical nature unless we collectively agree to—in actual practice—afford them to each other. There is a growing sentiment in America today that animals, too, have rights, and that we collectively should afford them, at the very least, more respect and consideration as the sentient, autonomous beings they clearly are. Of course, this flies in the face of Western civilization's stated assumption of man's dominion over the beasts. The way we resolve this conflict in our culture, or fail to, has much to do with who we are, who we will become, and the legacy we'll leave for generations to come.

Twenty-eight

❖ ❖ ❖

One has only to consider the life force . . . to lay the mind wide open to the mysteries—the order of things, the why and beginning. . . . One question leads inevitably to another, and all questions come full circle to the questioner, paused momentarily in his own journey under the sun and sky.

PETER MATTHIESSEN, *The Wind Birds*

O N A MAGICAL, heaven-hushed fall evening punctuated by the shuffles and grunts of bison and the fragile wail of coyotes, the luminous stars and colors of the northern lights streaked the skies above our home at Shadow Mountain. I witnessed the spectacle from the sage plain in front of our house where the ashes of our tiny son, lost in mid-pregnancy only months before, were strewn. That night, in the wake and wash of grief and the healing auroral wonder, a premonition fell like a star from the mysterious brew of radiance and hue that bathed the night sky—we would be given a daughter. Her brother, not destined for this earth, would guide her way into our world. Her name would be Aurora.

In another one of life's eerie synchronicities, I would learn less than a month later that I was pregnant. While researching the aurora borealis, I would discover that there are many mythologies associating the northern lights with fertility and conception. Candace Savage, in her beautiful book *Aurora,* describes how the Lakota Sioux believe the spirits of future generations waiting to be born create the aurora with their dance and how the central Asian Chuvash thought the lights were the goddess Suratan-tura (Birth-giving Heaven), believing the aurora was the sky giving birth to a son—thus the rolling and writhing shimmer—and she could be called upon to help women through labor. The Chinese believed that the aurora spectacle cast a fertility spell. Somewhat disconcerting, in light of my son's death, was the Iroquois belief that the aurora is the entry point into the Land of Souls, where the sky rises and falls to let spirits into the world beyond. In fact, the lights were seen as the spirits of dead ancestors by many aboriginal peoples. And so it would be that birth and death would be intimately entwined in the process of my pregnancy.

Fall surrendered to the onset of winter and the small life grew inside of me. The feeling of something "coming near" seeped through the chill of the November winds. We were heartsick to learn that my sister's cancer had returned, having spread through her lymph system and bones. Simultaneously, the wolves made their way down to the Tetons—they had been absent more than eighty years. The dark and mysterious parallel migration of the wild down the spine of the Rockies and through the slender backbone of my sister brought, with one, utter ecstasy and, with the other, blinding pain. The wild and its corresponding shadow seemed to be reaching ever deeper and more intimately into my life, forcing me to face its many forms of raw beauty, indifference, and cruelty.

When the wild comes near, something in us is called to attention, something jolts us into living each moment of life as it comes—precious, precarious, and fleeting. The arrival of wolves was greeted with a mixture of delight and dread in my home community. The mystery of their quicksilver presence, slipping in and out of the haze of winter frosts, the lingering notes of their howls, prompted hushed whispers and eager gossip. Everyone talked about where the wolves were, when, who had seen them. Sightings were considered privileged information, guarded greedily and shared pridefully. Even local ranchers, suspicious, reluctant, a little resigned, showed up with their binoculars at some of the overlooks where the wolves were frequently sighted. Few could resist the tingle, if not terror, of this new wild licking at our door. Three packs would ultimately trickle down from Yellowstone, pausing in the northern wilderness that rims the boundary of Grand Teton National Park before dropping down into the valley. I knew the place where they loitered—I had camped there illegally among dew-covered balsamroot on my first trip to Yellowstone twenty years before.

In the depth of winter the largest pack crossed through our yard in the middle of the night. Zany barked an excited greeting, I stirred, nestled deeper into the down nest of our bed, dreaming of long-legged canine silhouettes. My child, in utero, somersaulted in exuberant accompaniment to Zany's greeting. The next morning there would be tracks to confirm my dreams. I loved that the wolves came so near, nuzzling at the boundaries of our home, the dogs and my unborn child greeting them as they passed.

Sitting on the front porch in late April, rocking in a rain-damp cedar chair, I was telling stories and singing songs to my child (". . . if we could talk to the animals . . .") who cavorted like a playful seal inside my belly. The sun streamed down through a pocket of blue and I felt quiet and happy and sure of the world. The coyotes started howling; then a pair of sandhill cranes, who had only arrived the day before, joined their rippled cries to the coyotes' wails. Chickadees, downy woodpeckers, and myriad migrating warblers flitted through the still leafless aspens chirping with spring delight.

On an impulse I stood up and howled, a long, deep wolf howl, the first time I had howled since wolves arrived in the Tetons; just a statement to the world of my contentment and happiness. I sat back down on my rocker, my hands settled softly on my belly, satisfied, complete. A minute later an answer floated back. First one howl, then a second, a long, low moan. Distinctively wolf. I wanted to whoop and squeal and dance—a questionable undertaking for someone who looked like a very plump eggplant. I thumped on my belly and whispered urgently to my baby, "Did you hear that, did you HEAR THAT?" I howled again. Again I was answered.

Zany, a few yards away in her dog run, was frozen in rapt attention, her ears pricked hard to the east, her head slightly tilted in curiosity. Minutes passed, the air was heavy with silence. Only the birds twittered. Zany looked over at me and, catching my eye, she yowled, her version of a wink. I sat back down in my rocker, smiling, studying her studying me. I thought out loud, "At last I've found that dog a good home."

Siena Aurora Askins Rush was born on a late June morning. The light and shadows streaked across Antelope Flats, tumbling and taunting in a wild game of chase and charge reminiscent of the cinnamon-colored bison calves frolicking in the cool morning dampness. She came into the world with eyes beaming a dazzling feral blue and a dense crop of bison-brown hair tipped with wisps of blond as though she had been dipped in starlight. My sister, more beautiful and brave than ever, came to Wyoming to welcome her, to tell her about faith and fight and never giving in.

Less than a year later my sister Robin lost her long, brave fight against cancer on the night of May 10, 2000, at the age of forty-two. Only hours before, lying in her hospital bed, she held Siena, snuggling and whispering to her. Siena looked solemnly back at Robin, with the clear-eyed, fathomless gaze of newborn knowing, her little body pressed against the warmth of my sister's ravaged body in the way I remembered doing forty years before on a liver-colored Volkswagen seat. Looking at the two of them whom I love so dearly left me with an indelible image of life and death slipping by one another with a nod, and a knowing, to which I could only be witness. My sister died still fighting. She did not want to die, not one cell in her body resigned, but death took her, as deft and determined as a wolf taking its prey. I still can only reach for hope and bow to the wild's heart of darkness, while trying to bear "the unbearable knowing and knowing" that death teaches us. As Lorca wrote, "And yet hope pursues me, encircles me, bites me; like a dying wolf tightening his grip for the last time."

I am grateful my child was born into a world of wild things. Perhaps her first memories will be of sunlit meadows, of winking aspen leaves, and the puff-ball bark of antelope. Her childhood dreams will be filled with the guttural growl of rutting bison and the whispered whistle of raven's wings. There are so many things I look forward to sharing with this child—her first visit to an animal shelter, her first pony to roam the wilds of Wyoming, her first trip to Yellowstone.

About this time came the news we would have to leave Shadow Mountain. With the death of our landlord the homestead we occupied reverted back to national park ownership. The buildings will be removed or destroyed and, as it should be, the land will be given back to the animals. I will only visit this place on evening outings with my baby daughter by my side, perhaps nosing the car into the deep meadow grass as the sun's honey-warm rays sink behind the peaks.

The creatures will gather on the border of these lush aspen stands which sheltered me for the last decade. On those nights I will count the deer and elk for my child, telling her about the fawns and calves. Perhaps on the soft slope where four aspen trees bow together, we will see a young coyote with a faintly cocoa-colored ruff and snowy white chest who embodies a trace of my beloved Bristol. Perhaps on one of those nights we'll hear the low sweet moan of a single wolf, one of the granddaughters of the great matriarch of Yellowstone wolves. I will tell my daughter the story of a wolf named Natasha and what it means to keep a promise. And the sun will set, and the animals will fade like druids back into the trees and my story will drift into silence. Dark will descend, caressing the forests that fall like gleaming ebony hair down the shoulders of this place I love called Shadow Mountain.

Epilogue

Let the beauty we love be what we do.
There are hundreds of ways to kneel and
kiss the ground.

RUMI, NUMBER 82 IN *The Open Secret*
TRANSLATED BY COLEMAN BANKS

TODAY—LATE NOVEMBER 2001—at least 220 wolves in twenty-one packs roam the reaches of the Greater Yellowstone Ecosystem. Approximately 140 wolves in nine packs are inside the Yellowstone park boundaries, and another sixty in twelve packs are outside the park. This year all twenty-one packs had pups, totaling at least eighty.

In the fall of 1999 Natasha began her departure from the Rose Creek pack after her daughter, Number 18, became the alpha female. Number 8, Natasha's mate, died of natural causes the following summer. Natasha left and returned, left and returned, and then she left permanently. She wandered alone for a while, her black coat by then having fully given way to shadowed silver gray. Just about the time biologists thought she might have disappeared, she showed up in a remote area of Wyoming west of the park. She had been joined by a large, black uncollared male. They were christened the Beartooth Pair. They were later joined by one of Natasha's granddaughters, Number 19, who had three pups this year, elevating their designation to the Beartooth *pack*.

Natasha has more than answered my plea whispered to her back in Hinton, Alberta: she did indeed become "the mother of Yellowstone's wolves." In 1999, the last year for which data has been tabulated, 71 percent of the total wolf population in the ecosystem were her descendants.

Although exact current figures aren't available, today her lineage is represented in well over half of the wolves living in Yellowstone. (As the wolves split into new packs and disperse farther, they become harder to track and more blanks and question marks start showing up in the columns of data.) Her direct descendants lead five of Yellowstone's northern wolf packs and comprise parts of the Chief Joseph I and II, Leopold, Rose Creek, Druid Peak, Sunlight Basin, Absaroka, Swan Lake, Cougar Creek, and Mollie's packs. After Natasha arrived in Yellowstone, her deep black sleekness slowly shifted into patterns of silver, pewter, and ash, becoming lighter, moving through a gradation of shades of gray. Biologists say they are seeing the same pattern of coat color change in many of her offspring. Some of her progeny even reflect her physical carriage and manner of movement: strong, lean, ready—living evidence of how one animal, one turn of fate, can make a difference.

In 2000, a pack of wolves derived from the original Crystal Creek pack (Mollie had helped to carry the original alpha female into the Crystal pen, the first wolf to be brought into Yellowstone) was renamed Mollie's pack in honor of her contribution to Yellowstone wolf recovery. This pack also contains one of Natasha's sons and a grandson, which I'm sure would delight Mollie. In keeping with Mollie's wishes, we had scattered some of her ashes at the site the year after her death. This year Mollie's pack whelped six pups—all of which appear to have survived thus far, an auspicious sign that this memorial pack will flourish, a fitting tribute to my dear friend for whom they are named.

Recent news brought me great joy. After six years, the battery in Natasha's radio collar has just gone dead. No attempts will be made to recollar her. Her dense silver gray coat has now turned snow white except for a hint of black on her tail. Translucent swan-flight white, luminous burning white, as though she penetrated the colors of cream and fleece and pearl and ivory white to reach through to the steel blue on the other side. This is an earned white. From that fated day in Alberta—January 10, 1995—she has passed through all the complicated shades of gray, through death and grief in all of its manifestations, through the utter heart of darkness, and now she will at last be able to slip back into mystery, into the light and shadow from which she came, free of the meddling of our race, free from our good intentions. When the mother of the Yellowstone wolves dies, where she dies, and how, I hope we will never know; it should be that way. The wild's grace and mercy.

Select Bibliography

❖ ❖ ❖

The following list includes books I refer to in the text, a partial list of sources for this book, and various titles which have shaped my ideas and thinking over the years. This bibliography is by no means complete. I intend it as a convenience for those who wish to further explore the themes of *Shadow Mountain*.

Nadya Aisenberg, ed. *We Animals: Poems of Our World*. San Francisco: Sierra Club Books, 1989.

Henry Beston. *The Outermost House*. New York: Ballantine Books, 1928.

Robert Bly. *A Little Book on the Human Shadow*, edited by William Booth. San Francisco: HarperCollins, 1988.

David Clark Burks, ed. *Place of the Wild*. Washington, D. C., and Covelo, Calif.: Island Press/Shearwater Books, 1994.

Neil Evernden. *The Natural Alien: Humankind and the Environment*. Toronto, Buffalo, and London: University of Toronto Press, 1985.

Select Bibliography

Roger Grenier. *The Difficulty of Being a Dog,* translated by Alice Kaplan. Chicago and London: University of Chicago Press, 2000.

John Haines. *Living Off the Country: Essays of Poetry and Place.* Ann Arbor: University of Michigan Press, 1981.

Linda Hogan, Deena Metzger, and Brenda Peterson, eds. *Intimate Nature: The Bond Between Women and Animals.* New York: Fawcett Columbine, 1998.

Derrick Jensen, ed. *Listening to the Land: Conversations About Nature, Culture, and Eros.* San Francisco: Sierra Club Books, 1995.

Robert A. Johnson with Jerry M. Ruhl. *Balancing Heaven and Earth: A Memoir of Visions, Dreams, and Realizations.* San Francisco: HarperCollins, 1998.

Christopher Lasch. *The Culture of Narcissism: American Life in an Age of Diminishing Expectations.* New York: W. W. Norton & Company, 1979.

Barry Holstun Lopez. *Of Wolves and Men.* New York: Charles Scribner's Sons, 1978.

Federico García Lorca. *The Selected Poems of Federico García Lorca,* edited by Frederico García Lorca and Donald M. Allen. New York: New Directions, 1955.

Thomas J. Lyon and Peter Stine, eds. *On Nature's Terms: Contemporary Voices.* College Station: Texas A&M University Press, 1992.

Jim Mason. *An Unnatural Order: Uncovering the Roots of Our Domination of Nature and Each Other.* New York: Simon & Schuster, 1993.

Peter Matthiessen. *Men's Lives: The Surfmen and Baymen of the South Fork.* New York: Random House, 1986.

L. David Mech. *The Wolf.* Garden City and New York: The American Museum of Natural History, The Natural History Press, 1970.

Shierry Weber Nicholsen. *The Love of Nature and the End of the World: The Unspoken Dimensions of Environmental Concern.* Cambridge, Mass., and London: The MIT Press, 2001.

Gary Paul Nabhan and Stephen Trimble. *The Geography of Childhood: Why Children Need Wild Places.* Boston: Beacon Press, 1994.

Thich Nhat Hanh. *The Miracle of Mindfulness!: A Manual on Meditation.* Boston: Beacon Press, 1975.

Select Bibliography

Rainer Maria Rilke. *New Poems,* translated by J. B. Leishman. New York: New Directions Books, 1964. Also Stephen Mitchell, ed. and transl. *The Selected Poetry of Rainer Maria Rilke.* New York: Vintage Books, 1989. Also Robert Bly, transl. *Selected Poems of Rainer Maria Rilke.* New York: Harper & Row, 1981.

Paul Shepard. *The Others: How Animals Made Us Human.* Washington, D.C., and Covelo, Calif.: Island Press/Shearwater Books, 1996. Also *Nature and Madness.* San Francisco: Sierra Club Books, 1982. Also Florence R. Shepard, ed. *Coming Home to the Pleistocene.* Washington, D.C., and Covelo, Calif.: Island Press/Shearwater Books, 1998. Also *Traces of an Omnivore.* Washington, D.C., and Covelo, Calif.: Island Press/Shearwater Books, 1996. Also Paul Shepard, ed. *The Only World We've Got: A Paul Shepard Reader.* San Francisco: Sierra Club Books, 1996. Also *Thinking Animals: Animals and the Development of Human Intelligence.* Athens, Ga., and London: University of Georgia Press, 1978. Also *The Tender Carnivore and the Sacred Game.* Athens, Ga., and London: University of Georgia Press, 1973.

Donald Snow. *Inside the Environmental Movement: Meeting the Leadership Challenge.* Washington, D.C., and Covelo, Calif.: Island Press, 1992.

Gary Snyder. *The Practice of the Wild.* San Francisco: North Point Press, 1990.

Jack Turner. *The Abstract Wild.* Tucson: University of Arizona Press, 1996.

Connie Zweig and Jeremiah Abrams, eds. *Meeting the Shadow: The Hidden Power of the Dark Side of Human Nature.* New York: Penguin Putnam, 1991.

Sources, Resources, and Suggested Reading

❖ ❖ ❖

The following are books I recommend for readers who are interested in a comprehensive and detailed account of the Yellowstone wolf reintroduction effort.

Hank Fischer. *Wolf Wars.* Helena and Billings, Mont.: Falcon, 1995.

Thomas McNamee. *The Return of the Wolf to Yellowstone.* New York: Henry Holt, 1997.

Michael K. Phillips and Douglas W. Smith. *The Wolves of Yellowstone.* Stillwater, Minn.: Voyager Press, 1996.

Websites

❖ ❖ ❖

There are numerous websites that explore wolf issues. The following I've found to be the most accurate and up-to-date sources for information on the status of wolves in the greater Yellowstone ecosystem. The first two are official government sites and tend to offer straightforward statistics. The third site is coordinated by a private individual and at times the information presented is subject to interpretation, but overall I find it to be a valuable amalgamation of press stories, government statistics, informed debate, and personal anecdote.

National Park Service: www.nps.gov/yell/nature/animals/wolf

National Fish and Wildlife Service: www.r6.fws.gov/wolf

Ralph Maughan's Wolf Report: www.forwolves.org/ralph/index.html

To Help Support
Wolf Recovery

❖ ❖ ❖

The following organizations are good sources for information about wolves and wolf reintroduction, and are worthy of your support.

The Yellowstone Wolf Project
Yellowstone Center for Resources
Yellowstone National Park
P.O. Box 168
Mammoth, WY 82190
www.nps.gov/yell/nature/animals/wolf

Defenders of Wildlife
National Headquarters
1101 14th Street NW, #1400
Washington, DC 20005
Tel. (202) 682–9400
www.defenders.org

To Help Support Wolf Recovery

International Wolf Center
1396 Highway 169
Ely, MN 55731
(218) 365–4695
www.wolf.org

For people interested in Idaho wolf recovery:

Wolf Education and Research Center
418 Nez Perce
P.O. Box 217
Winchester, ID 83555
(208) 924–6960
www.wolfcenter.org

Notes

◈ ◈ ◈

CHAPTER 3

26 *"the deep current of pre-comprehension running silently"*: Paul Shepard, *Traces of an Omnivore* (Washington, D.C., and Covelo, Calif.: Island Press/Shearwater Books, 1996), p. 168. Throughout *Shadow Mountain* I reference Paul Shepard's work both directly, through quotation, and indirectly in the exploration of ideas related to our alienation from the natural world. For anyone interested in a rigorous and thorough examination of man's relationship with animals and wild nature, I highly recommend Shepard's work. The following titles are those I found most useful in my research: *The Others: How Animals Made Us Human* (Washington, D.C., and Covelo, Calif.: Island Press/Shearwater Books, 1996), *Nature and Madness* (San Francisco: Sierra Club Books, 1982), *Coming Home to the Pleistocene*, Florence R. Shepard, ed. (Washington, D.C., and Covelo, Calif.: Island Press/Shearwater Books, 1998), *The Only World We've Got: A Paul Shepard Reader*, Paul Shepard, ed. (San Francisco: Sierra Club Books, 1996), *Thinking Animals: Animals and the Development of Human Intelligence* (Athens,

Notes

Ga., and London: University of Georgia Press, 1978). *The Tender Carnivore and the Sacred Game.* (Athens, Ga., and London: University of Georgia Press, 1973).

For those interested in an excellent overview of Shepard's ideas, I recommend the August 1997 (vol. III, no. 3) "Paul Shepard Remembered" issue of a little-known but superbly crafted nonprofit publication called *Wild Duck Review,* edited and published by Casey Walker. Many of the topics addressed by *WDR* in its wide-ranging investigations of today's cultural, environmental, and scientific issues parallel the ideas probed in *Shadow Mountain.* I urge anyone interested in original, provocative, well-informed discourse on the cutting edge of environmental thinking to check it out. Wild Duck Review, P.O. Box 388, Nevada City, CA 95959; tel. (530) 478–0134; www.WildDuckReview.com.

CHAPTER 4

31 *Our forefathers didn't just want to control wolves*: Barry Holstun Lopez, *Of Wolves and Men* (New York: Charles Scribner's Sons, 1978). Lopez explores this phenomenon of projection and displacement with tremendous insight and thoroughness on pp. 137–152 and 167–199.

31 *In fact we spend over half a million of our tax dollars*: Wildlife Damage Review. The review is a credible nonprofit watchdog organization that provides much-needed scrutiny of federal Wildlife Services (formerly Animal Damage Control) programs administered under the U.S. Department of Agriculture. It is an excellent resource for information on predator control issues as well as waste, fraud, and abuse within the ADC wildlife management programs. Wildlife Damage Review, P.O. Box 85218, Tucson, AZ 85754; tel. (520) 884–0883; wdr@azstarnet.com. Another good source for similar materials, especially related to the northern Rockies, is the Predator Project, P.O. Box 6733, Bozeman, MT 59771; tel. (406) 587–3389; predproj@avicom.net.

32 *Goodness will reign in the world*: Andrew Bard Schmookler, "Acknowledging Our Inner Split," in *Meeting the Shadow: The Hidden Power of the Dark Side of Human Nature,* Connie Zweig and Jeremiah Abrams, eds. (New York: Penguin Putnam, 1991), p. 191.

33 *The word* wild *is like a gray fox*: Gary Snyder, *The Practice of the Wild* (San Francisco: North Point Press, 1990), pp. 9–11.

33 *Too often "wildness" is a glib*: Jack Turner, *The Abstract Wild* (Tucson: University of Arizona Press, 1996), pp. 28–29. Although I only quote *The Abstract Wild* directly in a couple of places in the book, the influence of Turner's writing and ideas has been very significant in the creation of *Shadow Mountain.* I urge anyone interested in the concept of "wildness" to review Turner's work. From conservation biology to grassroots activism, philosophy to applied science, the issues related to wildness that Turner raises are both original and potent, and

306

have already begun to affect the basic assumptions and theories upon which our ecological thinking is based.

35 *Jung referred to it as holding*: Connie Zweig and Jeremiah Abrams, eds., *Meeting the Shadow: The Hidden Power of the Dark Side of Human Nature* (New York: Penguin Putnam, 1991), p. 271.

CHAPTER 6

53 *The theory that our childhood contact with the natural world and animals is critical*: Gary Paul Nabhan and Stephen Trimble, *The Geography of Childhood: Why Children Need Wild Places* (Boston: Beacon Press, 1994). Nowhere have I seen this concept more beautifully explored than in *The Geography of Childhood*. Nabhan and Trimble invoke the ideas of Edith Cobb, Paul Shepard, Jean Piaget, and Robert Cole, and translate them into an accessible and personal stroll through the philosophies of childhood development and the effects of the natural world on child rearing in the developed nations. I'm drawn to their stories because they address a fundamental ingredient to the success of future conservation—an examination of child-rearing practices and the importance of childhood exposure to the natural world and animals. Also, they tell their own stories of childhood enchantment that led to lives devoted to the preservation of the wild. Although the academic theories are relevant in establishing context, it is our own shared stories that will ultimately offer example and guidance in restoring a healthy relationship with the natural world.

57 *The wilderness is out there*: John Haines, "Notes from and Interrupted Journal," in *Place of the Wild*, David Clark Burks, ed. (Washington, D.C., and Covelo, Calif.: Island Press/Shearwater Books, 1994), p. 111.

58 *The elegance of Shepard's thinking*: Shepard, "A Posthistoric Primitivism" and "The Wilderness Is Where My Genome Lives," both in *Traces of an Omnivore*, pp. 165–214 and 215–221.

59 *There is a profound, inescapable need for animals*: Shepard, "The Ark of the Mind" in *Traces of an Omnivore*, p. 3.

CHAPTER 8

81 *The coincidences and themes that have repeated*: Robert A. Johnson with Jerry M. Ruhl, *Balancing Heaven and Earth: A Memoir of Visions, Dreams, and Realizations* (San Francisco: HarperCollins, 1998). The ideas and insights presented in this book were very helpful to me in trying to understand and articulate a pattern of remarkable "coincidences" that occurred during the next fifteen years, many of which are chronicled in *Shadow Mountain*. Johnson, a

renowned Jungian scholar, explores the notion of "fate and coincidence" in his provocative work that traces the story of his extraordinary life. The book explores the mysterious forces that guide us and shape who we are, something he calls "the slender threads of synchronicity," the patterns that give meaning to our dreams and what seem to be preordained experiences.

CHAPTER 15

157 *We need another and wiser and perhaps a more mystical concept*: Henry Beston, *The Outermost House* (New York: Ballantine, 1928).

CHAPTER 16

163 *Thich Nhat Hanh had been speaking*: Thich Nhat Hanh, *The Miracle of Mindfulness!: A Manual on Meditation* (Boston: Beacon Press, 1975). The story quoted is by James Forest and appears on pp. 102–103.

CHAPTER 17

172 *But rather than chronicling the endless political battles*: The political details of this period are in Hank Fischer's excellent book, *Wolf Wars* (Helena and Billings, Mont.: Falcon, 1995).
174 *Effective protest is grounded in anger*: Jack Turner, "The Abstract Wild" in *On Nature's Terms: Contemporary Voices,* Thomas J. Lyon and Peter Stine, eds. (College Station: Texas A&M University Press, 1992), p. 89.

CHAPTER 24

242 *In spite of numerous monitoring flights:* I am deeply indebted to Tim Eicher for the documents he supplied and the extensive telephone interviews he granted me in reviewing the details of the McKittrick story. I also would like to credit the excellent on-site research and record of these events chronicled by my friend Tom McNamee, first in *Outside* magazine and later in his excellent book *The Return of the Wolf to Yellowstone* (see suggested reading), which informed this chapter.

CHAPTER 26

266 *Shepard's denouncement of pets has rocked the ranks*: Shepard, *The Others: How Animals Made Us Human,* pp. 140–152.

Acknowledgments

❖ ❖ ❖

FROM THE TIME of making my promise to Natasha, through the years
of fulfilling it, to interpreting its meaning in the pages of this book, the
arc of this story, this passion, has spanned a twenty-two-year period.
This book is the product of conversations, collaborations, and the blessings of
having lived among a fertile community of friends who are thinkers and activists, all of whom have contributed to its content. I passionately believe in
the power and importance of naming names and offering credit where it's
due. It's a very difficult, if not impossible, undertaking to adequately acknowledge all the people who have supported me both professionally and
personally over those years, but I will try. I thank the many who are un-
named, and for any omissions or oversights, I offer my sincerest apologies.

It is to my parents, Raymond Askins and Christine Ehrhart, that I owe the
greatest debt, for their sacrifice and far-reaching wisdom in choosing to rear
their children in the north of Michigan. That choice had a profound impact
on my life. I am grateful, too, for the support and encouragement they and

my stepfather, Gerald Ehrhart, gave me throughout the writing of this book. To Charles and Elisabeth Askins I owe the glee of having been an adored grandchild. Your gifts of love and laughter I will carry my whole life. To my sister, Robin Askins, who taught me how preciously fleeting life can be—it was my honor to bear witness to your burning faith and courage. You are my angel and this book was immeasurably deepened by your irascible and unstoppable spirit. I love you. And without my brother Craig, my guiding star, this book would not exist. The gods showered me with immeasurable blessings in granting me your presence as a brother.

The bright spirits and quick wit of my stepsons, Benjamin and Richard Rush, have lit the long path of my work with wolves and with writing. To my son Mikhail: I know your spirit is woven through these words like a bright color stitched through a quilt. From you I learned tenderness, and for that I am thankful. To my dear daughter, Siena Aurora—it is for and because of you, and your fierce, intrepid spirit, my little one, that I wish and am able to offer these personal pages for others to read. This book is, at its heart, a prayer for the world in which I want you to grow up. I hope you will always have wild places and wild creatures for your solace, and that they will hold you, help you, inspire you, and nourish you as they have me.

I thank my extended family for their support of my husband and me through the rigors of shared parenting and independent creative careers. My beloved late mother-in-law, Mollie Rush, a stalwart conservationist, was a source of much inspiration. Susan, Bobby, and Andrea Rush, and my sister-in-law, Janet Whelan, supplied good humor, delectable meals, warm beds, child care, and endless encouragement.

I thank Ms. Anne Sykes Ekstrom, Dale Parsons, Rick Casper, and Bob Wollenberg, whose skill and enthusiasm had great influence on me. I am greatly indebted to Dr. John Mark Thompson, my advisor at Kalamazoo College, who cleared the way for my senior thesis on wolves. I also thank Dr. Lewis Batts and Dr. Kim Cummings for their guidance and support, and the late Bill Pruitt, who facilitated the opportunity for me to go to Africa. For the experience that ignited the passion to pursue my work I offer my sincere gratitude to Dr. Erich Klinghammer, Ms. Patricia Goodman, Monte Sloan, and all the other committed people at Wolf Park, and I also thank Colleen Cabot at the Teton Science School for her leadership.

I thank Rod Drewien, Dave Mech, Frank Craighead, and Mardy Murie for living their passions of infinite curiosity about the ways of the wild, and in so doing teaching the rest of us. Thanks goes to my dear friend Jeff Foott, who, after so many others had taught me how to look for wild creatures in wild places, taught me how to actually *see* them. I thank Steve Kellert, Joe Miller, and the teaching staff at the Yale School of Forestry and Environmental Studies, my writing teachers at Yale, especially Leslie Moore, who made me believe a good metaphor could change the world, and Ed Ricciuti for his big heart and patient instruction. A deep bow to Peter Matthiessen for his example as conservationist, writer, teacher, and friend. His integrity as a human being, his passionate belief in the worth of words well-crafted, and his discerning toughness and compassion as a writing teacher have all benefited this book. I thank him for his friendship, which has been a guiding light in my life, and has served as inspiration, navigation, and illumination throughout The Wolf Fund's work and the writing of this book. While I was at Yale I received an Edna Bailey Sussman Fund grant and the Outdoor Writers of America Bodie McDowell scholarship, both of which provided much needed funds for attending Yale and significantly enabled my writing studies. I thank those organizations and their supporters.

Without the vision, guidance, time, energy, and resources of the people who served on The Wolf Fund's board and advisory board, that little feral organization would never have existed: Thomas Campbell, Susie Cannon, Glenn Ekey, Gordon Glover, Arvid Nelson, Tom Rush, Martha Schoonover, Laura Snook, Sue Barton, Michael Bean, Luigi Boitani, Yvon Chouinard, Carolyn (Scotty) Dejanikus, Barbara (Bargo) Fargo, Harrison Ford, Curt Gowdy, Dr. Stephen Kellert, Edward H. (Ted) Ladd, George Lamb, Dr. David Love, Peter Matthiessen, Thomas J. P. McHenry, Dr. L. David Mech, Margaret (Mardy) Murie, Robert Redford, Dr. George Schaller, Ted Turner, Caroll L. (Sonny) Wainwright, John Weaver, P.A.B. (Pete) Widener, and Ted Williams.

A small cadre of exceptional people assisted as The Wolf Fund's staff, satellite consultants, and volunteers *extraordinaire*. Collectively they moved mountains and it was my great honor to work alongside them. My deepest thanks go to my core crew over the years: Jill Welter, Nicholas Lapham, Ellen Leventhal, Mollie Frantz, Eve Throop; I would also like to thank Libby Crews, Laura Henderson, Pricilla Marden, Joe Marshall, Sidney Smith, Susan Stone, Rob Underwood, Brian Whitlock, and Jennie (Wood) Sheldon for their time, effort, and talent.

Acknowledgments

There were several people whose independent work was such an integral part of The Wolf Fund that I can't imagine it having existed, functioned, or succeeded without them. Susan Alexander from the Public Media Center was both a cherished friend and fiercely effective press agent for our mission. A special thanks to Robert Redford for his narration of The Wolf Fund's public service announcement, which introduced millions to our work. Sue Barton, our fiery godmother and volunteer publicist, guided and helped us, single-handedly introducing half the country, if not the world, to the issue. And Adrienne and Jeff Pollard, the designers of all The Wolf Fund's materials, who understood on every level what I meant when I said, "It will be poetry, not politics, that will bring wolves back to Yellowstone." Jeff and Adrienne worked so hard for so long and for so little that no words can possibly encompass all the dimensions of my gratitude for their work, their spirit, their constancy, and most of all, their dearly held friendship. I would also like to offer tribute to our legal angel, Kim Cannon, who deftly and precisely delivered the essential legal argument for Yellowstone wolf reintroduction at a pivotal moment.

My thanks to E. Geoffrey Verney, Debbie McGilvery, and the staff at Monadnock Paper Mills, a small company in the foothills of New Hampshire that provided recycled paper for nearly all of The Wolf Fund's printed materials. Their commitment to beauty, quality, and a sustainable environment exemplified the possibilities for collaboration between commerce and conservation.

Over the years a number of writer and photographer friends shared their work to support The Wolf Fund's, allowing us the use of their photographs, poems, articles, editorials, essays, or creating new work for our publications. Many of these people have also been very supportive and offered patient encouragement for my own writing, both this book and efforts that preceded it. I owe a great debt to Rick Bass, Wolfgang Bayer, Wendell Berry, Jon Bowermaster, Jim Brandenburg, Bill Campbell, Bruce Davidson, Nicholas Dawidoff, Garth Dowling, Jeff Foott, Jim Harrison, Hanna Hinchman, Bob Landis, Barry Lopez, Tom Mangleson, Peter Matthiessen, Tom McNamee, William S. Merwin, Richard Nelson, Geoff O'Gara, Brenda Petersen, David Quammen, Susan Reed, Tim Sandlin, Monte Sloan, Gary Snyder, David Swift, Mary Tall Mountain, Jack Turner, Maryanne Vollers, Ted Williams, Terry Tempest Williams, Art Wolfe, and Ted Wood.

For their friendship, their support of The Wolf Fund or the wolf issue, and for their contributions to our work I would like to offer special thanks to the following people and organizations: Bob Anderson, Gene Ball, Alexandra Ballantine, Rocky Barker, Pat and Janie Beattie, Thom Beers, Nick Boxer, Gertrude Brennan, Carl and Susi Brown, Lee Bynum and Betty Miller, Denise Casey, the Liz Claiborne and Arthur Ortenberg Foundation, Tim Clark, John and Barbara Cleveland, Roger Cohn and Patty Brown, Coldwater Creek, Wendy Condrat, Conservation International, Bob Crabtree, Marcia Craighead and the Craighead Family, Susan Crosser, Paul Dolan, the Dornan Family, Libby Ellis, Environment NOW, Lil Erickson, Bob and Linda Ewing, Bronson and Melinda Fargo, the Fingerhut Foundation, the French Foundation, Valerie Gates, the Geraldine R. Dodge Foundation, Gretchen Glickman, Bruce Gordon, Michael Grieco, Guilford Travel, Jim Halfpenny, the Harder Foundation, Geneen Haugen, John and Hillary Hemmingway, the Homeland Foundation, Alan Horn, Bill and Joffa Kerr, Beedee Ladd, George Lamb, Tony and Burks Lapham, Robert and Betty Lidner, Manuel and Debra Lopez, Rick Luskin, Andrew Melnykovych, Esther Margolis, Thayne and Kathleen Maynard, Robbyn McFadden, Scott McMillion, David Mills and Stephanie Lynn, Michael Milstein, Clark and Veda Moulton, Dan Neal, the Norcross Foundation, Roger and Lyn O'Neil, Gil and Margaret Ordway, John Passacantano, Patagonia, Inc., Leigh Perkins, Doug Pope, Project Lighthawk, the Public Media Center, Burt and Meg Raynes, Richard Reagan and Sonya Manzano, Charlotte and Rich Reid, the Rex Foundation, Peter Richardson, Allison and Peter Rockefeller, Laurance Rockefeller, Steven Rockefeller, Sheila Sandubrae, the late Len and Sandy Sargent and the Cinnebar Foundation, Gary and Beth Schuler, the Schumann Foundation, Pete Seligman, Gerry and Imagine Spence, Emily Stevens, David and Joan Stokes, Pete Stranger, David Swift, Gary Tabor, Paul Tebbel, Colleen Thompson, Angus Thuermer, David Titcomb, Judith Tukitch, Laura Utley, Lucy Waletzky, Mark Walters, Joyce Weldon, Sibyl and Tom Wiancko, Todd Wilkinson, and Paul Winter. To the many more who have not been named, I thank you for the myriad ways you sustained and facilitated our work.

A special thanks to Penny Maldonado and Corrine O'Brien at the Moose Post Office, for care and kindness above and beyond the call of duty; the staff at The Valley Bookstore, who were always ready to accommodate urgent reference needs; and the excellent staff at the Teton County Library for their support of The Wolf Fund's requests and for their assistance in the research phase of this book. There were also many members of the print and broadcast media whose evenhanded treatment of a contentious subject brought Yellowstone wolf recovery into the national consciousness. I sincerely thank you.

It was a great privilege to work with so many talented conservationists from the broad array of nonprofit groups involved in wolf recovery. The knowledge, talent, tenacity, and patience of my friend and colleague Hank Fisher from Defenders of Wildlife inspired me and taught me much. His Defenders teammates, past and present, deserve tremendous credit, among them Evan Hirsche, Cindy Shogan, Rupert Cutler, Roger Schlickeisen, and Dick Randall. Tom France of the National Wildlife Federation provided legal guidance and cool-headed strategic planning thoughout the twenty years of battle, as did coworkers, particularly Tom Dougherty and Steve Torbitt. The tireless efforts of Pat Tucker and Bruce Weide and their organization, Wild Sentry, made (and continues to make) a significant contribution to wolf education. I would like to thank Tom McNanee, fellow writer, activist, and hell-raiser, for his good work and collaboration on many fronts during the long battle. I thank Whitney Tilt and the National Fish and Wildlife Foundation for their critical support of the wolf recovery effort. His sage wisdom and strength of character was a beacon through the long, shadowed years of politics and legal maneuvers. My debt to Michael Bean of the Environmental Defense Fund both personally and professionally is enormous.

There were so many conservationists who worked hard on this project, on both the local and national levels, that it is impossible to name them all. Those who happened to be in The Wolf Fund's orbit include Suzanne Laverty of the Wolf Education and Research Center; Michael Scott, formerly at the Wilderness Society; Terri Martin and Brien Culhane, formerly at the National Parks and Conservation Association; Wayne Pacelle at the Humane Society; Nichole Evans at Alaska Wildlife Alliance; Betsy Buffington and Liz Howell at the Wyoming Chapter of the Sierra Club; all the folks at the Predator Project, the Greater Yellowstone Coalition, National Audubon Society, the Fund for Animals, the Idaho Conservation League, the International Wolf Center, Mission Wolf, Wolf Haven, and Sinapu.

Wolf recovery would not have been possible without the courage and integrity of Bruce Babbitt, secretary of the interior during the Clinton administration, who changed the course of history. Babbitt's stellar staff was

Acknowledgments

exceptional. Particularly key were the roles of Tom Collier, Don Barry, Brooks Yeager, Molly Poag, and Keven Sweeney. They made all the difference. I would also like to acknowledge the contribution of Congressman Wayne Owens (Democrat from Utah) and thank him for his leadership on wolves in the late 1980s.

At the National Park Service, William Penn Mott, director during the Reagan years, was the first to advocate the return of wolves to Yellowstone. He was a hero. Within the ranks of the National Park Service, Bob Barbee served as superintendent of Yellowstone during the long, embattled years of garnering public support and building a political foundation for the vision of wolf reintroduction. I owe Bob tremendous thanks for all the ways in which he supported both the work of The Wolf Fund and me personally. For information and insight, for guidance and mentoring, I owe great thanks to John Varley, director of Yellowstone Center for Resources, and to Wayne Brewster, his deputy director. I also offer my gratitude for the contributions the entire Yellowstone National Park staff, particularly Norm Bishop, Paul Schullery, Marsha Karle, Amy Vanderbelt, Dan Sholley, Mark Johnson, and Ginny and Dave Cowen, made to wolf recovery.

The credit for the extraordinary success of the actual reintroduction goes to Yellowstone's courageous (and, sadly, recently departed) superintendent Mike Finley, and to the wolf project leaders, Mike Phillips and Doug Smith. The wolves could not have been appointed better guardians. I also thank Mike, Doug, and their gallant assistant, Deb Guernsey, for sharing information vital to this book.

In the U.S. Fish and Wildlife Service (USFWS), the other primary government agency charged with the recovery of wolves, the directors during the period were John Turner and Mollie Beattie, who are discussed in the preceding chapters; after Mollie's death Jamie Clark succeeded her. Jamie deserves great credit for her excellent oversight of the project. USFWS Washington staffs, regional directors, and field personnel also deserve credit for sharing the vision and implementing it.

In his capacity as the federal point person on wolves there was no one who gave more of himself (and continues to do so) than USFWS wolf project leader, Ed Bangs. It was Bangs's expert leadership and unflappable manner on the ground that led his agency to victory. Hundreds of times he assisted The Wolf Fund with everything from basic policy and legal background informa-

315

tion to detailed biological insights and explanations that guided our efforts. USFWS personnel whom I would especially like to thank include Doug Crowe, Joe Fontaine, Dale Harmes, Mike Jimenez, Ralph Morganwick, Sharon Rose, and Carol Tenney. I am indebted to Tim Eicher, the USFWS special agent from the Division of Law Enforcement whose good work led to the McKittrick conviction, for his help in researching that portion of the book. There are a number of wolf biologists I would like to thank individually: Steve Fritts of the USFWS for his role in planning the reintroduction logisitics; Carter Niemeyer from Wildlife Services for his role in both the reintroduction and recovery efforts; John Talbott and Jay Lawson of Wyoming Game and Fish, who helped bring the state and federal entities together; and Jay Gore and Timm Kaminski, both of whom were involved in the parallel wolf recovery efforts in Idaho.

Those to whom I owe the greatest debt are, of course, Dr. L. David Mech and John Weaver, whose roles are described in the text. I consider it a great privilege and honor to have fledged with the wings their guidance and training gave me. I am also grateful to my dear friend Luigi Boitani, one of the world's premier wolf biologists, whose friendship was a poetic refuge during endless discussion on management and control. I thank him and his lovely wife, Stefania Bartoli, and daughter, Caterina, for their warm hospitality at Pentolina, Italy, nestled in the clay-colored hills outside of Siena, where Tom and I basked during our honeymoon, healing from the long years of wolf wars—a place so nurturing and beautiful that our daughter bears its name.

This book is rooted in friendship and enabled by the generosity and kindness of many people. I am particularly indebted to a number of people whose intervention, support, and encouragement made it possible for me to complete this book. I feel privileged to have Dr. Bruce Hayse as a friend and physician, a person of great capacity, compassion, and endurance. You have seen me through. I thank you. I also am deeply indebted to Dr. Don Counts for the remarkable gift of his generosity and his efforts on my behalf. My wholehearted thanks also go to Dr. Lisa Brady, Dr. Brent and Tika Eastman, Jerry Fussell, Rebecca Hawkins, Jan Hayse, Noreen Heidleman, Martha Hunter, Dr. Ken Lambert, Frank Lowen, Carol Mersereau, Dr. Dirk Noyes, Nola Peacock, and Dr. Anthony Venbrux.

There is no gift greater to a mother's writing than the trusted care of one's child. I thank my parents for their generosity in that capacity; Billee Jean

Acknowledgments

Brown; Bill and Maryanne Campbell; Lyn and Jan Dalebout; Heidi Harrison; Deanna Ingram; Brooke Kastelic; Susi Kneeland; Susan, Andrea, and Cuyler Rush; Lisa Samford; Danielle Shapiro; Sarah Tollison; Janet Whelan; and Leigha Wilbur.

So much of this book has been informed and enlightened by my beloved dogs. I thank Pam Boyer for her benevolent heart, her insight into animal behavior, and for taking care of my dogs when I couldn't. I also thank Dan and MJ Foreman, Kathrin Luderer, Deb Tomkinson and the staff at Spring Creek Animal Hospital; also Deena Welch, Mocha's guardian angel. I am grateful for the friendship of Sophie Craighead, Barb Larkin, Ellen McKee, Mary Lee Nitschlje, Cheryl Smith, and Sandy Strout, and for helping me learn to learn from our canid guides.

For providing at different times a home or a place to work, or both, for my family and me I owe a debt of thanks to Jeannie Anderson and Pete Wales, Henry Baldwin, Sarah Jane and Michael Chelminski, the Dornan Family, Jeff Foott, Christian Guier, Clark and Vita Moulton, Tom and Sybil Wiancko, and Bob and Anne Yarnall.

I would like to thank Bill Campbell and Maryanne Vollers for being there, always, in every way, as friends *extraordinaire*. I thank my oldest and dearest friend in the Tetons, Lyn Dalebout, who had lived this story and has accompanied me through so much with a poet's clairvoyance, a lasting friend's truth, and a residing belief in goodness and the grace of the earth and its wisdom. Her comments on the manuscript made a crucial difference in the final text. I thank Kimberly Hewitt Lohr for her love, wise counsel, and encouragement in the last twenty-five years, and for being there at precisely the right moment (as is her way) after the birth of my daughter. A formative part of my life was defined by the friendship of Julie (Martin) Wilhelm, and her parents, Marion and Larry Martin, who provided a second home for me, alight with laughter and wacky revelry that glitter my teenage memories. Many dimensions of our experiences and friendship informed this book. I hold dear the lifelong friendship of Jennie Lyn Moody, and the calm, courage, and wisdom of her lovely husband, Gary Hawk. Together you have taught me the faith and ferocity of lasting friendship and its enduring wealth.

I thank Jack Turner for the breadth and abundance of his love and friendship, and for all the ways he has accompanied, supported, defended, enabled, informed, counseled, nurtured, and assisted my family and me over the last twenty years. Many of the ideas contained in this book evolved from long discussions and debates I've had with Turner, and its pages are seasoned with the clarity, wisdom, force, and influence of his intellect. From escorting me to "death threat" lectures (his Glock inconspicuously tucked under his uncharacteristically genteel tweed jacket) to his tender tending of Siena with his lovely partner, Dana, he has been refuge, confidante, collaborator, and a most helpful and candid manuscript reader. I am blessed beyond words by this friendship.

I thank Terry Tempest Williams and Brooke Williams for their wide, wild friendship that has stretched through so many years. Terry's example, her ferocity, her passion, and her fierce belief in the "sorcery of literature" has informed and guided my work. Our conversations and her comments have been crucial to *Shadow Mountain*'s development; after reading the manuscript, as a friend, and as an artist, she asked for more, and I think this is a far better book because of her guidance.

I am deeply blessed by the friendship of the following people who are touchstones in my life: I thank Marcia Casey for the poetry, compassion, and friendship she has offered me; Joanne Dornan for her nimble wit and inquisitive, roaming mind; Beth McIntosh for the rich refuge of her gardens, which reflect the delight and calm of our friendship; Shira Musicant for her deep, bright spirit and expansive soul; Arvid Nelson for his unquenchable curiosity and superlative enthusiasm; Jeff Pollard for his example of being human and wholehearted, and for his tireless efforts on behalf of this book and its design; Adrienne Pollard for her delight and embodiment of delicacy, beauty, and simplicity; Mimi Rich for her easy laughter and great soul; Bob Schuster for his big heart, fierceness as a friend, and wise counsel; Laura Snook for her feral spirit and her readiness, always, to remind me of the simple, delicious joy of picnics; Sarah Tollison, for her sprightly young spirit and deep, fathomless soul; and Ted Williams for his dear, unflinching friendship and his courageous example.

My friends, my tribe, my community (many of which are mentioned in the text or preceding pages) I send showers of blossoms to you all: Denise Ackert, Steve and Anne Ashley, George and Chebela Ayoub, Grove Burnett, Cate Cabot, Merideth Campbell, Nancy and John Carney, Chris Clark, Story Clark and Bill Resor, Jamie Clark, Virginia and Jim Dean, Kaidi Dunstan, Angie and Jeff Foss, Helene Gordon, Stephen and Marilee Gordon, Greg and

Acknowledgments

Judy Houda, Elisabeth Hughes, Karen Jerger, Kirk Johnson, Jean Jorgensen, Susan Juvielier, Ted Keresote, Sandra Lambert, Gardiner and Nick Lapham, Paul and Joan Lawrence, Michael and Jackie Lessac, Jamie Lohr, Kathy McCance, Dana Meitz, Mike and Alex Menolascino, Robin Moore, Georgie, Wendy, and Lisa Morgan, Mark Musicant, Mary and Hank Padula, Patty Pappas, Doug and Andrea Peacock, Tracy Penfield, Alex Pitt, Lisa Ridgeway and Jim Little, Phil Round, Lisa Samford and Wally Ulrich, Rick Schwolski, Nancy and Jack Shea, Laura Simms, Dottie and Palmer Smith, Jeff Springett, Sarah Sturges, Julia Thorne and Rich Charlesworth, Thekla Von Hagke and Callum Mackay, Casey Walker, Jocelyn Slack Wasson, Jean Weiss, Holly Welles, Judith and Tom Wiancko, Donna Williams, and Jack Zajac.

I owe much to my adored and decidedly plucky agent, Kris Dahl, for the time and effort she has put in on my behalf. Her patience, steadfastness, and humor have meant much to me, and her skill as agent has benefited this book in countless ways. I also thank Jud Laghi at ICM for all his help. I thank my first editor and cherished friend, Betsy Lerner, at Doubleday. This book exists because of her. Her editorial insights and suggestions on the first draft were astute and transformative, and helped to birth this book in its most generative stage. After Betsy Lerner's departure, Amy Scheibe offered excellent insight and guidance in shaping the final manuscript, and Stephanie Land's enthusiasm and logistical and artistic assistance in shepherding the book through production was invaluable. I also thank Chris Litman, who was a wonderful and trusted helper throughout. Finally, I thank Bill Thomas for granting me the time to complete the manuscript and for his effort to honor and accommodate my ethical and aesthetic concerns around the physical presentation of this very personal story.

To my husband, partner, and collaborator, Tom Rush, I owe my deepest gratitude for his all-enabling love. Through all stages of my work, from the early years of The Wolf Fund to the finalizing of this manuscript, he has accompanied me, never without his wry wit, lifesaving humor, and a song that could dispel even the darkest shadows. During the writing of *Shadow Mountain* he served many roles: first-line editor, adviser, dinner chef, dog wrangler, lullaby lyricist, and—the role I most cherished—floral elf. My work desk was adorned with an ever-changing blessing of fresh flowers: lilacs, lilies, poppies, honeysuckle, tulips, forsythia, and gardenia blossoms that suffused my writing cabin with fragrance. The intent and tenderness of those blossom offerings

Acknowledgments

sustained me and enabled the completion of this work. Tom helped me wrestle the manuscript into final form, staying by my side through far more all-nighters than I am able or wish to recall. I am honored and humbled to have my name beside his in life, marriage, and the mystery of learning to love. My dearest, you are my bedrock.

My final thanks is to my family of canid "others": Tammy, Skye, Bristol, Zany, Mocha, Rye, and Roo, the creature companions that have shared my life. And to Natasha, whose manifestations and potent spirit have so deeply informed and graced my life. This book is my humble offering, a record of a promise kept and a wolf pup's life that made a difference.